Advanced C Programming

Advanced C Programming

John Thomas Berry
The Waite Group

A Brady Book
Published by Prentice Hall Press
New York, New York 10023

Advanced C Programming

A Brady Book
Published by Prentice Hall Press
A Division of Simon & Schuster, Inc.
Gulf + Western Building
One Gulf + Western Plaza
New York, New York 10023

Manufactured in the United States of America

2 3 4 5 6 7 8 9 10

Library of Congress Cataloging in Publication Data

Berry, John Thomas 1947–
Advanced C Programming.

Includes index.
1. C (Computer program language) I. Waite Group.
II. Title.
QA76.73.C15B47 1986 005.13'3 85–14996
ISBN 0–89303–473–8 (Paper Edition)

Special volume discounts are available by contacting the Special Sales Department, Brady Company, Simon & Schuster, Inc., Gulf + Western Building, One Gulf + Western Plaza, New York, New York 10023

To my wife Nancy and my daughter Rebecca for their infinite love and patience.

Contents

1 Introduction 1

1.1 What Is This Book About? **2**
1.2 What You Must Know **3**
1.3 How We Will Proceed **3**
1.4 The C Preprocessor **4**
1.5 Summary **8**

2 Structured Programming in C 9

2.1 Writing Modular Programs **10**
2.2 Design Considerations **10**
2.3 A Typical Problem Breakdown **11**
2.4 Levels of Functions **14**
2.5 Functions and Modularity **15**
2.6 Using Scope **20**
2.7 Building Modules **25**
2.8 Function Libraries **32**
2.9 Summary **34**

3 Using the Standard Library 35

3.1 Theoretical Considerations **36**
3.2 Writing Data to the File System **39**
3.3 Opening and Closing a File **42**
3.4 Device Files **44**
3.5 Character I/O **45**
3.6 Character Conversion **48**
3.7 Formatted I/O **51**
3.8 Additional File Manipulation Functions **56**
3.9 Summary **61**

4 Using Structured Data Types 63

4.1 The Mapping Relation **64**
4.2 Arrays **69**
4.3 Character Strings **73**
4.4 Structures **80**
4.5 Combining Structured Data Types **87**

4.6 Initializing Structures and Arrays **89**
4.7 The Union and Enum Data Types **91**
4.8 Summary **93**

5 Pointers 95

5.1 Pointers and Memory **96**
5.2 Declaring a Pointer, Address-Of, and Indirection **102**
5.3 Using Pointers **107**
5.4 Using Pointers with Structured Data Types **112**
5.5 Linked Data Structures **117**
5.6 Pointers to Functions **126**
5.7 Pointers and the Register Storage Class **129**
5.8 Summary **130**

6 Calling the Operating System 131

6.1 Dealing with the Operating System **131**
6.2 Accessing System Commands **134**
6.3 The File Management Subsystem **135**
6.4 Making the Connection: open(), creat(), and close() **136**
6.5 Accessing the Values: Read() and Write() **139**
6.6 Error Checking **148**
6.7 Summary **149**

7 Bit Manipulation 151

7.1 Twiddling the Bits **152**
7.2 The Complement and Shift Operators **154**
7.3 The And, Or, and Exclusive Or Operators **158**
7.4 Using the Bit Manipulation Functions **162**
7.5 Bit Fields **165**
7.6 Summary **167**

8 A Data Base Manager 169

8.1 Using C **169**
8.2 Data Bases **171**
8.3 The Data Dictionary **173**
8.4 Functional Decomposition **175**
8.5 Using Pseudocode **178**
8.6 Source Code **192**
8.7 Summary **205**

Index 207

Preface

There are several points that make this particular book unique.

—It really is an advanced book; it deals with problems and techniques that presuppose a prior familiarity with the C programming language.
—It discusses C in context; it doesn't just present it as a series of commands and data structure forms but as a dynamic problem solving tool that can be used to explore a problem set and structure it so that a solution can be found.
—It shows C as it is used. C programming has a style and this book both shows it and show why it is good. Structured programming concepts are not abandoned, but we show them in a C context rather than torturing the syntax to fit some theoretical preconception.
—Finally, some new structured concepts are introduced. These constructs are easily implemented in C, but are not possible in many other languages. Most notably, we use the scope and storage class rules in conjunction with independent compilation of files to create program modules with very low connectivity—a desirable trait in structured programming.

Many C programming texts offer a description of the syntax and a few simple-to moderate examples. Their aim is to familiarize the reader with the mechanics of programming in C and to offer an overview of the language. This book, in contrast, has been designed with two aims:

—to introduce advanced techniques especially as they appear in realistic programming problems, and
—to introduce the reader to the environment in which C programming exists—the tools available as well as the kinds of problems it is best at solving.

This book will help the reader internalize the C programming language as a problem solving tool.

1

Introduction

This chapter serves as a general introduction; it consists of two sections. The first section sets the stage for the remainder of the book. It details what the goals of the text are:

—what knowledge you need
—how these goals can be accomplished

A brief description of the topics and the projects covered in this book are also included.

The second section covers the macropreprocessor facility, a characteristic that C has in common with some assemblers. Because the preprocessor is an important aid to the structuring of our C programs throughout the book, we are presenting its basic concepts here. The preprocessor contains several statements that function as meta-commands to the compiler. These statements are an invaluable tool for the C programmer, as they can be used to facilitate the writing of portable and easily maintainable programs. This chapter should demonstrate these commands in their full power within a realistic context and should show you how they can be used to implement structured software design techniques.

Goals:

- To understand what prior knowledge is necessary to profit from a reading
- To understand the format of the book
- To understand the preprocessor phase of the compilation

1.1. What Is This Book About?

The C programming language is emerging as one of the most important contemporary mediums for software development. Its size, its popularity in academic institutions, and its position as an intermediate level language—high enough to support structured program constructions, but low enough to implement algorithms that must directly interface to the hardware—has guaranteed it a place in every serious programmer's repertoire. Additionally, C spans the full range of computing and is found on machines ranging from very large mainframes down to the smallest personal computer. Much of the most exciting and popular application software for small to medium size business computers is coded in C. It is growing in popularity each day.

Many introductory books on the C programming language are available. These books typically cover the syntax of the language, including some of C's more exotic and difficult constructions. However, a book that attempts to cover all of a complex topic such as a programming language, must leave out many details to keep its length at a reasonable level. This is not a failing of these books, but it is a necessary consequence of the subject matter. This book attempts to discuss precisely those advanced topics that tend to get only limited attention in these texts.

C is neither a particularly difficult language to learn nor an obtuse tool in which to program; but neither is it a simple language such as BASIC. Compromises have all been made on the side of adding power to this programming language and not on the side of "user friendliness". Historically, C is a working language, created initially not as an instructional device, but, rather, to solve real-world problems; it has its share of idiosyncracies and even inconsistencies. And the kind of programming that it permits deals with a part of the machine where operations are often obscure. In sum, C is a complex—not simple—tool.

We shouldn't dwell too much on the negative side. C is actually better than most programming languages. It's

- more consistent
- more logically structured, and
- more portable than most modern programming languages

Like any complex tool, it takes a little time to master.

Our task in this book will be to take the individual who has gone through the preliminary steps of learning C, who knows the syntax of the language and has written small to medium size programs using it, and to move them to the next level of understanding. We will concentrate not on the elements of C but rather on the use of C in problem-solving situations.

Our ultimate task is to make C into an internalized problem-solving tool, to enable you to actually see solutions through C rather than by applying C, as some kind of foreign agent, to the solution of problems. Our aims are ambitious, but if we can just point you in that direction, they will be fulfilled.

1.2. What You Must Know

This book is not an introductory text for C language. You are expected to be familiar with the syntax of C. We assume this familiarity. We freely use any C statement or construction in an example even before we engage in a lengthy discussion of its usage. The basic core statements are not discussed at all except in the context of examples, and, only then, if they are involved in an interesting or unusual construction.

It is further assumed that you are familiar with the use of editors, compilers, computer operating systems and their utilities, and with some of the more common concepts of computer science such as stacks and linked lists. However, expert status is not assumed. You should be able to use the computer as a tool and not find it as itself a problem. Nor is expert knowledge of computer science required; only a general understanding of the underpinnings of programming is necessary.

This book is aimed at those who have exhausted the elementary educational resources for C and who desire to push their understanding of this programming language to a more professional level. We are speaking to the individual who wants to internalize C as a problem-solving tool.

An important secondary goal of this book is to expose you to the kind of problems that professional programmers face, problems that lack the self-completing features of instructional materials. We hope to show you what kinds of compromises between elegance, structure, and getting the job done are necessary and how to make those compromises in the least damaging way. Quite unashamedly, we will be showing you tricks and shortcuts that might be expurgated from a more theoretical text as too unstructured or as bad programming style. This action should not be construed as an attack on these principles but only as another aspect of our desire to show programming as it really is. Perhaps nothing is quite as frightening as the first time you face a "real" problem in the context of the "real" world. If we can ameliorate that fear, this book will have succeeded.

1.3. How We Will Proceed

Our plan of action will be to devote a chapter to each advanced topic.

- Chapter 2 will explore the tools of modularity available in C: scope, separate compilation, and function definition.
- Chapter 3 will turn its attention to the Standard Library concentrating on the input and output functions.
- Chapter 4 will discuss the use of structured variables: arrays and structures.
- Chapter 5 focuses on the ubiquitous pointer, one of C's most powerful constructions.
- Chapter 6 discusses direct interfacing between the operating system and a program.

- Chapter 7 covers bit manipulation.
- Chapter 8 contains the discussion, design, and implementation of a small data base manager.

In each chapter, we focus on these items not as independent mathematical entities but as elements that can combine together with other elements to produce a program. Our primary interest is in statements, operators, functions, and data structures all working together and interacting with one another, sometimes in untidy ways. Realistic examples are used in each chapter to make the discussion concrete.

In Chapter 8, we design and implement a small data base management system; this chapter is an attempt to draw together the material and concepts discussed in the book into a reasonably large-scale project. Just as the examples explore the complexity created by the interaction of the elements of C, so here we show the additional complexity created by a large and complete set of programs.

We hope, in this book, to create not only an understanding of all aspects of C programming but also to create a context for C. By studying how the elements of C interact with each other and with the problem elements, we can develop in this context, a feeling for how a given problem will be solved with C: what elements of C, what data structures to use, even a notion of how to design the algorithms. This kind of insight distinguishes the mature programmer from the novice. We hope this book will have this effect on you.

1.4. The C Preprocessor

Before the C compiler begins to scan the source file, it makes a pass with a macro processor. This often underappreciated and underutilized preprocessor stage can be a significant aid to structured programming and top–down design. Macros and macro processors are utilities more familiar to assembly language programmers than to those who most often work in high-level languages. This may be why this stage of the C compiler is so often neglected.

The first operation that the preprocessor can do for us is to allow the inclusion of external text files in our source file just prior to compilation. This preprocessor command is one everyone who has ever written a C program has used:

```
#include <stdio.h>
```

This command must be in the program source file, usually near the beginning. It instructs the preprocessor to insert, at this point, the contents of the file, stdio.h. The angle brackets indicate where the file is to be found, in a standard directory.

```
#include "stdio.h"
```

will accomplish the same goal but will look for the file in the same directory as the program source.

The "#" character indicates a command line for the preprocessor, it must be placed in the first column of the line. Note further that there is no semicolon at the end of the line. Unlike the C program proper, the preprocessor is oriented to the physical line. End-of-line terminators are not needed. Preprocessor commands can be continued on the following line by using a "\" as the last character on the line.

The #include command helps us to modularize our programs. Text lines, such as definitions and variable declarations that are common to many files, would best be put in a file of their own and then could be included in each file where their presence is required; this action will lead to fewer transcription errors. The use of #include will make our source file easier to follow. It will allow us to give a name to a set of objects and hide the details from view. Program Listing 1-1 illustrates this point. The file, adr_decl, hides the details of these declarations from the main program, thus leading to a cleaner, more understandable listing. Note that the #include only works for text files. Connecting compiled files is a different process.

```
struct name  {
  char lname[81],
       fname[81],
       mname[81];
  };
struct address  {
  char street[30],
       city[30],
       state[2];
 };
struct  {
  struct name pname;
  struct address paddress;
 }entry;

              (a) Contents of file adr_decl

#include "adr_decl"

main()
{
  :
  :
```

Program Listing 1-1. Illustration of the use of the #include command.

The preprocessor also provides us with a facility for doing straightforward textual substitution. We can give a name to a value and then use that name throughout the file. The preprocessor will substitute value for name consistently. The command

```
#define RATE 1.5
```

will cause the character string, RATE, to be replaced by 1.5. Traditionally, the name field of a #define is capitalized to distinguish it from a variable.

Values that will remain constant throughout the program run, but which may change from time to time, should be defined at the beginning of the file with the

#define command. This will make it easier to consistently change a value throughout a file (*see* Program Listing 1-2).

```
#define RATE .065

main()
{
 double cost,price;

 printf("enter item cost:");
 scanf("%lf",&cost);

 printf("total cost is %lf\n",cost+cost*RATE);

}
```

Program Listing 1-2. Illustrating a simple use of the #define command.

The #define command can also do substitutions that require an argument. The command

```
#define MAX(a,b)    ((a) < (b) ? (b) : (a))
```

will create a new statement, MAX, that will take two arguments and return the larger one. The dummy arguments a and b should be replaced by the actual values used during an invocation of the macro. Thus,

```
t=MAX(x,y)
```

will replace a with x and b with y. What distinguishes this macro definition from a true function is that the macro's statements are actually put into the program wherever it is invoked. The function code appears only once. If we call MAX() 10 times, there will be 10 copies of MAX() in the program. The trade-off is calculated on the size of the code. Below a certain number of lines the overhead involved in a function call must yield to the simplicity of the macro definition. Note the extra set of parentheses around the dummy variables.

To complement the #define, a command that will undo such a definition is available:

```
#undef MAX
```

will destroy the definition that was associated with this character string. Program Listing 1-3 illustrates the complementary use of these two commands. Just as with the #include, these commands can be used anywhere in a file; but, unlike the #include, there is frequently reason to use them at other places than the beginning of the file.

The C preprocessor supports conditional compilation with the #if family of commands. The most basic of these is the simple #if; this evaluates a constant expression and will compile the statements that follow only if that evaluation yields a nonzero value. Thus,

```
#define ORD(a,b)    ((a) > (b) ? (a) : (b) )

largest(x)
int x[];
{
 int i=0,max;
 max=x[0];
 for(i=1;i<10;i++)
    max=ORD(x[i],max);
 return(max);
}
#undef ORD
#define ORD(a,b)    ((a) < (b) ? (a) : (b) )

smallest(x)
int x[];
{
 int i=0,min;
 min=x[0];
 for(i=1;i<10;i++)
    min=ORD(x[i],min);
 return(min);
}
```

Program Listing 1-3. Illustrating the complementary use of #define and #undef.

```
#if SWITCHON
int x=0;
#endif
```

will allow the integer variable, x, to be declared and initialized to 0 only if SWITCHON is nonzero. Note the use of #endif to define the region over which the #if is effective. A #else command is also supported. Program Listing 1-4 diagrams the relationships created by the use of #if, #else, and #endif. Program Listing 1-5 shows a typical use for these commands: To enhance portability, we must recognize that not every C compiler supports void. We can write our code by using functions declared as this data type and yet keep its portability by putting this #if section at the beginning of the file. By adjusting the constant NOVOID to an appropriate value, our function will work with both kinds of compilers.

The #if family also contains #ifdef and #ifndef. These commands test for a previous macro definition. The command

```
#ifdef MAX
```

will be true only if MAX has previously appeared in a #define command line. The command

```
#ifndef MAX
```

will be true if MAX has not yet been defined. Both these commands work with #else and #endif.

One additional preprocessor command, the #line command, forces the file to take on a foreign format so that it can be used with other macro processors. The command

```
#if <constant_value>
        :
        :                          compiled only if <constant_value> is non-zero
        :
#endif


#if <constant_value>
        :
        :                          compiled only if <constant_value> is non-zero
        :
#else
        :
        :                          compiled only if <constant_value> is zero
        :
#endif
```

Program Listing 1-4. Illustrating the use of the #if, #else, and #endif commands.

```
#define NOVOID 1

#if NOVOID
typedef int void;
#endif

void function1()
      :
      :
      :
```

Program Listing 1-5. A typical use for the conditional compilation command.

```
#line 99 'fileA'
```

will force the next line to be line 99 and will change the input file name to "fileA". This command is of limited value.

1.5. Summary

This chapter has served two goals. The first part introduced the reader to the book and the book's method. We have delineated the presuppositions and assumed background of the reader. We have also briefly outlined the topics covered and the methods used to focus on those topics.

In the latter part of the chapter, we explored the preprocessor commands. Although common in assembly language programming, C is unique among high-level languages in having this macro-processing facility. We have seen its values as a tool for structuring data and enhancing portability. We will be using some of these commands throughout this book.

2

Structured Programming in C

In this chapter we explore modern programming techniques as they are implemented in C. Although much has been made of the universality of structured programming and design principles, it still makes sense to study them in context. A structured FORTRAN program is quite different from the same algorithm implemented in C. The similarities are there and are obvious; but, the differences are both dramatic and sometimes subtle. Our focus is on the multifaceted relationship between a program and its functions, files, and the variables that connect them.

The main tools for modularization in C are the function and the file. A function is a subprogram that performs one of the tasks necessary to accomplish the task set by the program design. A file consists of function definitions and variable declarations and may be compiled independently of any other file. Files are linked by the scope of variables. A program—a considerably weaker notion than in most programming languages—is a collection of functions defined within various files. Data abstraction and hiding are implemented by the scope rules that control the visibility and changeability of variables.

Goals:

- To understand the theory and techniques of structured modular design
- To understand how to implement structured designs using C
- To understand the relationship between functions, files, and scope

Review:

- The rules of scope
- The extern storage class
- Function definition
- The mechanics of separate compilation and linking

2.1. Writing Modular Programs

The terms *structured programming*, *top–down design*, and *modular design* are used frequently within the context of programming and software development. Very much like the word *ecology* or *natural*, these concepts have taken on an almost holy aura and are used more to pass judgment than to help produce better software. For example, Pascal is the epitome of a "structured language," BASIC is its antithesis. Strong data typing is a "structured" technique. Global variable declarations are not. The list can grow endlessly when each individual adds his or her share of anecdotes and mythology. Like any poorly understood, but useful, body of knowledge, the concepts of structured programming become oversimplified absolutes, such as, you mustn't use global variables, and you mustn't use unconditional branching.

We must recognize two points about structured programming. Its principles are substantially correct. Modular programming is better programming,and top–down design is a better programming technique. But, we must also consider these principles in light of the tools that are being used. Good, maintainable programs can be written in any programming language, and they all follow the same general principles of design. Pascal and C are different programming languages, and the implementation of a given algorithm would be different in each one but perhaps more similar than to that same algorithm as set in BASIC. All three programs could be good, well-structured ones. As we shall see, C is an excellent vehicle for producing such software.

As in any activity that involves human design, each language results from a series of often mutually conflicting trade-offs. Sometimes these differences can be exploited to advantage. C is a programming language that lacks many of the features commonly thought to add structure to a program. C is not a strongly typed language—conversions between data types are easy and fluid. Nor does C support a hierarchical block structure—there is only one level of function definition, and functions cannot be defined within functions. Yet C cannot only be used to write easily maintained programs, but, it is also an excellent vehicle for rapid software development. In fact we shall see in this chapter that C, through its highly developed set of scope rules for variables and its support of separate compilation of functions, adds an additional layer of structure, thus enhancing the design process. Just as we can decompose a program into functions that are autonomous and have well-controlled entry and exit operations, we can create modules of sets of functions in C that allow us to create tighter, even more well-behaved functionalities. Our task in this first chapter will be to explore these structured techniques and to develop a feeling for C as a tool with which to design good programs.

2.2. Design Considerations

The most efficient way to tackle any but the shortest problem is to break it down into subproblems that are easier to solve. This process is iterative. Each of these simpler problems is further divided until we finally arrive at a set of problems whose solution is trivial. This technique, frequently called functional decomposition, partakes more of common sense than esoteric science; yet, it is still at the heart of any program design.

How we go about this decomposition depends on many factors; chief among these factors are personal style and the programming medium in which the solution will be coded. Ideally the problem is analyzed into its component parts, which are then coded in algorithmic form, and the most appropriate programming language is chosen for implementation. Other factors usually dictate the choice of system software and even hardware components. A problem is usually not characterized as "write an accounting system" but more often "write an accounting system in C to run on the XYZ computer". Even when a programmer has a free hand, the programmer will often pick hardware and software resources on a personal basis independent of the problem at hand. This is not an unreasonable approach; the business of programming is to get the job done well and quickly. We all have our preferences usually for things we know well and can work with effectively. Most modern programming languages are sufficiently general that this rarely becomes a problem.

It is useful to discuss design technique and theory within the context of a particular programming language. Not only does C strongly support and even encourage such function-based design, it has several components that offer unique and powerful ways of accomplishing this goal. The C elements we will be exploring in this chapter are

- function definition in more than one file
- scope relations
- the separate compilation of functions

But before we turn our attention there, let's consider a concrete design example.

2.3. A Typical Problem Breakdown

The Box shows a problem that is typical of many applications written in C. It's also useful as a model for a large class of similar problems. The aim is to write a program that will analyze an arbitrary piece of text and display some interesting values associated with that text. The problem is small enough that it could be coded as one massive function, but this temptation must be resisted. A large function would involve some tricky programming—difficult to do, error-prone, and almost unmaintainable. If, however, we break the problem into a series of functional units or modules it becomes quite an easy programming task. In fact the separate functions are already part of the problem. It is useful to think of these problem-based functionalities as defining different regions of the program. What leads to tricky and oblique programming is trying to separate these functional units in the program code without using any of the tools that C provides, tools such as function definition. It is just the use and definition of these tools on which this discussion will focus.

Statement of the word problem

Problem: Design a program that will accept as input a paragraph of text and will display the following statistics based on that paragraph:
total number of words
frequency of four-syllable words
frequency of three-syllable words
frequency of two-syllable words
frequency of one-syllable words

As an aside and an admonition, if you are still tempted to code these small "quick-and-dirty" programs all within main(), consider this: Small utilities are usually the most long-lived and persistent of all programs. The word-counting program we write today might still be with us, with all of its surprising bugs, for a long time to come. Good design always pays off even in the face of seemingly faster techniques.

Figure 2-1 is a graphical representation of a first pass at functional breakdown. The three main things the program must do are accept the text into the machine, process it, and display the results. The processing stage is further divided into two distinct steps: counting the words and calculating the frequency table. There are two things to remember when viewing this diagram. First, it is not a flowchart or a graph; it is only a rough breakdown of the problem. A lot of factors affecting the final design do not appear in this diagram. A big problem with teaching program-

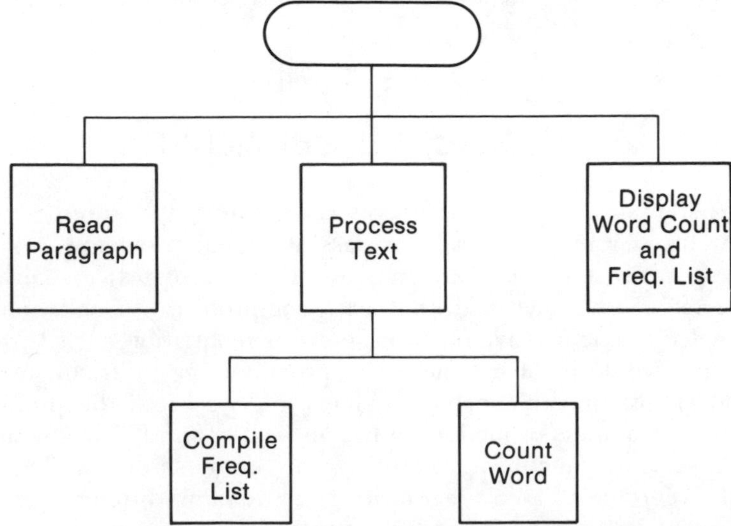

Figure 2-1. A first pass at a functional decomposition of the problem.

ming design is that we tend to fall in love with the design process and its tools while losing sight of the program that is the aim of all this effort. In any case, the diagram does not yet represent a form that shows an easy transition to a C program. It is to produce such a transition that we go to the trouble of producing such a diagram. Further analysis is necessary.

Consider the further breakdown of the problem in Figure 2-2. In this diagram we've begun the process of delimiting and naming the functions that will be used to implement our program. For each of our three main divisions, we have a corresponding C function: Read paragraph is text_in(), process text is text_count(), and display word count and frequency list is display(). Now we would probably be ready to start coding the program. The design stage is not yet over, but it's now necessary to deal with the specifics of the programming language and to abandon the comforting generality of the graphic display.

It is important to realize that the design phase is not over. For one thing, it is an iterative process and although the structure and number of functions we have sketched out looks complete and intuitive, we may yet find that changes will be

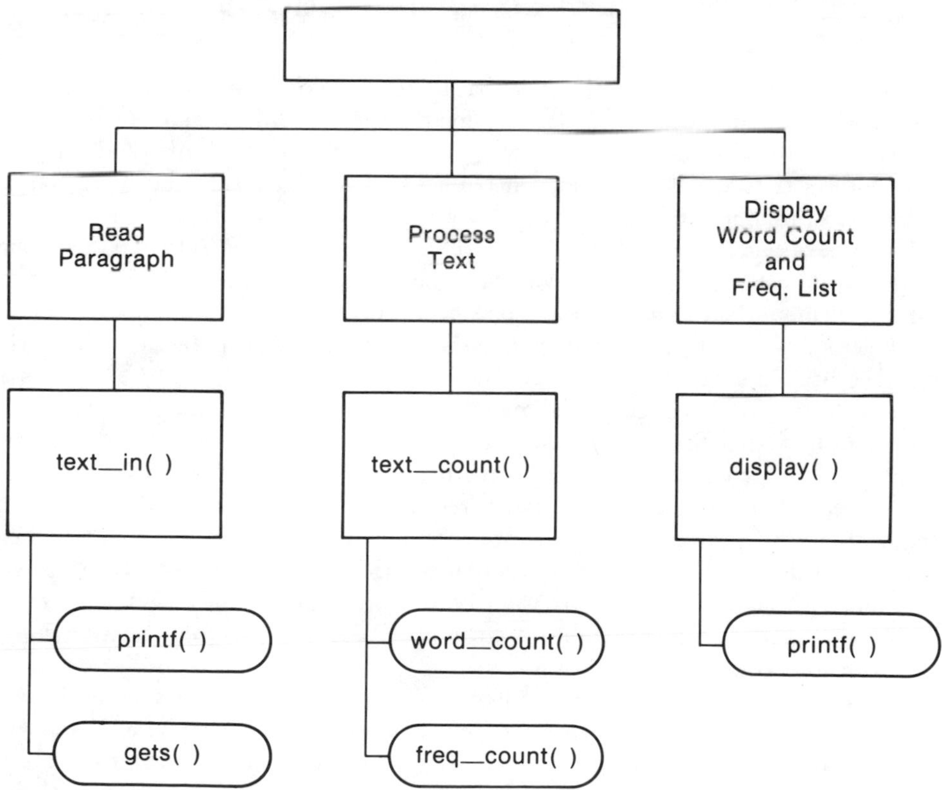

Figure 2-2. A second pass at functional decomposition for the word-counting problem.

necessary. Some functions may be combined or additional ones may be necessary. How far we take this process is a function not only of the complexity of the problem at hand but also of our familiarity with it and with the facilities of C.

The process that we've put forward here is an informal one; it can be and has been made more formal. On a large multiprogrammer project, more structure is necessary so that each person's creation will be sufficiently alike to be compatible. Smaller projects need not go to these lengths, but some kind of plan is necessary even for the programmer working alone. Everyone at some time has indulged in creating a program by just sitting down at the terminal and writing; but by eschewing design, we arbitrarily limit ourselves to programs that can be completed in one sitting. Our only weapon against complexity is design. Designing need not be the formal and stilted process so often called structured programming, but it should be some kind of structured process.

2.4. Levels of Functions

Look again at Figure 2-2 and notice that there are two distinct levels of functions. Text_in(), text_count(), and display() define the three broad divisions of functionality that the program exhibits. Below are the standard functions printf() and gets() and two additonal (somewhat self-evident) functions word_count() and freq_count(). These latter functions represent the actual working functions. The former, high-level functions are aggregations of these low-level routines. The ideal is to export as much of the work of the program as low as possible. These high-level functions are typically little more than a series of function calls connected by a broad, logical structure or skeleton. We might even characterize them as execution lists because they bring into execution a series of lower-level functions.

What does all this theory and planning mean to the working programmer? This kind of structure is pervasive among problems amenable to a computer solution. The process of becoming a mature programmer is largely one of learning to recognize these common structures in the heap of data and specification that reflects the early stages of a project. The sooner such a disheveled heap becomes ordered, the sooner the eventual solution can be planned. We shall also see shortly that this kind of division of the program meshes well with the C language—that the implementation structures bear a one-to-one relationship to this kind of problem decomposition.

Let us interject a note of caution here. We must be particularly careful not to be overcome by the mathematical simplicity of the diagram; we can refine, expand, and redefine it to infinity. We could even expand it beyond the ability of C or any programming language to implement; this is a danger with any graphic technique and tends to limit its usefulness. We must keep squarely in mind that our only purpose in doing any analysis at all is to aid us in writing programs.

Our analysis to this point leaves unanswered questions. The general structure of a program into high- and low-level functions certainly makes sense, but it still leaves us in the dark about the details of these functions: How big are they, what should and should not be included, and at what point should a task be divided into more than one function. A flip answer might be that this is where the "art" of programming takes over from the science. Let's see if we can explore and elucidate some of these artistic principles.

One of the first criterion for a function definition is one of size. A function definition should never exceed a page in length. This definition is persistent and attractive, but we must be skeptical in the face of its arbitrariness. This size measure might serve as a rough check on our design, but it cannot really guide us. Functions in C do tend to be short. This is not a full criterion.

A better design criterion is directly related to our earlier functional decomposition. The ideal function does one, and only one, task. In the case of the standard library routine, gets(), the function returns a pointer to a just entered character string, word_count() will return the number of words in the paragraph and so on; this almost always leads to short and concise functions but not to ones of an arbitrarily given size. Note too that while our discussion seems to apply only to the low-level functions, it is just as applicable to the higher-level ones. Here it is a matter of keeping our execution list small and unified—I/O functions here, core processing functions there, and so on.

Other factors also affect the functional decomposition of a problem. Those aspects of the problems that are likely to change over time,such as an array size or a specific value,should be kept in a separate function. Those factors that depend on the specific hardware parameters or on special features of the implementation are best isolated (for example hardware addresses). Anything that affects the portability of the program should be given this special isolation treatment so that it can be changed easily if the need arises.

2.5. Functions and Modularity

Our previous discussion of design principles and technique leads us into a discussion of their implementation in C. But, before we can do this, we must develop an understanding of what a C program is. We shall find that it is quite different from the traditional programs found in languages like Pascal.

Most modern programming languages are taught with emphasis on some kind of modularity. This modularity usually takes the form of subprograms—subroutines, functions, or procedures—that help break the program's task into more manageable pieces. These subprograms are said to be autonomous units but they are all subdivisions of the program and cannot exist apart from it. This is most explicit in Pascal where all functions and procedures must be predefined before the main program. The situation is quite different in C. The notion of a program is weaker in C than in most modern languages. C puts more emphasis on the notion of a fully independent function.

A program in C is really a collection of functions. A few functions may be from the standard library, a few may be unique to the program, and some may have been shared across many programs. The very structure of the language with its preprocessor commands and variable scope rules not only facilitates the reuse of functions but actively encourages it. The defining mark of a program, main(), is really only another function. C was one of the first languages to drop the notion of strict compartmentalization of functions into discrete programs. Perhaps because of its early bias toward systems programming, C looks to an environment of execution where the distinctions between operating system and program break down even further. This is most clear when using C under Unix where the operating-system calls easily merge into the programming language. This is quite a departure from more traditional programming languages, such as Pascal, where each program is a world unto itself, and, only with difficulty, does it communicate with other programs and with the operating system. C's emphasis on functions and not on specific programs also offers a bridge to other modern programming languages. Lisp is a language that is radically different from most programming systems, yet it shares with C this functional emphasis.

What practical lessons issue from all this high-level theorizing? The primary one is that we must take a much more radical approach to modularization than is necessary or even practical in other programming languages. C's very structure forces us to break our programming projects down into their simplest components and then to construct a program by combining these basic building blocks. Furthermore, there is a bias to produce general purpose functions that can be used and reused to build other programs (*see* Figure 2-3), to add these functions to the environment. We are continuously redefining the operating system and the programming language itself to make them both even richer and more convenient to use.

The tools that we have to work with are functions, files (and separate compilation), and the scope of variables. We'll leave the files as a tool of modularity. Here we'll concentrate on the use of functions as building blocks.

The most obvious use of functions is to simplify our code. Sometimes this simplification can be quite dramatic. Consider a program to find and display the prime numbers within an interval. Our first version (*see* Program Listing 2-1) is written all within main(). As can be seen from even a perfunctory glance at the code, it is an involved program. We have an outer loop that presents each number in the interval as a candidate for "primeness" and an inner loop that does a series of trial divisions on each of these numbers. A flag value is set or not depending on the result of the trial divisions. If a candidate fails the test, there is no need to continue to process it, so we execute a break statement to return control to the outer loop where we decide whether or not to print out that value. Contrast the second program (*see* Program Listing 2-2), where we create a function, is_prime(), that accepts a number and tests it for primeness. Main() consists solely of a loop that steps through the interval and a single decision statement driven by the is_prime() function. Program Listing 2-2 is shorter and has a structure that is clearer and more obvious.

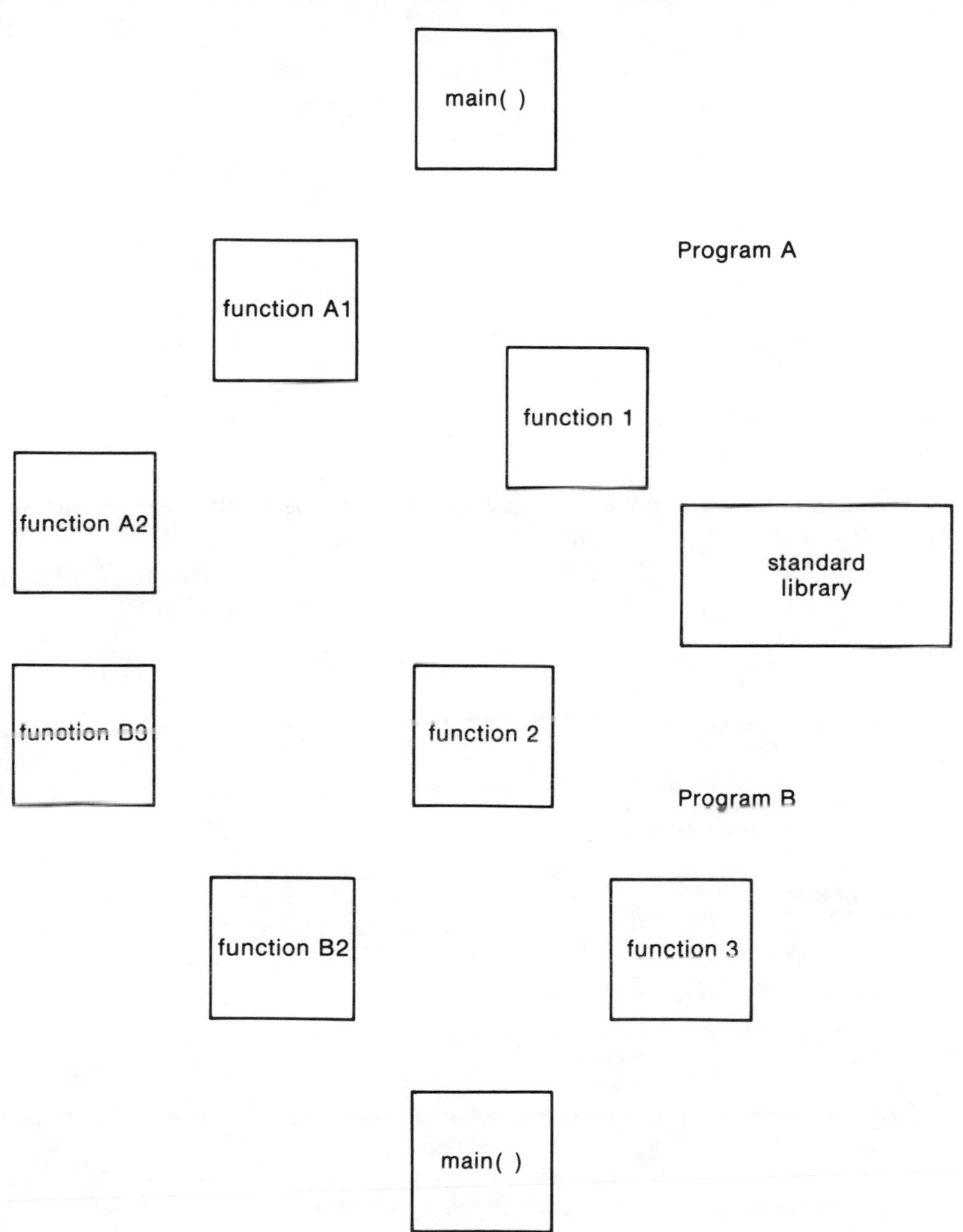

Figure 2-3. A C program is a collection of functions, some of which are shared with other programs.

```
main(argc,argv)
int argc;
char *argv[];
{
 int begin,end,loop1,loop2,flag;

 begin=atoi(*++argv);
 end=atoi(*++argv);

 for(loop1=begin; loop1<=end; loop1++)
 {
  flag=1;
  for(loop2=2; loop2<=loop1-1; loop2++)
   if(!loop1 % loop2)
   {
    flag=Ø;
    break;
   }
  if(flag)
   printf("%d\n",loop1);
 }
}
```

Program Listing 2-1. A program to display prime numbers within a given interval without using functions.

```
main(argc,argv)
int argc;
char *argv[];
{
 int begin,end,loop;

 begin=atoi(*++argv);
 end=atoi(*++argv);

 for(loop=begin; loop<=end; loop++)
  if(is_prime(loop))
   printf("%d\n",loop);
}

is_prime(x)
int x;
{
 int loop;

 for(loop=2; loop<=x-1; loop++)
  if(!(x % loop))
   return;
 return(1);
}
```

Program Listing 2-2. A program to display the prime numbers in an interval using functions.

The second program is the better of the two, but why? The most obvious and perhaps most important answer is that it is easier for us to grasp. A straightforward design that is clear and easy to understand means that we, as programmers, will make fewer mistakes and that we can tackle tougher, more involved, and more complex problems.

Where did the complexity go? How are we able to write a simpler program? Some of it is probably an even trade. We replaced part of our algorithm's complexity with the overhead of a function call. It was a good trade-off for us on two counts. First, the compiler optimizes the necessary calling code, which it probably cannot do for our other statements. Second, and most importantly, the details of this calling code are hidden from us. Also, some of the complexity simply disappeared when we divided our task into two simpler ones: Loop through the desired numbers and test for primeness and put them in an ordered execution list. The details of is_prime() are hidden from main(). This technique, called data hiding, is central to all advanced programming and is one of our main themes throughout this book.

The technique of data hiding, or more properly data abstraction, allows us to keep deferring the details of an algorithm from function to function. Each function handles some of the details and expects to be served by the functions it calls. Eventually, so few details are left that the algorithm is easy to implement.

Consider Program Listing 2-3. This simple program calculates the mean of a set of real numbers. Three functions are really at work here. In main(), we simply recognize the existence of a function, mean(), and print out its value. All the details of where the numbers come from and how the mean is calculated are left to mean(); it performs a service for main(). Mean(), in turn, expects get_val() to supply it either with a new number or a special end-of-input marker; it contains all the details of totaling up the numbers, doing the proper division, and passing the number back to main(). Get_val() takes responsibility for doing all the input and any necessary conversions; it checks each character string entered for the end-of-input value and sends an appropriate flag value to mean(). Otherwise, it converts the input from its ASCII character format to its proper numeric format and sends it to mean().

```
main()
{
 float mean();

 printf("%f\n",mean());
}

float get_val()
{
 double atof();
 char *ch;

 while((gets(ch)!="stop")
  return(atof(ch));
 return(-1);
}

float mean()
{
 static float total=0.0;
 static int k=0;
 float y;

 while((y=get_val())>=0)
 {
  total+=y;
  k++;
 }
 return(total/k);
}
```

Program Listing 2-3. Program to calculate the mean of a set of entered numbers.

This example serves to illustrate and clarify our earlier point. At each function some details are handled but others are given to other functions to handle. This kind of design breakdown allows the programmer to tackle problems of reasonable size and to build even more complex ones by decomposing their complexity into a series of simple building blocks.

2.6. Using Scope

Unlike many other programming languages, the concept of a variable's scope—where that variable is accessible in the program—is an active ingredient of the C design process. Where most languages offer a distinction between local and global variables, in C we can define these variables plus variables global to a set of functions, local variables that retain their values between function calls, and, as will be seen in greater detail later, variables that are global to only one file. The richness of the scope rules in C is often bewildering to the novice programmer, but it is an important tool that must be mastered if the full power of C is to be exploited.

We can manipulate scope to connect functions in controlled ways. Consider a variation on our earlier mean program (*see* Program Listing 2-4). An array of floats is defined in the main() function. Both get_val() and mean() are passed this array, which serves as the bridge that connects these two functions. The array, pile[], is local to main(), but it is passed by reference to each function in turn, thus tightly binding them together (*see* Figure 2-4). All three are tightly coupled.

```
main()
{
 float pile[100], mean();
 printf("%f\n",mean(get_val(pile),pile));
}
get_val(x)
float *x;
{
 double atof();
 char *ch;
 int k=0;

 while(gets(ch)!="stop")
 {
  k++
  *++x=atof(ch);
 }
 return(k);
}

float mean(k,x)
int k;
float *x;
{
 float total;
 int loop;

 for(loop=0; loop<=k; loop++)
  total+=*x++;
 return(total/k);
}
```

Program Listing 2-4. A Pascal-like implementation of the mean program.

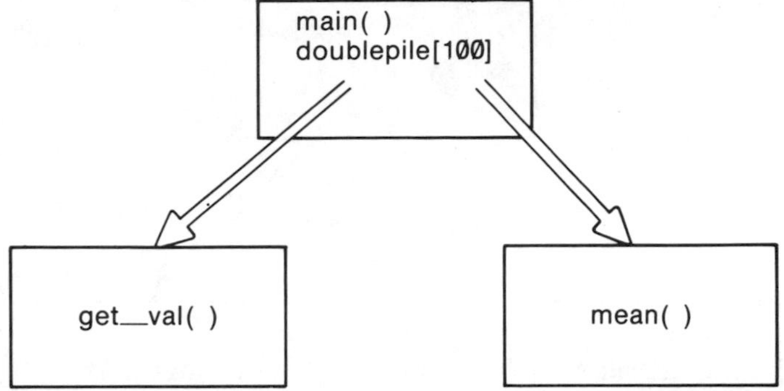

Figure 2-4. The array pile tightly couples the two functions get_val( ) and mean( ) to main( ).

Program Listing 2-4 illustrates a very Pascal-like program where the variables defined in main() are treated as if they are global to the entire program; this is neither desirable nor typical of C. It's necessary to couple get_val() and mean(), but not main(); main() should serve only as an entry point to the program, calling mean(), and expecting an appropriate value back.

Consider a third revision of this program (*see* Program Listing 2-5). Here mean() and get_val are again connected by the array pile[], but the existence of this array is hidden from main(). Mean() and get_val() are tightly coupled, but main() is only loosely connected. This relationship is illustrated in Figure 2-5.

```
main()
{
 float mean();

 printf("%f\n",mean(get_val());
}

float pile[100];

get_val()
{
 double atof();
 char *x;
 int k=0;

 while(gets(x)!="stop")
  pile[++k]=atof(x);
 return(k);
}

float mean(k)
int k;
{
 float total=0.0;
 int loop;

 for(loop=0; loop<=k; loop++)
  total+=pile[loop];
 return(total/k);
}
```

Program Listing 2-5. An implementation of the mean program in a more traditional style.

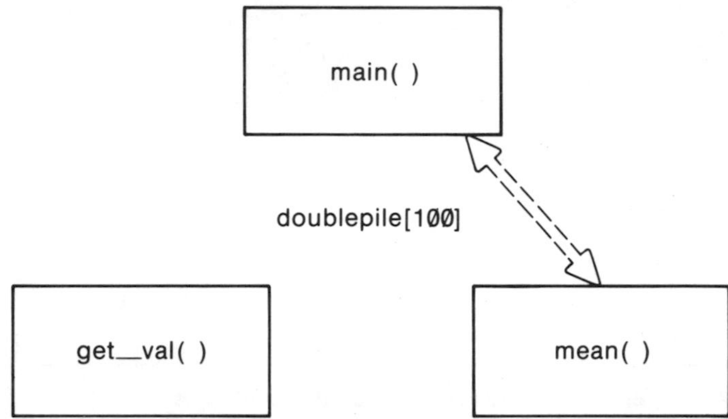

Figure 2-5. Mean( ) and get_val( ) are tightly coupled through the array pile.

Why not just couple all three functions tightly? Because using global variables always involves the possibility of side effects. By keeping the coupling well controlled, we minimize some of this danger. Futhermore, main() is a poor function to be included in such a relationship since it will interact directly or indirectly with most of the functions that define the program. The advantage of C is that we can define variables as global to a small region of the program. This way we can get the benefits of this simple and straightforward connection while minimizing the risks.

Program Listing 2-5 is also a more stylistically acceptable one. C is not a block-structured language, and good C programming style reflects this. Block-structured languages, like Pascal, require and encourage a programming style in which subprograms participate in an hierarchical relationship. In contrast, the typical C program has a flat structure, one in which each function is on the same level of definition. C programs can be written in such a way as to work counter to the preferred style, but there is little incentive to do so. The flat structure facilitates the design process and makes the relationship between program elements stand out more clearly. Compare Program Listing 2-4—very Pascal-like implementation—to the more traditionally designed code in Program Listing 2-5.

Let's draw some of these topics together in another example. Program Listing 2-6 is the listing of a simple RPN calculator program. This program contains four functions divided into three functional groups (*see* Figure 2-6). Although it might seem to be a case of analytic overkill with such a small program, it is important to get in the habit of doing such division. Almost every program shares this structure; it is a helpful model during the design phase.

Every program has a central core of functions that represent a direct translation of the algorithm in question into C. In our current example this is the main() function. Branching off from this core are two sets of support functions. The interface functions interact with the world outside the program's domain. Here next_in() accepts and converts user input. The low-level support routines are typically where the detailed processing is done. Push() and pop() fulfill this role in the example.

Understand that these divisions are a design tool and not some structure required by the C language. The process of translating an algorithm into a program is an

```
#include <stdio.h>
#define MAX 1Ø
#define BRK  Ø
main()
{
 double x,tØ,t1,push(),pop();

 for(;;)
  switch(next_in(&x))
  {
   case Ø:
    push(x);
    break;
   case 1:
    printf("%f\n",push(pop()+pop());
    break;
   case 2:
    printf("%f\n",push(pop()-pop());
    break;
   case 3:
    printf("%f\n",push(pop()*pop());
    break;
   case 4:
    tØ=pop();
    t1=pop();
    if(t1!=Ø)
     printf("%f\n",push(tØ/t1);
    else
    {
     push(t1);
     push(tØ);
    }
    break;
   case 5:
    exit();
  }
}
next_in(x)
double *x;
{
 double atof();
 char ch[8Ø];

 gets(ch);
 if(isdigit(ch[Ø])|| isdigit(ch[1])
 {
  *x=atof(ch);
  return;
 }
 else
  switch(ch[Ø])
  {
   case '+':
    return(1);
   case '-':
    return(2);
   case '*':
    return(3);
   case '/':
    return(4);
   case BRK:
    return(5);
```

Program Listing 2-6. A simple calculator program.

```
    }
}

double stack[MAX];
int top=0;

double push(x)
double x;
{
 if(top<MAX)
  return(stack[++top]=x);
}

double pop()
{
 if(top>0)
  return(stack[top--]);
}
```

Program Listing 2-6 (continued).

iterative one, starting out on a high level, such as this example, and moving back and forth between levels of abstraction and detail. This list of divisions might grow and shrink during the design process; it is never hard and fast. C, more than any other language, defies such neat categorization.

Significant to our current discussion is the way both push() and pop() are tightly bound. The array stack[] is declared just prior to the definitions of these two functions. From the scope rules, we realize that this makes it global to these two but unknown to main() and next_in(). These latter functions only know that they can push a number onto a high-level data structure called a stack and pop one off. How this is all accomplished is known only to push() and pop() (*see* Figure 2-7). Note that we used the scope rules as a part of the design to hide the internal structure of our push and pop commands. Later, if it is necessary to change the way we implement the stack, we can do so with a minimum of disruption to the rest of the program. Also it is clearer to a reader of the program what is being done and what data

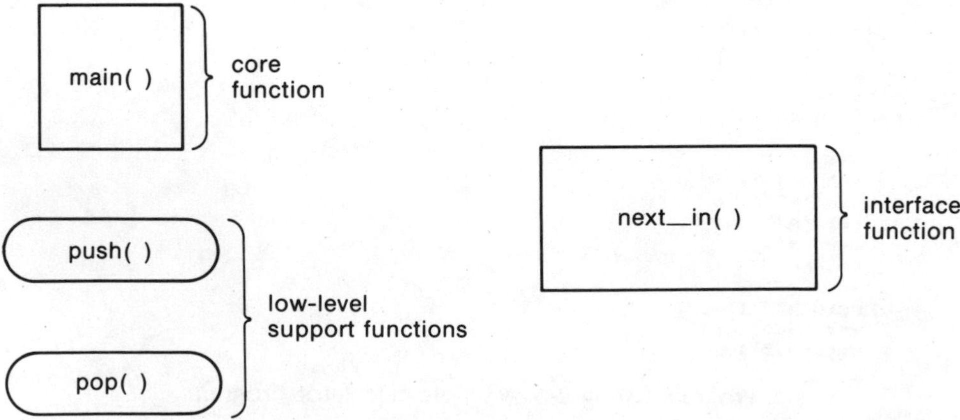

Figure 2-6. Functional grouping of the calculator program.

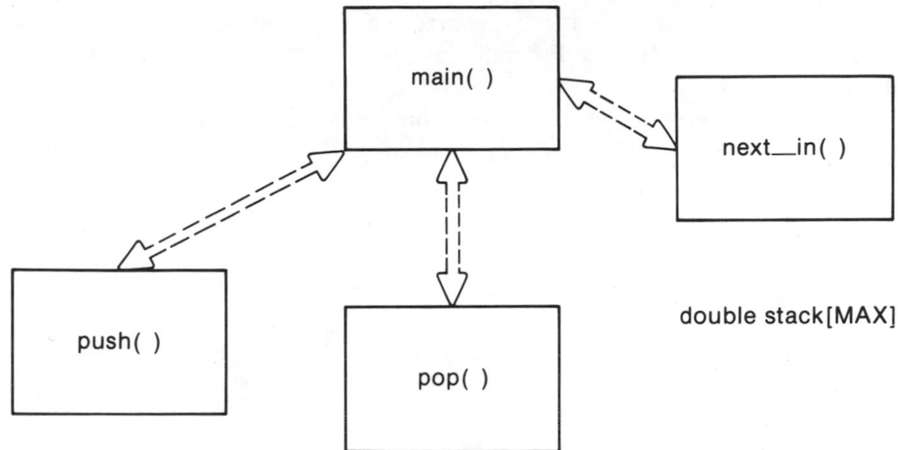

Figure 2-7. Scope relations within the calculator program.

structure is being used. Neither one of these goals would be met if this section of code were buried in some monolithic program.

2.7. Building Modules

C supports the notion of separate compilation. A function can be compiled independently of any particular program, and the object code so created can then be linked in as needed. This is a great convenience because it encourages the creation of function libraries; these libraries are organized sets of functions specialized to a particular task. But this facility goes far beyond mere convenience. As we have seen, scope rules can be applied not only to functions within a file but to the file itself. As we shall shortly see, this capability will allow us to use the file itself as a design tool. An entire file, as well as a function, can define a module, with well-controlled input/output (I/O) and private data types and structures.

Let's briefly review the C storage class "extern". Recall that when we were defining functions within a single file, we could declare variables whose scope was not a single function but the entire file or a good portion of it. This declaration was outside of any function definition. The scope of this variable extended from its point of declaration to the end of the file; it was global to a portion of the file.

The storage class of such a global variable is extern. With a single file containing all of a program's parts, this distinction is not too important, but as soon as we start breaking a program into more than one file, it can become a significant factor in our planning and design.

Look again at the calculator program in Program Listing 2-6. The declarations are both global variables of storage class extern. Recall that these two variables connect the functions push() and pop() but are invisible to the rest of the program. Functions are by default of class extern.

We can enhance the modularity of this program by exporting the push() and pop() functions to a separate file (*see* Program Listing 2-7). What have we gained here? Push() and pop() define their own functional region of the program. We've mapped that region onto a separate region in the computer. Contrast this with the original, one file listing. The multifile version more adequately reflects that regional division.

```
#include <stdio.h>
#define MAX 10

double stack[MAX];
int top=0;

double push(x)
double *x;
{
 if(top<MAX)
  return(stack[++top]=x);
}

double pop()
{
 if(top>0)
  return(stack[top--]);
}
```

Program Listing 2-7. The contents of the file stack.c.

The primary medium of this separation is the scope of stack[] and top. In the original program the scope of these two variables was the tail end of the source file; it was only imperfectly separated from the rest of the functions. If we had had two such separable regions, we would have had trouble because there was no way to limit the scope of a variable except by restricting it to a function, and then it can't perform its connective function. There is no fence character to limit an externally declared variable. But, with a separate file, the file itself is the barrier. The reach of stack[], for example, can stretch only as far as the end of its own file. The only connections to the program are those we explicitly make—in this case calls to push() and pop() (*see* Figure 2-8).

The situation is still not perfect. The two variables stack[] and top are still available to the rest of the program; they can be declared as extern and accessed. These variables could even be accessed as a side effect. If we redeclare them in the main file, the compiler will reconcile the reference to the original set. It will assume that we meant these variables to be global to the entire program; in a large program with many such relations, this is a distinct possibility.

Consider Program Listing 2-8. By declaring our two global variables static, we restrict their scope only to the home file. They are hidden from the rest of the program and, most importantly, hidden from any undesired side effects.

Program Listing 2-9 is the source code for the improved calculator program, calc.c. Notice that we had to declare push() and pop() in the main function. Although technically an extern declaration is required, the default storage class for functions is extern; so, consistent with C programming style, we left it off.

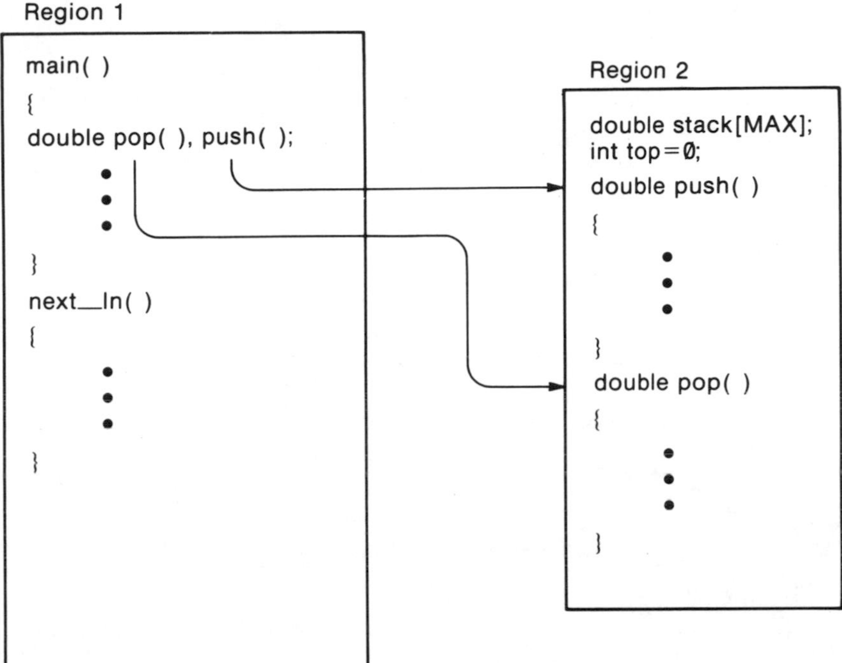

Figure 2-8. A diagram illustrating the connectivity of the two-program region.

```
#include <stdio.h>
#define MAX 1Ø

static double stack[MAX];
static top=Ø;

double push(x)
double x;
{
 if(top<MAX)
  return(stack[++top]=x);
}

double pop()
{
 if(top>Ø)
  return(stack[top--]);
}
```

Program Listing 2-8. The file stack.c with enhanced data hiding.

By declaring these functions in main(), we restrict their scope within the file calc.c to this function, which is a reasonable thing to do. Because they will only be used here, their scope need extend no further that this function. The smaller the region over which a function or variable has effect, the less chance of side effects. Figure 2-9 diagrams the somewhat complex relationships found in our calculator program.

```
#include <stdio.h>
#define BRK Ø

main()
{
 double x,tØ,t1,push(),pop();

 for(;;)
  switch(next_in(&x)
  {
   case Ø:
    push(x);
    break;
   case 1:
    printf("%f\n",push(pop()+pop());
    break;
   case 2:
    printf("%f\n",push(pop()-pop());
    break;
   case 3:
    printf("%f\n",push(pop()*pop());
    break;
   case 4:
    tØ=pop();
    t1=pop();
    if(t1!=Ø)
     printf("%f\n",push(tØ/t1);
    else
    {
     push(t1);
     push(tØ);
    }
    break;
   case 5:
    exit();
  }
}
next_in(x)
double *x;
{
 double atof();
 char ch[8Ø];

 gets(ch);
 if(isdigit(ch[Ø])||isdigit(ch[1])
 {
  *x=atof(ch);
  return;
 }
 else
  switch(ch[Ø])
  {
   case '+':
    return(1);
   case '-':
    return(2);
   case '*':
    return(3);
   case '/':
    return(4);
   case BRK:
    return(5);
  }
}
```

Program Listing 2-9. Contents of the file calc.c.

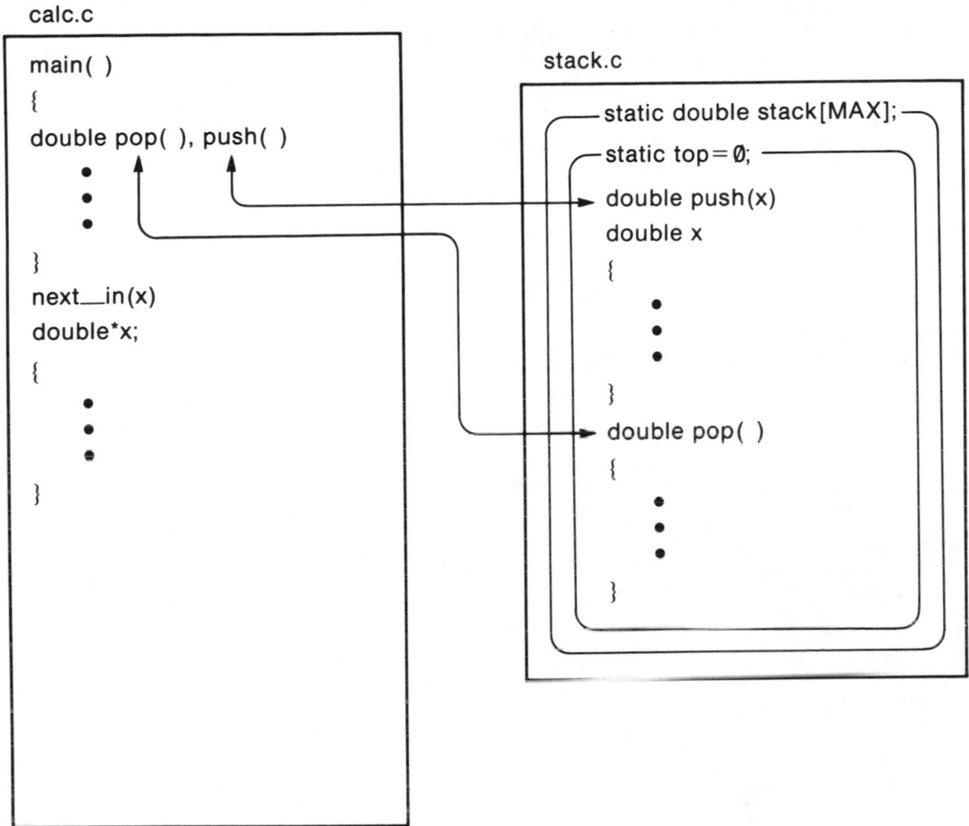

Figure 2-9. Illustrating the scope relations of the two-file calculator program.

Stop and look back now. Our most important point has been that through a judicious use of the scope rules and C's capacity for independently compiling and then linking functions, we can develop a new tool for structuring a program. As we pursue this topic further we shall see that this tool is powerful indeed.

Program Listings 2-10 through 2-12 list a program that will evaluate one-line arithmetic expressions—expressions of the form 23+46*3/2. This is a very simple-minded program; evaluation is strictly left to right and no parentheses are allowed. This program will illustrate the notions of data hiding and also show some of the practical benefits of these techniques.

Aside from main(), there are two core functions, get_input() and eval(). Get_input() is a boolean function that signals main() to either end the program or start the evaluation of the expression. Within get_input() each character is accessed as it arrives. Digits are accumulated into num[] until an operator is reached. This operator is pushed onto the operator stack, and the number, after suitable conversion, is pushed onto the operand stack. The process is repeated until an equals sign is entered or until the [break] key is pressed. Control is then returned to the main() function.

```
#include <stdio.h>
#define BRK Ø
#define CONTINUE 1

main()
{
 double eval();
 while CONTINUE
  if(!get_input())
   exit();
  else
   printf("%f\n",eval());
}

get_input()
{
 char num[8Ø],ch;
 int mark;
 double push(),atof();

 while CONTINUE
 {
  mark=-1;
  while(isdigit(num[++mark]=getchar())
     ;
  opush(ch=num[mark]);
  num[mark]='\Ø';
  push(atof(num));
  if(ch=='=')
   return(1);
  if(ch==BRK)
   return(Ø);
}
double eval()
{
 double push(),pop();

 while CONTINUE
  switch(opop())
  {
   case '+':
    push(pop()+pop());
    break;
   case '-':
    push(pop()-pop());
    break;
   case '*':
    push(pop()*pop());
    break;
   case '/':
    xØ=pop();
    x1=pop();
    if(x1!=Ø)
     push(xØ/x1);
    break;
   case '=':
    return(pop());
  }
}
```

Figure 2-10. The relationships between the various regions of the evaluator program.

```
#include <stdio.h>
#define MAX 10

static double stack[MAX];
static top=0;

double push(x)
double x;
{
 if(top<MAX)
  return(stack[++top]=x);
}

double pop()
{
 if(top>0)
  return(stack[top--]);
}
```

Program Listing 2-11. Operand stack functions for the arithmetic evaluator program—file stack.c.

```
#include <stdio.h>
#define MAX 10

static stack[MAX], top=0;

opush(x)
int x;
{
 if(top<MAX)
  return(stack[++top]=x);
}

opop()
{
 if(top>0)
  return(stack[top--]);
}
```

Program Listing 2-12. Operator stack functions for the arithmetic evaluator program—file ostack.c.

Eval() works its way down through the operator stack and takes operands off the operand stack and pushes the result back onto it. Eventually the only thing left is the final value which is then returned to the main function. Note how the left-to-right evaluation is directly supported by the logic of this function.

Main(), get_input(), and eval() are all contained in the file evaluate.c. This file defines the program—these are the high-level core functions. We have two additional files that are also part of this program, stack.c and ostack.c, which contain the stack operations for the operand and operator stacks, respectively. Note that both of these files are very similar. They both have an array, stack[], and a cursor for that array, top. Both array and cursor are private to the file. Both files contain a function that will put a value onto the stack and a function to remove a value. The data types of the variables and functions are different to reflect the kind of data being dealt with, but the functionality is the same.

Here we've got the situation we just discussed: two sets of functions defining disparate regions of the program. The scope of the operator stack and that of the operand stack need not and should not overlap. The only practical way to do this is to define them in separate files as we have done. Figure 2-10 diagrams the relationships between the various parts of the evaluator program.

Stack.c and ostack.c offer a service to the program. To efficiently implement the algorithm, we need to have a stack data structure. In this case we need one to hold real numbers and another to store operators. The chief advantage of a stack is that it is not defined by storage strategies inside the computer but by the operations push and pop. There are many ways to implement this data structure, but in order to design the program, we really don't care about the "how," just that we can use it. It would be best if it were a built-in command, and in a sense, that's what we've done here. How the values are stored is private to each of these files, unusable by any other part of the program. Only the two commands, push and pop, are available. Compiling these functions in separate files is the only way this can be accomplished.

There are practical advantages to the programmer from separate compilation. By using two files for the two stacks, we can create an almost exactly parallel structure, which means easier design and less chance of errors derived from slight differences and incompatibilities. Of course this structure also simplifies maintenance. Changes and improvements can be restricted to small regions of the program. For example, we could easily change our implementation of the stack—perhaps use a linked list—without altering the rest of the program. Indeed it would not even be necessary to recompile any more than the file in question and then relink the program. The "human interface" issue, while less theoretical, should be considered just as important.

2.8. Function Libraries

Modularity is a persistent metaphor throughout the C language; it even extends to matters of programming style. The bias toward small and highly specialized functions leads to the common practice of combining sets of these functions into specialized libraries. This technique enhances both programming productivity and the programmer's working environment.

Two factors come together to make function libraries a C metaphor. C is an extendible language; it has a core of defined commands and operators but all of its I/O statements and many of its high-level operations are exported to collections of functions, the standard libraries. So, for example, the string manipulation functions, most of the mathematical operations beyond simple sums and multiplications, and file I/O are all done by functions that have been supplied with the compiler but are not defined within the language itself. The programmer is free to change these functions to fit a new situation or to write entirely new ones. The value of this option is perhaps most clear in the case of input and output. There is nothing so exotic, strange, and unexpected as the operation of a peripheral device. Because I/O statements are functions written in C, it is easy to extend coverage to new devices by writing a new function to cover its requirements and protocols.

The other tendency in C is not to approach programming as a traditional task of man versus compiler versus machine; instead the approach is to view the computer as

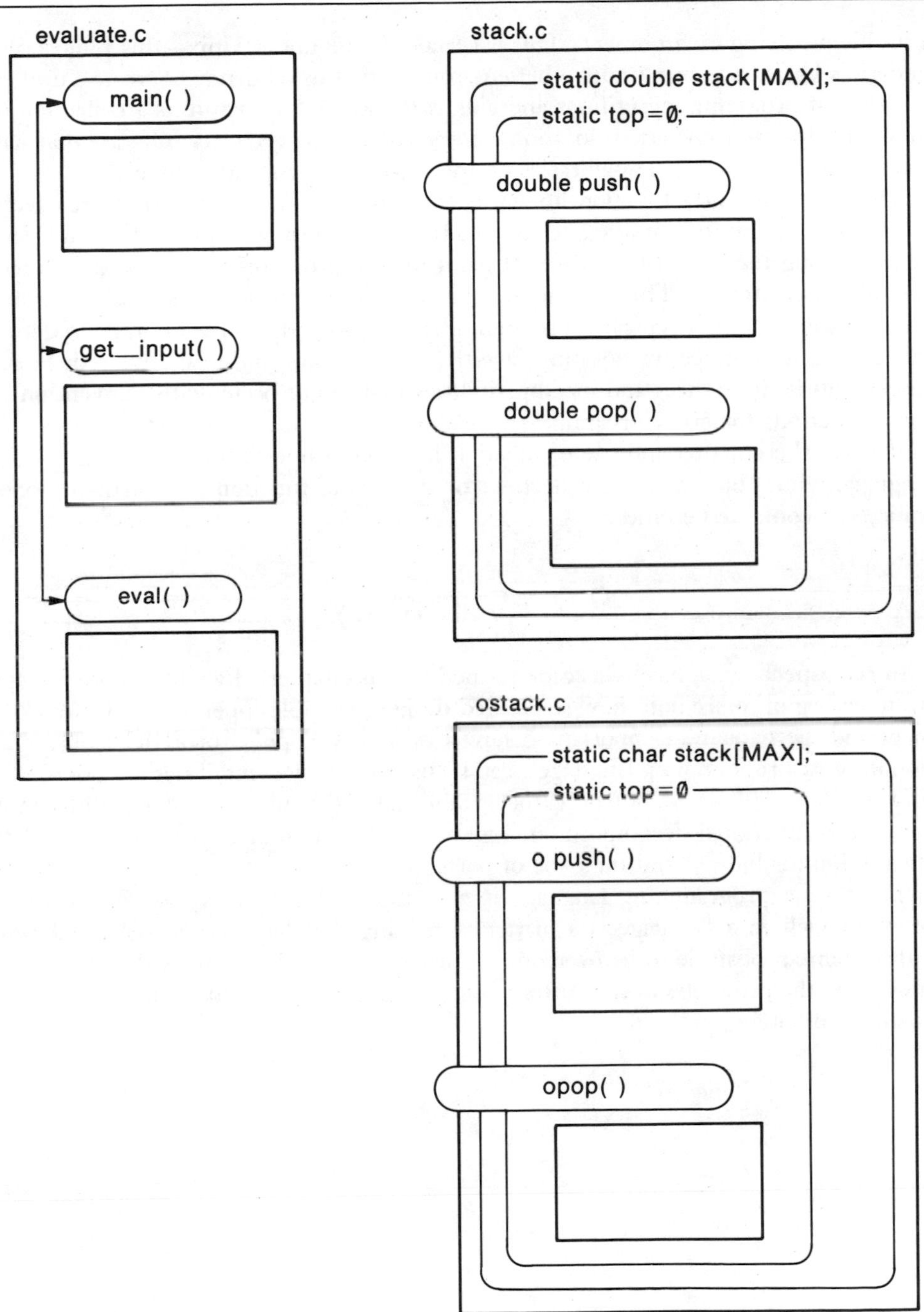

Program Listing 2-10. Arithmetic expression evaluator—file evaluate.c.

a problem-solving environment. This is certainly true under Unix—this philosophy underlies Unix. But even under other environments, this tendency to create a unified network of programming utilities and aids is found. A C program is a collection of functions drawn from various locations. Some compilers even offer software that will combine functions into new libraries on the model of the standard ones.

The advantage of a function library is the same as that of any structured technique. We can write a unified set of functions, create new commands in the language, debug them, and have them at hand for the programs that depend on these special circumstances. This technique is particularly useful where several programs are interconnected—a typical C programming situation. By using a library to define this common interface we not only save the time it takes to do this, we reduce the risk of subtle differences and incompatibilities that might occur with reinvention of these functions for every program.

Finally, the creation and use of function libraries supports the notion that C is a language whose programs are collections or systems of functions rather than monolithic, self-contained entities.

2.9. Summary

In retrospect, what have we accomplished in this chapter? Two important things: we have begun to see both how structured design principles operate in a C environment and, perhaps most importantly, how a variable's scope, a theoretical consideration in most programming languages, can be used as an element of design. Along the way we have discussed not only the syntactical mechanics associated with these concepts—functional decomposition, function size and connectivity—but also data abstraction (or hiding) and the issue of portability.

To learn a programming language is a matter of learning syntax. To learn to program well in a language is a matter of making that language a tool for design rather than an obstacle to be overcome. Throughout this book, we will continue to show how the principles of structured programming can be put to use in the practical business of solving problems.

=3=

Using the Standard Library

One of the unique characteristics of C is the flexibiltiy of its input/output structures. There are no built-in I/O commands or statements, but all communication to the outside world is done via functions: either user supplied to fit the present occassion or supplied through the standard I/O library. This chapter introduces you to this library and creates an understanding of the trade-offs involved with handling I/O in this fashion. The library itself is rich and varied. We concentrate on two areas to press home our point about the flexibility of this approach: disk file I/O and terminal I/O. Our choice of topics is driven by common sense: Both disk file access and terminal I/O are prime components of many if not most real projects.

Most devices that communicate with a computer have a one character-at-a-time orientation; this is true even for some extremely sophisticated computers such as graphics terminals. Indeed, the ubiquitous formatted I/O statements are built up from more primitive character-oriented ones. In this chapter we explore the nature of such character-oriented functions. We will review, in context, getc(), putc(), ungetc(), getchar(), and putchar(). Our goal is to give you a feeling for the way this kind of I/O is handled—how information flows into and out of the computer.

Goals:

- To understand the nature of character-oriented peripheral devices and how to deal with them
- To review the important character I/O functions in the standard library
- To develop a feeling for how high-level I/O functions can be created with primitive I/O functions
- To understand the trade-offs involved when exporting the I/O routines to a library of functions rather than defining them as part of the language
- To review and explore the formatted I/O functions—printf(), scanf(), sscanf(), sprintf(), fprintf(), and fscanf()—and their associated format tokens
- To understand the standard library functions that support direct file access

The first and still most difficult problem that a programmer must face is dealing with the outside world. The computer is a neat, well-ordered universe of mathematical precision dominated by numbers. The outside world, in contrast, is dominated by characters. The notion of character conversion, thus, will become another area of focus.

We will review some of the practical considerations involved in converting back and forth among different simple data types along with the conversion functions in the standard library. We will introduce you to the notion of formatted I/O and to the formatting functions within the standard library. Special emphasis is placed on the two most common I/O functions in C, printf() and scanf(). Through a set of realistic examples, the power of these I/O functions is explored.

Formatted file I/O is also discussed within this same context. You will finish this chapter able to handle the multivariate nature of machine-world interface. Additional disk file functions are also discussed including opening and closing of a file—fopen() and fclose()—as well as those functions that support direct access—ftell() and fseek().

3.1. Theoretical Considerations

Most programming languages include, within their repertoire of statements, commands which communicate with the outside world. In Pascal it's readln and writeln, in FORTRAN it's READ and WRITE, and in BASIC, it's INPUT and PRINT. These statements are part of the syntax of their respective languages. C, in contrast, has no such built-in command. No input or output statements are built-in to the core syntax of C. All such facilities are add-ons, built up as functions, and gathered together into what is commonly called the Standard Library. These functions represent an under-utilized resource both for what they can themselves do individually and what they can do together. It will be our task in this chapter to explore some of this potential. But before we jump, head-down, into this exploration, you need to have a better understanding of some of the broader issues and considerations.

The first question you might ask is "What is the trade-off?" What do we gain in C that we lose in the more traditional languages, and what do we lose in C? Flexibility is the main gain. By not defining the I/O statements in the core of the language itself, we are free to meet the demands of any new peripheral device that we many need or desire to interface. No matter how strange, unexpected, or unanticipated an interface protocol might be, we can deal with it. We need only, after all, write a simple—or not so simple—C function. It is no more exotic than that. The more traditional languages, in contrast, have built right in to their syntax the protocols for the devices common at the time their final design was frozen. Thus only with great difficulty can these languages be made to deal with new situations; it usually requires a redesign of the language or an awkward interface to assembly language subroutines. All of this is only too obvious to anyone who has used FORTRAN IV in an interactive environment or come across the common bug in Pascal that has the read statement—a supposedly direct access command— wait for an end of line character to be entered.

C is more flexible in its dealings with the outside world; it has removed the most changeable aspect of programming from the syntax, but what has it lost? On a macroscopic level, probably nothing. On a microscopic level, perhaps a bit of efficiency has been sacrificed: We have the overhead of a function call plus the inefficiencies inevitably built-in to the general purpose C statements that are used to code these functions. The built-in statement, in contrast, has machine code specific to and optimized for its limited operation. All this must be conceded, but the fact remains that on a macroscopic level, all of these problems are swamped by other, more significant inefficiencies. From an economic point of view, the greatest problem is programmer productivity. Few pieces of hardware or software are as expensive as a programmer. Wasting a programmer's time is the greatest inefficiency. From a personal point of view, no one, no matter how dedicated, can work efficiently with ill-fitting tools. The flexibility enjoyed by the C I/O library enhances productivity by allowing the programmer to fit the tools precisely to the job. The question of efficiency on the machine code level is usually a "strawman" argument anyway, viable in only a few specialized cases such as digital signal processing where real time response is critical. Even here, C's well-designed syntax can hold its own against assembly language.

By exporting I/O to a function library, C also enhances the portability of programs. Anyone who has written more than two programs knows that dealing with the outside world causes the biggest problem when moving a program from one computer system to another. The C function library acts as a barrier between the relative "real world" of the computer system, with all its idiosyncrasies, and the reasonably pure realm of the program logic (Figure 3-1). Since the I/O commands are really functions, they can be rewritten to fit the contingencies of the new situation whether it be hardware or software. Good programming practice dictates that the interface to the program remain the same. Portability, in light of this capability, becomes nonproblematic.

By not building I/O into the language, C becomes the best choice for interfacing to any future peripheral devices. Interfacing, not only directly to a device but also to other programs and software systems, is more easily and naturally handled by C than by any other programming language. Two examples of this kind of interfacing might be a graphics subsystem and a data base manager. In both cases, a set of interrelated functions is required rather than the single character-by-character protocol converter typical of a simple I/O function. The graphics routines would include scaling and other transformations as well as output to the appropriate peripheral device. A data base manager includes many kinds of transformations, sorting routines, and the creation and deletion of disk files.

The last two examples are good because they are indicative of the kinds of problems that C programmers typically face. A computer is really a collection of subsystems, both hardware and software. The I/O facilities are no exception. The days when a terminal would simply plug into a computer and the same central processing unit that did the calculating would also handle the operation of that terminal are fading memories even in the world of small microcomputers.

Today, we are almost always dealing with a multilayered subsystem that is a subtle marriage of hardware elements and software routines. Indeed, as research progresses, what once was wired into the hardware moves over to software, and

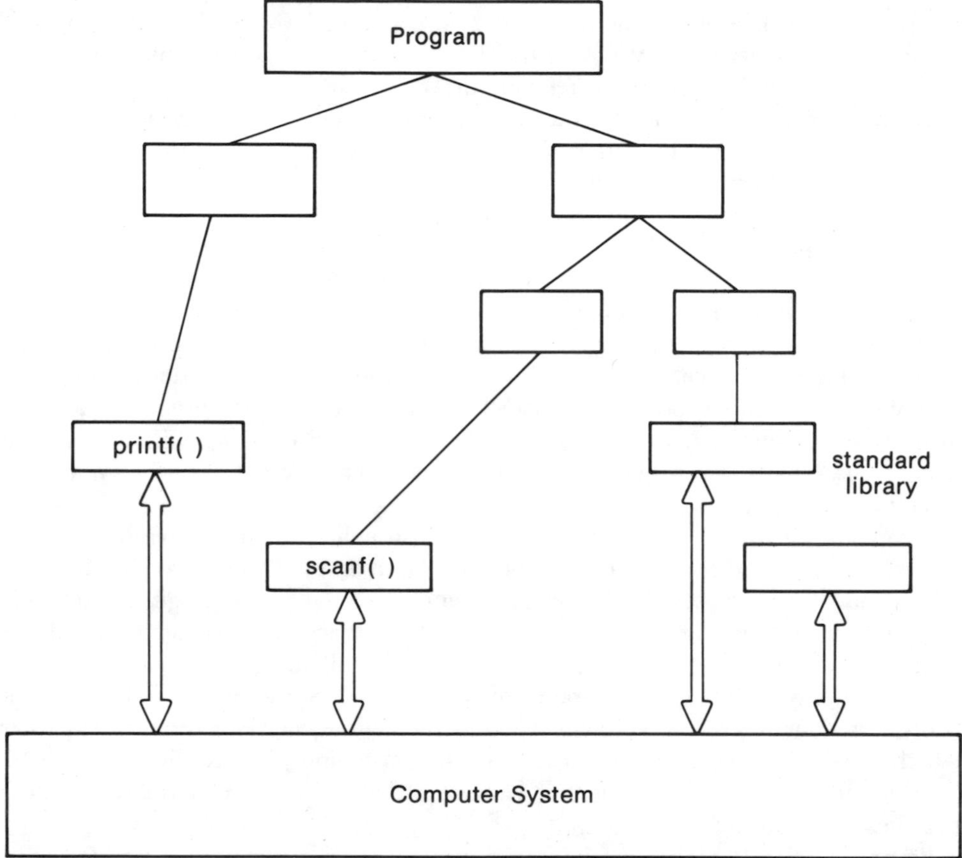

Figure 3-1. The standard library acts as a portability barrier between the program and the computer system.

software routines are recoded as firmware. The boundaries between the machine and its attendant software are not at all clear. The trade-off is a real one—increased performance and the ability to easily integrate new devices and situations.

With increased flexibility and performance, however, come increased complexity. This complexity, in turn, is subject to subtle and difficult problems. C is in a unique position to deal with these difficult design tasks. The modularity of its I/O subsystem reflects the structure of computer I/O subsystems. The interface is a direct one: C connects to the computer at the lowest level of system call. There is no need to step outside the language to an assembly language subroutine to deal with a new device. C's bias toward highly modularized porgrams is also an asset when dealing with this extremely complex situation.

The major division of the I/O subsystem separates the disk I/O from that of the devices—printers, terminals, and such—that are also attached and available to the system. In an important sense, this is an illusory division. The design of most modern operating systems, particularly Unix, tries to unify these two seemingly disparate realms of activity. Devices are treated as if they were files. All interfacing can then have the same format. This method is another way to deal with the complexity of this subsystem. C reflects this design philosophy in its own set of I/O functions. As we shall see, it attaches the user terminal, probably the most common I/O device, to three standard files: stdin, stdout, and stderr. By using these file identifiers, any file function will work as well for a terminal as for a disk file. It should be noted, however, that the standard library also includes I/O functions specific to the user terminal.

3.2. Writing Data to the File System

Although rarely covered in depth in a beginner's text, a program's interaction with the file system is one of the most important interfaces to the computer. Without the ability to save data and results from one run to another, the power of our programs would be significantly cut. In most modern operating environments, this need is even greater since all input and output, even that sent to terminals, printers, and other physical devices, is file oriented; devices are simply specific kinds of files.

There are two ways to accomplish this file system interaction. We can directly call the service routines of the operating system. These functions perform only a basic service for us. All details of the interaction would have to be handled by the program, which is sometimes called unbuffered I/O. The other possiblility is to use the file definition and access functions supplied to us within the standard library. It is these functions that we will focus on. The unbuffered I/O discussion is saved for a later chapter.

What is a file? There are a lot of different answers to this question depending on the context in which it is asked. At its minimum, a file is a named location on the secondary storage device, usually a disk drive. Physically, the file consists of a group of locations on a particular platter which, in turn, is in a particular unit (Figure 3 2). There is an area somewhere within that disk drive unit that could be pointed to as the file. These physical locations are themselves divided into logical entities called sectors (or sometimes blocks or even records). These sectors are numbered sequentially from the first one in the disk drive through the last one; this numbering system gives a file's address. At its most basic level, then, a file consists of a group of sectors linked together only by the fact that we wish to include them together. The operating system, or more properly, the file management subsystem, which is part of the operating system, keeps a record of these sector addresses in another location sometimes called the Volume Table of Contents. (Parts of this may be kept within memory for faster access but it is itself stored in a file.) It is here that each file is given a name. This name is the connection between the program (or any other software that might need access to it) and the physical file on the disk. Figure 3-3 illustrates this relationship.

The file name is, in a rough sense, the demarcation line between the hardware and the software notions of a file, (do not put too much into this neat division). The line is fluid and partly depends both on the hardware capabilities

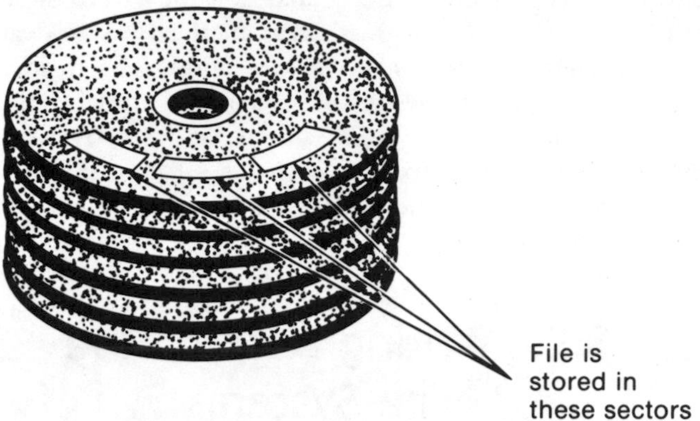

Figure 3-2. A file is a set of locations on a particular platter within a particular unit.

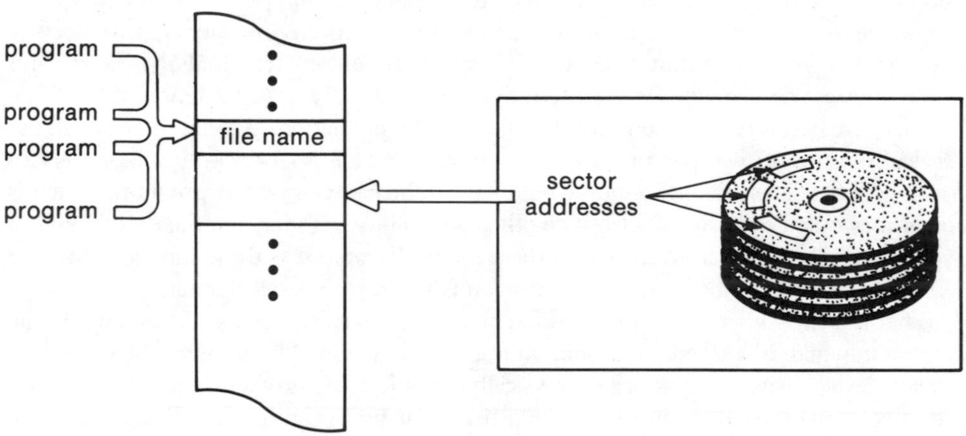

Figure 3-3. The file name represents the physical sectors on the disk drive.

themselves—some disk drives are "smarter" than others—and on the configuration of the computer system—where the designer chose to put that particular aspect of the processing power.

Our view so far of the file management system is oversimplified. This part of the operating system can do much more than merely name areas of the disk drive media. At the very least, we must be able to read and write specific values to a file. Other necessary functions include allocating more space on the disk, creating a new file name, and removing a file. An additional oversimplification comes from the fact that we only sketchily described the very basic level of interaction with the disk drive. A typical modern operating system adds an additional layer of organization in the form of a directory structure. This organization can be simple or complex, but it isolates the program by interposing another layer between it and the actual device (Figure 3-4).

So far we've talked about the file from the system's side. What we have defined is a named location of indeterminant size on the secondary storage device to which we write values and from which we can read them. What does a file look like from the program side? What kind of structure is inherent to a file? Many programming languages define several types of files. Pascal, for example, allows the programmer to specify an individual file as a storage repository for a particular data type. Thus, we could have a file of characters or a file of integers, even a file of complex, structured data (the Pascal "record" analogous to the "struct" data type in C). Other languages may allow numeric data to be stored in a binary format. These languages are adding yet another layer of structure onto the basic file entity. These compilers and interpreters automatically, and quite transparently to the programmer, produce the necessary code to convert the program data into the form desired. The actual nature of the file and the format of the data storage scheme are hidden from the programmer. In C there is only one kind of file, a file of characters. Indeed, a file is nothing more than a long string or "stream" of characters. Structure can still be added to a file in C, but it must be done explicitly through the program code.

This philosophy of simplicity in the file system, which C shares with its close companion Unix, is consistent with the design philosophy of the C language itself. C is sometimes described as a "mid-level" language because it lacks many of the features of

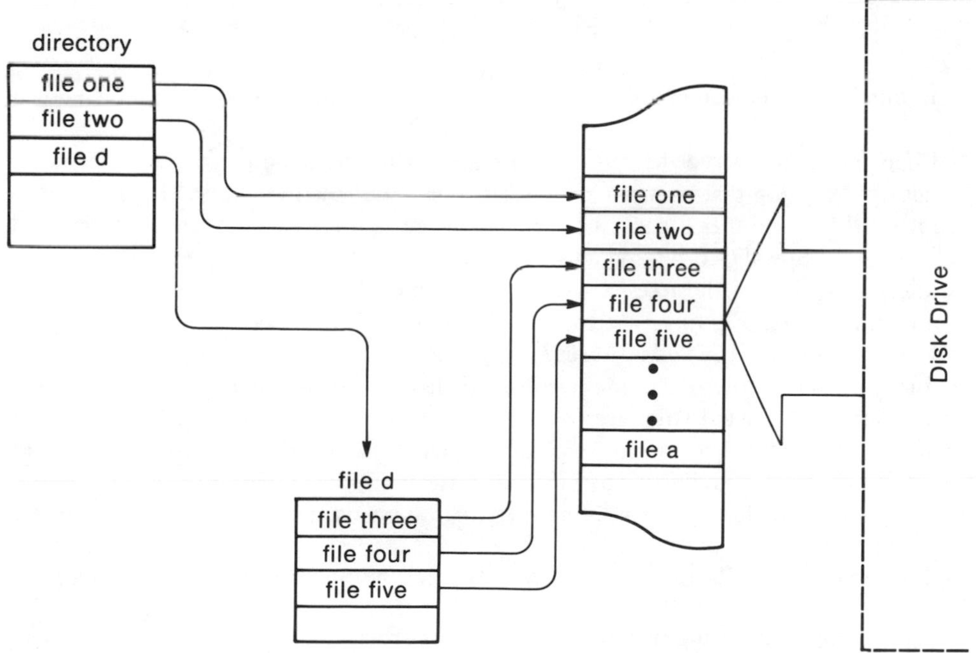

Figure 3-4. Most operating systems add a layer of organization between the user/program and the file management system.

more traditional "high-level" languages like Pascal. Whether or not this observation is fair, it is consistent with the overall design of the syntax which always attempts to offer the maximum flexibility to the programmer. The file structure is no exception, and certainly, for a large class of applications, this is not a defect but rather an asset.

Why is it important to take note of the structure that is added to a file or even the bare structure of a file that serves as a building block? If we are going to use a disk file as a problem-solving tool, we have to understand how to represent our real-world data in the proper form.

3.3. Opening and Closing a File

To access and utilize a file in C, we must make use of the file manipulation functions. These functions represent a rich subset of the I/O library. These functions all require as a parameter, a file variable (called a "stream" variable in the Unix documentation). Our first task then is to create this variable. The next point in any access is to actually open the file in question and assign it to the file variable. These two interrelated tasks are accomplished by a declaration and by the execution of the fopen() function.

A file variable is actually a pointer to a location of type FILE. The fopen() function also returns a pointer to a location of this type. Both must be declared before they can be used:

```
FILE *file_variable, *fopen()
```

It might be advantageous for us to pause and discuss the nature of the FILE data type.

FILE is actually a typedef statement found in the file, stdio.h. It is made up of a structure definition that contains certain key data about the individual file. These data are needed by the other functions to be able to access the file in a straightforward and reliable way. Specifically, it contains a buffer for the file data, the position of the file pointer in that buffer, the access mode to the file, and a link to the file control block (fcb) maintained by the operating system. This latter concept is important.

For every file that is "open"—ready for some kind of I/O—the operating system maintains a data structure in memory called the file control block. This data structure contains the details that are necessary to send values to the file, receive values from the file, or to perform any other kind of access. The FILE data type is linked to this fcb but does its own structuring and buffering independently of it. Indeed, on many systems, including Unix-based systems, no buffering, at least none useable by the program, is provided.

The first step to file I/O is to attach or "open" the file. This process involves:

- allocating and setting up the internal FILE structure
- requesting that the operating system create an fcb and attach it to the file in question—or create a new file and attach one
- connecting these two structures

All of these services are performed by the fopen() function:

```
file_pointer=fopen(file name,access_mode);
```

where file name is the name as it appears to the operating system—the name that is displayed by a directory command—and access mode is one of three ways of dealing with the file:

- `w` opens the file for writing. Any previous data in the file are destroyed.
- `r` opens the file for reading.
- `a` opens the file for appending. New data are added on to the end of the file without disturbing any previous contents.

Both file name and access_mode are character strings. It is particulary important to remember this about access_mode because it is a string containing only one character. The size and format of the file name are dependent on the system and personal whim.

If fopen() attempts to open a file that doesn't exist, the result depends on the access mode. If the command was for a write or append, a new file is created and then opened. If the access was "r", an error has occurred, and fopen() returns the NULL pointer value to signal this situation. Other error conditions will also cause this value to be returned. NULL is defined in stdio.h.

Just as a file must be opened before use, it must also be closed after the program is finished with it. Normal termination of an executing process will automatically close all files, but this is sloppy programming practice and should be avoided. Failure to close a file can lead to unexpected results. Most commonly, information supposedly written to an unclosed file may be lost. In most cases of file I/O, the values going to the file are held in a buffer. Each time a value is sent, it is put into that buffer, and when it is full, it is transferred to the file—we say delicately that the buffer is "flushed". If the program is interrupted while the buffer is only partly filled, these values may not be written to the file even though the program thinks they were. Another consideration with unclosed files is the limitation on the number of open files permitted to a program. The operating system considers the area holding its file control blocks to be a scarce resource, and it limits the number allowed to any program. Values range from 12 to 32 and are system dependent. Although this limitation is serious to only a small class of applications, it is always best to be tidy about closing files.

The function that will take care of this task is

```
fclose(file_variable);
```

It takes file_variable from a previously opened file as a parameter. The function fclose() is of type int so it need not be declared. It must be called, in turn, for each open file. An error condition causes the function to return EOF (also defined in stdio.h). The two most likely errors are:

- failure to transfer values from the buffer.
- an open file was not associated with file_variable.

3.4. Device Files

Access to peripheral devices such as printers and terminals is also modelled on file I/O. As we already discussed, each such device is considered an individual file on the system. Such files must be opened and closed just as a disk file must. Significant differences of operation between different devices are hidden by the operating system.

Every C program automatically opens three files:

`stdin`	accepts data from outside the program
`stdout`	is where values produced by the program are sent
`stderr`	an output file to collect any error messages generated by the program's execution

These are file variables, and each one is attached to the user's terminal (or console on single-user systems). We can use these values anywhere a file variable would be appropriate.

These device assignments are adequate for a great many situations—that's why they were chosen as the default values— but other options are available to us. Simplest, perhaps, is to take advantage of operating system facilities for redirecting input and output. Unix has this capability, but so do other operating systems where C is used. The format of redirection is system dependent. Note that redirection usually leaves stderr attached to the terminal. This is a design decision to ensure that error messages don't get lost. C also offers us a way to reassign these files within a program: We can perform our own redirection.

The function

```
freopen(file name,access_mode,file_variable)
```

will close a current file assignment and reassign file_pointer to file name; this is a way to change the file I/O from one file to another. A reasonable use for this function might be to reassign stderr to a disk file to make a permanent record of the error messages generated during a program's execution. Program Listing 3-1 shows a function that will accomplish such a redirection. Like fopen(), freopen() will return NULL if it was unable to open the file named in err_file. If, however, it is successful, the function makes the reassignment and returns the value of the old file variable assignment. Our function, too, will return these same values—NULL in case of an open failure and the old value if the operation is successful. We retain this value in case we wish the program to return stderr to the terminal at some future time during the program's run.

```
FILE *save_err(err_file)
char err_file[];
{
 FILE *olderr,*freopen();

 if( (olderr=freopen(err_file,"w",stderr))!=NULL)
  return(olderr);
 return(NULL)
}
```

Program listing 3-1. A function to redirect error output to a disk file.

C allows the programmer to open other devices besides the three standard ones; these devices, however, are usually handled by a set of more primitive I/O functions. (These will be discussed in Chapter 6 which deals with interfacing directly to the operating system.) Now we'll concentrate on accessing these files that we've opened.

3.5. Character I/O

Perhaps the most basic form of input or output is character oriented. Most devices attached to a computer are either one-character-at-a-time devices or can be dealt with, through proper buffering, as such devices. Also we can use this character-based input as a building block to create more complex schemes of I/O; this is just what has been done to create the formatted I/O functions printf() and scanf().

The first character-oriented I/O task is to take in a single character. This can be done with

```
getc(file_variable);
```

This function returns the next character in the file associated with file_variable. Actually, what is returned is an integer value rather than a true character. This output is necessary in order to capture all the possible values that might come through getc() and that are not in the ASCII character set. For example, the EOF (end-of-file mark) returned by getc() in case of an error or the end of the file is typically (but not always) a -1. This integer/character crossover is possible because of the special relationship between integers and characters in C.

The ASCII character set assigns a small integer value to each of its defined tokens. There are, in fact, 128 ASCII characters. The first 33 are nonprinting "control" characters, the rest have some graphical representation. Recognizing that characters are really small integers, C allows the distinction between integers and characters to break down. Integer values can be output as characters, and arithmetic can be done on these character values. This latter capability turns out to be quite a useful one particularly when dealing with peripheral devices directly.

To send a character out to the next position in the file, we can use the function

```
putc(character,file_variable);
```

This function puts character in the next position in the file. Putc() returns the character value it just put on the file. In case of error, the function will return EOF. Both getc() and putc() are typically defined as macro calls. This means that during the preprocessor phase of compilation, they are expanded into in-line code rather than being a true function call. fgetc() and fputc() are true functions whose operations are nearly identical to getc() and putc(), respectively.

Two additional macro definitions are available in the standard library that often prove useful: getchar() and putchar(). Getchar() returns the next character on the file stdin—essentially the next character typed on the keyboard. Putchar(character) sends characters out to stdout—usually the display screen. These commands are equivalent to getc(stdin) and putc(character,stdout). Although not strictly necessary, getchar() and putchar() recognize the primacy of the standard files stdin and stdout.

We've discussed a fair number of functions that are available to us from the standard library. Let's put them to work. Program Listing 3-2 is a simple function that will

- Get the next character from stdin
- If it is lowercase it will shift it to uppercase
- If an end-of-file mark is entered, it will replace it with a newline character
- All other values will pass through unchanged

```
get_upper()
{
 int ch;

 if( (ch=getchar())==EOF)
  return('\n');
 if(ch>='a' && ch<='z' )
  return(ch-('a'-'A');
 return(ch);
}
```

Program listing 3-2. This function will switch all alphabetic input to uppercase.

We can freely mix integers and characters in this function. This kind of intermixing is convenient and really necessary to a programming language that is designed to interact closely with the operating system. Converting from lower- to uppercase is also convenient. Because a character is just an integer, we can simply subtract an offset to produce the desired result. Even the offset is easy to calculate once we remember that the alphabetic characters are in lexical order. We just subtract the lower- from the uppercase integer. Each lowercase letter is just this offset distance from its uppercase cognate.

Before we push on to another example, consider a matter of style within the operation, get_upper(). By design, we are testing for three situations:

- an end of file mark
- a lowercase letter
- all other cases

The temptation might be to use a switch or an if-else-if construction here. This would add an unnecessary complication to this function and obscure its operation.

Our design is simpler and more concise; it takes advantage of the fact that we can specify a return and return value in the function.

Let's write something a bit more ambitious. Program Listings 3-3 and 3-4 detail a program that will

- read through a file
- convert all lowercase alphabetic characters to uppercase
- convert all control characters (ASCII 0-31) into a printable format
- display the result

```
put_new(f)
FILE *f;
{
 int ch;

 while( (ch=getc(f))!=EOF) {
   if(ch>='a' && ch<='z' )
    putchar( (ch-('a'-'A'));
   if(ch<=31) {
     putchar('^');
     putchar( (ch==0)?'@':(ch-'A'));
    }
   putchar(ch);
  }
 putchar('\n');
}
```

Program listing 3-3. This function will read a character from a file, process it, and display it on stdout.

```
#include <stdio.h>

main(argc,argv)
int argc;
char *argv[];
{
 FILE *f,*fopen();

 if( (f=fopen(*++argv,"r"))==NULL)
  exit();
 put_new(f);

}
```

Program listing 3-4. The main function for the convert program.

Admittedly this is a somewhat arbitrary set of operations, but ganging conversions together like this is a very common kind of processing task.

In Program Listing 3-4, we have the heart of the program. Taking a previously opened file, this function will read each character, do the appropriate processing and conversion, and put it out to stdout. Program Listing 3-5 lists the main function for this program. Note that in the case of the control characters, we first output a caret, "^", and then we use the ASCII value as a kind of index into the printable characters—ASCII 1 is control A, so a special case must be made for the 0 value.

```
make_a_num(ch)
int ch;
{
 static buf[80],where=-1;
 int num,loop;

 if(ch>='0' && ch<='9') {
   buf[++where]=(ch-'0');
   return(-1);
  }

 for(loop=0;loop<=num;loop++)
  num+=(num*ten_pow(where);

 return(num);
}

ten_pow(x)
int x;
{
 int loop,total=1;
 for(loop=1;loop<=num;loop++)
  total*=10;
 return(total);
}
```

Program listing 3-5. A function that will convert a string of digits into a number.

3.6. Character Conversion

A great deal of I/O is subject to one kind of conversion or another; most conversion is between a string of digits and the binary representation of the number they represent. Other reasonable conversions include to upper- or lowercase and even to more specialized character types, particular sets of characters, or, like our final example in the last section, where we created a printable form for the set of control characters. Program Listing 3-5 shows a function that will convert a string of digits—the characters 0,1,..,9—into a number. The function will accumulate digits up to the first nondigit character and then will start processing. Note how we can use the static storage class to implement this accumulation. This is not an entirely happy design—it only works for positive integers of moderate size—but it will serve to illustrate the kinds of conversions typical of C.

Consider a more practical example. In dealing with dollars and cents we rarely can use the float or double data type even though these are, strictly speaking, real, valued quantities. The problem is that even a double-precision value suffers from an inherent error; an error that can build over the course of a series of calculations. In most financial contexts, any such error would be unacceptable.

Many solutions to this dilemma are available. One possibility is to manipulate money as an integer value—the total number of pennies. This is usually not practical in most programming languages because of the upper limit on the size of the integer data type. But in C, we have available the long integer type which makes this a practical alternative for situations involving financial data.

Even admitting the propriety and wisdom of using integer values for money amounts, it still would be nice to be able to enter values in the familiar dollars and cents format. We certainly don't want to force the program user to have to enter money amounts as a large integer value. Further reflection reveals this is nothing more than a conversion problem. Data enter the computer as a string of digits and must be converted anyway to numeric format; thus allowing a decimal point should pose no particularly exotic or difficult problem. Program Listings 3-6 and 3-7 illustrate two complementary functions that will deal with this kind of input.

```
long take_dollar()
{
 int buff[15],where=-1,loop,ten=1,ch;
 long num=0;

 while( (ch=getchar())>='0' && ch<='9')
  buff[++where]=(ch-'0');
 if( (ch=='.') {
   if( (ch=getchar())>'0' && ch<='9')
    buff[++where]=(ch-'0');
   else
    buff[++where]=buff[++where]=0;

  for(loop=where;loop<=0;loop--) {
    num+=buff[loop]*ten;
    ten*=10;
   }
  return(num);
}
```

Program listing 3-6. A function that will accept dollars and cents input.

```
give_dollar(x)
long x;
{
 int ten=1,buff[15],where=-1,loop;

 while( (x/(ten)>0)
   ten*=10;

 for(loop=ten;loop=1;loop/=10) {
   buff[++where]=x/loop;
   x=x-(x/loop)*loop ;
 }

 for(loop=0;loop<=where;loop++) {
   putchar(buff[loop]+'0');
   if(loop=(where-2))
    putchar('.');
 }
}
```

Program listing 3-7. A function that will convert a long integer to a string of digits with a decimal point in the appropriate spot.

In Program Listing 3-6, take_dollar() accepts characters up until the next nondigit input. If this input is not a period, it appends two zeroes onto the end of the digit string. If the character is a period, it looks at the next two entries. If both are digits, they are appended to the string; but, if either character is a nondigit, two zeroes are put in their place. Note that each character is converted to a number and stored in an array buff[]. Conversion requires that we add each number in the array after multiplying it by its appropriate power of 10.

Program Listing 3-7 reverses the process. Here we must strip off each digit, convert it to the proper ASCII character value, and send it out to stdout. First, we find the largest power of 10 that will divide the number and leave a nonzero value. Starting at this value, we work our way down, stripping off each digit and, for the sake of convenience, storing it in a buffer. Conversion to the proper character value is done at the time the value is output. The location of the decimal point is found by a simple, straightforward calculation.

As a slight digression, let's discuss certain points of programming style that come up in the definition of these last two functions. In Program Listing 3-6, note the construction

```
buff[++where]=buff[++where]=0;
```

This construction shows the capacity of C for concise yet noncryptic coding. An expression built by using the assignment operator will return the value yielded by the right expression. In this case, we can use it to elegantly and, what's more important, clearly, initialize these two values on the same line. In both program listings we see again how the close relationship between characters and integers allows us to write efficient code. Because we can treat an ASCII character as its numeric code, we can easily convert between character and number. The conversion factor is the offset from the value for "0". By subtracting this value from the digit, we get a number. By adding a number to the "0" value, we get the digit associated with that number. This not only shows an instance of "sensible" arithmetic operations on characters, but it also illustrates an important programming technique. By using the value "0" instead of the actual ASCII number assigned to this digit, we make our function just a bit more portable. In fact, it will work with any character set that defines the digits 0-9 as contiguous characters.

Character conversion is not something new just discovered by us. The standard library contains a number of conversion functions. Toupper() and tolower() will return a letter shifted to upper- or lowercase, respectively. Nonalphabetic characters and those already in the proper case are passed through. These are not, strictly speaking, functions but are, rather, macro definitions usually found in a file called ctype.h. Keep this in mind because there are some operational differences between functions and macros. A particularly useful set of conversion functions are those that will convert a string of digits—and other appropriate characters—to one of the numeric data types:

`atoi()` will convert a digit string to an integer.
`atol()` converts a string to a long integer.
`atof()` converts a string to a double.

These functions will accept leading spaces or characters as well as a sign. atof() will also accept a decimal point. The standard library also contains a set of testing macros; these produce a boolean value that indicates the broad type of character that is being dealt with. Included in this group are

`isalpha()`	returns 1, if the character is alphabetic.
`isdigit()`	returns 1, if it's a digit.
`islower()`	returns 1, if it's lowercase.
`isupper()`	returns 1, if the character is uppercase.

There are other macros available to cover every category represented in the ASCII character set.

We can use these functions to simplify our take_dollar() function. Program Listing 3-8 illustrates the improved version. Note that the use of isdigit() and atol() from the standard library has greatly simplified the code. It is necessary to append the null character "\0", because atol() expects to be given a character string (we'll talk more about character strings and their manipulation in Chapter 4). The algorithm is the same as that in the first version of this function. We buffer character input until we reach a nondigit input. If this nondigit is not a decimal point, we add two zeroes and the end of string mark,"\0". Otherwise, we look at the next two characters entered, if either one is not a digit, we also fill the string with zeroes. If the next two characters are digits, they are appended and passed to atol().

```
long take_dollar()
{
 long total,atol();
 int ch,where=-1,flag=0;
 char buff[20];

 while( isdigit(ch=getchar() || ch=='.')
  if(ch!='.')
    buff[++where]=ch;
  else
    flag=1;

 if(!flag)
  buff[++where]=buff[++where]='0';

 buff[++where]='\0';

 total=atol(buff);
}
```

Program listing 3-8. An improved dollar and cents input function.

3.7. Formatted I/O

We have covered character-oriented I/O and its cognate operation, character conversion. These two operations come together in a family of functions in the standard library—the formatted I/O functions. It's a safe bet that anyone who is at all familar with C will have come in contact with its two most prominent members: printf() and scanf(). These two alone account for a large proportion of all input and output in C. They allow us to specify I/O across the full range of simple data types, from single characters up to large, double-precision floating-point numbers. Most C programmers would agree that these are enormously powerful functions; but even at that, their power is often underutilized.

The basic form of the printf() function—indeed of the whole formatted I/O family—is

```
printf(format_string,expression_list)
```

The expression list is any combination of variables, constant values, or expressions built up by using the various arithmetic operators. The format string contains, most importantly, the conversion formats for the values in the expression list. It also contains characters that are simply passed through to the output unchanged. These latter characters typically serve as prompts, titles, or identification for the values on the expression list. The output formats are indicated by the use of special characters or tokens:

%d for integer values
%f for single- or double-precision real numbers
%c for a characters value
%s for a character string

These are the most commonly used formats. There is one other special group of characters that is frequently found in the format string: the escape characters. These are typically characters that send control signals to the peripheral device. With the printf() function, the newline character, "\n", is the most commonly used of these escape characters.

The simplest use of the printf() function is probably

```
printf("hello world\n");
```

which is the contents of the beginning C programmer's first program. This use survives in more advanced programs in the form of the printing of input prompts such as

```
printf("enter value-> ");
```

Note that with this last example, the cursor will stay on the line until the presumed input function is executed. There is no particular argument against using printf() even for relatively simple output such as this; it has a simple, straightforward syntax—simpler than any function we would have to write to output even this simple prompt.

Used in its simplest form—without specifying anything more than the type of output—printf() will display the values on its expression list with sufficient space to accommodate the value: a number will leave just enough space to print out its digits plus a negative sign as the situation warrants; a character always takes up a single space; and a character string takes up as many spaces as are sufficient. We can, however, add a width specifier as a preface to the format specifier; this will indicate the number of places on the display medium allocated to that particular value. Note that this is a minimum value.

If the number is smaller than this allocated space, it will be right justified within it. If, in contrast, the number is too large for it, the space will be expanded to fill it. Program Listing 3-9 illustrates this relationship.

```
printf("%3d\n",12)      ===>  _12

printf("%3d\n",123)     ===>  123

printf("%3d\n",1234)    ===> 1234


printf("%3s\n","ab")    ===> _ab

printf("%3s\n","abc")  ===> abc

printf("%3s\n","abcd")===>abcd
```

Program listing 3-9. Illustrating some relationships between format specifications and their outputs.

A second parameter that can preface the format character is the precision; this is separated from the width specifier by a period. The precision has two distinct uses:

- With a floating-point number, it indicates the number of digits after the decimal point.
- With a string, it indicates the number of characters within the string to be printed (counting from the left).

The precision field has no meaning for character or integer formats. Left justification can be indicated by a negative immediately following the "%" marker. This is the basic operation of the printf() function, but more power awaits us.

Both the width and the precision of a format specification can be dynamic. By replacing either or both of these fields with an asterisk, their value can be obtained from the expression list. Program Listing 3-10 lists a function that will center a string expression. Using a string manipulation function, strlen(), that returns the number of characters in the string x, we calculate how many characters must be printed over the midpoint of the page (for convenience, we assume this midpoint to be column 40). By making the field wide enough to reach this point, we assure that the string will be centered (*see* Figure 3-5). The expression that indicates the field width must precede the expression that contains the value being formatted.

```
center_it(x)
char x[];
{

 printf("%*s\n",(4Ø+strlen(x)/2),x);

}

Note:    strlen() return the length of x--the numbers of characters
         up to the end of the string marker '\Ø'.
```

Program listing 3-10. A function to print a string centered on the display medium.

Modified integer values can also be specified in the format string:

`%ld` indicates a long integer value.
`%o, %x` will display an octal or hexadecimal integer (the "l" modifier may also be used here).
`%u` indicates an unsigned integer.

In the %u case, no space will be left for a possible sign value. Finally, there are two additional specifiers for floating-point numbers:

`%e` will print the value of a real number in scientific notation.
`%g` will display a number in either scientific or real format, whichever will occupy the fewest number of display columns.

This then exhausts the options available for the format string. As we shall see shortly, these same format characters, with some slight variation, are used across the entire family of formatted I/O functions.

Scanf() is the input function, complement to the printf(); it has a similar format

```
scanf(format_string, variable_list)
```

where format_string contains the specifier for each variable in the list. This list, in turn, is actually a list of pointers to variable locations. The same format characters used here were used earlier in the printf() function; however, there are slight variations that must be noted.

The "l" modifier must be prefaced to the "f" or "e" format for a double-precision floating-point number. The nonformat characters in the format string perform a different function as well; they indicate the expected delimiter characters.

```
scanf("%d/%d/%d", &mon, &day, &year)
```

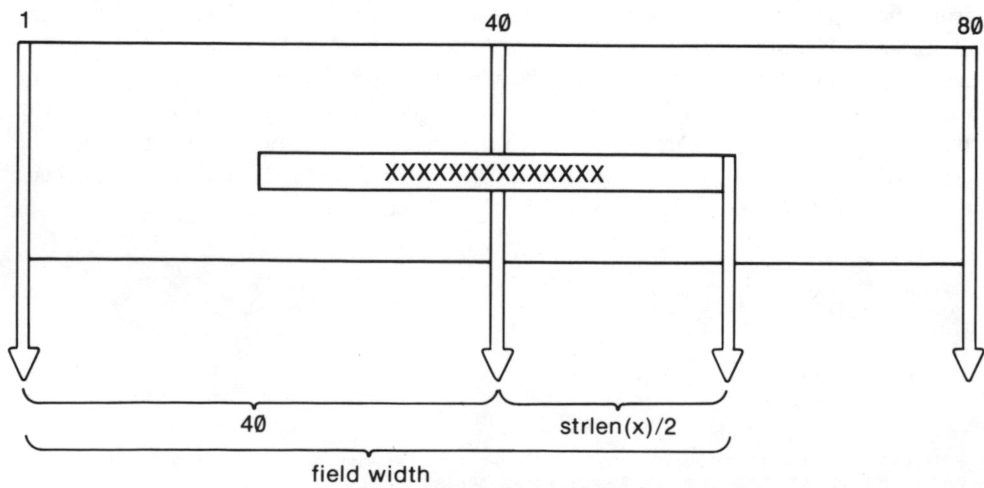

Figure 3-5. A diagram illustrating the calculation for centering the string.

will expect input of the form mm/dd/yy—for example, 01/25/85. The slashes are part of the input—it is an error not to include them. This capability allows us to add another layer of formatting to the input. White space—tabs or spaces—used as a delimiter acts generally accept any characters to separate the input values. The width specifier indicates the number of characters or digits to be entered. An asterisk preceding the width specifier indicates that no input is to be taken but a number of characters will be skipped equal to the field width whether specified or default.

Ordinarily a character string input is delimited by white space—typically a blank. Thus

```
scanf("%s",line)
```

will accept all characters up to the first blank space or tab character; this makes it difficult to use the scanf() function to enter an entire line of text unless that line contains nothing but letters, numbers, or other printing characters. However, the syntax of the format string does allow us a way around this problem. We can define a set of characters that will govern the input of the string. This capability is only defined for the characters string. The format for this kind of specification is

```
%[xxx..xxx]
```

where each x represents a character to be included in the set. When a scanf() function evaluates this type of format, it will start accepting input and will continue to accept it as long as the entered character is one that is contained in the specified set. Leading white space is not ignored. Well-defined ranges of values can be specified by connecting the first and last elements of the range. Thus

```
scanf("%[0-9A-Za-z ]",line)
```

will accept a line of alphanumeric data including spaces but excluding any control or punctuation characters. If the first character in the specification is a circumflex (caret), "^", then the set performs the complementary function: It accepts all input until one of the specified characters is entered.

```
scanf("%[^\n]",line)
```

will accept all characters up to a newline character—the entire line. Note that this format will do more than the previous one. It is often easier to specify a wide range of possible values using the circumflex. We can also specify a field width in addition to a set of acceptable characters.

Printf() and scanf() deal with stdout and stdin. Within this family are also two pseudo-I/O functions; these perform the same kinds of conversions we've been talking about but within main memory. Sprintf() puts its converted output into a string variable. sscanf() takes values from a character string and puts its converted values into one or more variables whose addresses are found on its variable list. The general forms of these functions are

```
sprintf(out_string,format_string,expression_list)
sscanf(input_string,format_string,variable_list).
```

The syntax rules for the format string are identical to printf() and scanf(). These two functions are valuable because they allow us to do in memory what is not easily or cleanly done in any other way. For example, they also make it possible to create printer or screen images that can be saved and then displayed all at once rather than piece by piece as they are being built. Capabilities like this make for a better user interface.

Program Listing 3-11 lists an improved version of our earlier function to print out a dollar and cents amount. The function is much simpler with the use of sscanf() and printf(). The only processing necessary is to move the last two digits over to make room for the decimal point. We do not use the increment or decrement operator when manipulating the character array, dollars[]. The variable "where" is being used as an anchor value—as something to count against—not as a cursor. We want to set the value at the end of the string and count from there, not move from there. With C it is sometimes as important to know when not to use powerful features as when to use them.

```
give_dollar(x)
long x;
{
 int where;
 char dollars[15];

 sscanf(dollars,"%ld",x);

 dollars[(where=strlen(dollars)+2)='\Ø';
 dollars[(where-1)]=dollars[where-2];
 dollars[(where-2)=dollars[where-3];
 dollars[where-3]='.';

 printf("$%s\n",dollars);

}
```

Program listing 3-11. An improved version of give_dollar.

3.8 Additional File Manipulation Functions

At the beginning of this chapter we sketched out some basic techniques of disk file manipulation: how to open and close a file and basic character-by-character I/O. The standard library offers us a selection of additional, more advanced, file-oriented functions to supplement our basic repertoire. Even though the C file system is conceptually simple, with the additional capabilities provided by these functions, we can build upon it, any arbitrarily complex data storage system.

The formatted I/O family of functions is represented by two file-oriented members: fprintf() and fscanf(). These two functions operate in the same way as the rest of this family, the only difference is that they are directed to a file rather than to stdin, stdout, or a memory location. The general forms of these functions are

```
fprintf(file_variable,format_string,expression_list)
fscanf(file_variable,format_string,variable_list).
```

File_variable is a pointer variable created by a previous call to fopen(). Formatted input and output is easier, particularly if we are manipulating objects larger than a single character. It is also useful to produce printer or display images on disk for later processing.

A series of macro definitions in the stdio.h file will aid us in determining and dealing with some common error conditions that may occur during file processing. While not strictly an error condition, feof(file_variable) will indicate whether or not an EOF mark has been read in the file pointed to by file_variable. Ferror(file_variable) will indicate the presence or absence of an error condition during the process of accessing the file in question. An error condition must be cleared by using clearerr(file_variable) or it will last until the file is closed; this could give an erroneous result masking subsequent errors.

Finally, the standard library offers us support for direct access to files. Direct access—sometimes called, paradoxically, random access—allows us to move to an arbitrary position in the file and start processing from there. This action is in contrast to sequential access where each object in the file must be accessed in turn, and to get at the *n*th object, you must access all the objects from the first through *n*-1. This kind of direct access is at the basis of most data storage systems.

Two complementary operations need to be done to create and maintain a direct access file. We have to be able to locate our current position in the file, and we have to be able to move to a particular place in that file. Ftell() performs the former function, and fseek() performs the latter function.

```
ftell(file_variable)
```

returns the current position of the file cursor in the file. This position is the number of bytes from the beginning of the file.

```
fseek(file_variable,position,direction)
```

positions the file cursor a number of bytes equal to position from the reference point. The direction parameter indicates the location of this reference point:

If it's equal to	*The reference point is*
0	the beginning of the file,
1	the current position of the file cursor, and
2	the end of the file

We can illustrate the use of some of these functions with an example.

One way to aid in retrieving data from a file is to create one or more index files. In its simplest form, an index is a file that contains one of the fields from the main file as well as the position in that file of the rest of the data associated with that particular field. Figure 3-6 illustrates this relationship. The arrows are a traditional graphical device to illustrate connections between entries in the index and the main file. The chief advantage of this kind of organization is ease of access. The index file is smaller and can be searched more rapidly. Frequently, indices are sorted, and, since it is possible to have an index on any field in the file, we can create the functional equivalent of a file sorted on all of its fields—taken to this extreme, such a file is said to be fully inverted.

Program Listings 3-12 through 3-15 illustrate a program that will allow the user to enter address data—name, street, city, and state—into a file and then build an index for that file on the name field. The program is defined across four files, one for each functional unit. The main() function is simply an anchor point to call the add_data() or build_index() functions as desired by the user. The file opening function, newfile(), may be considered a bit thin to have a module of its own, but we must remember that the file system functions are the most dependent on the underlying implementation and are also most frequently subject to enhancement and optimization. Thus, they are the most volatile functions in a program.

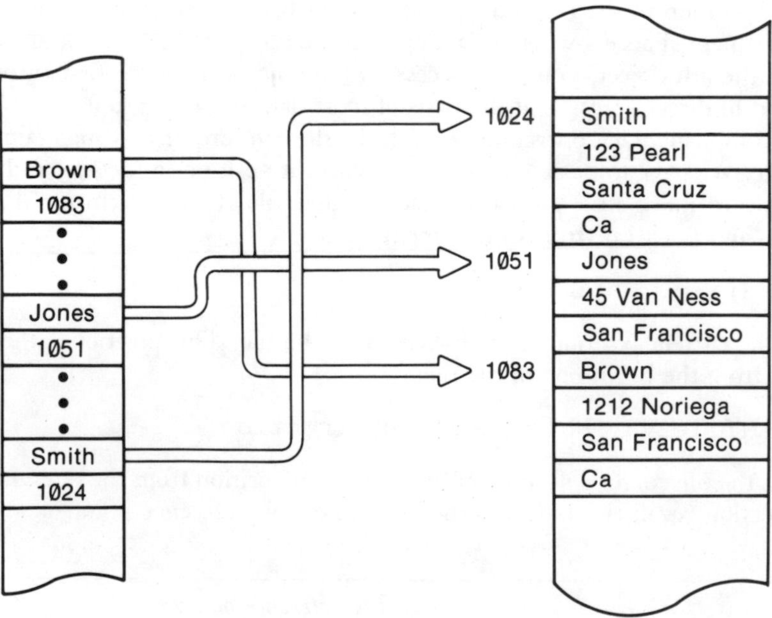

Figure 3-6. A diagram illustrating the relationship between a file and one of its indices.

```
#include <stdio.h>

main()
{
 int ch;

 while( (ch=menu()) )
  switch (ch) {
    case 'e':
     exit();
    case 'a':
     add_data();
     break;
    case 'b':
     build_index();
     break;
  }
}

menu()
{
 int ch;
 printf(" e(xit)\na(dd data)\nb(uild index)\n-->");
 scanf("%d",&ch);
 return(ch);
}
```

Program listing 3-12. Contents of file main.c containing the main function and the menu function for the program.

```
#include <stdio.h>

get_record(nam,str,city,st)
char nam[],str[],city[],st[];
{
 printf("name...");
 gets(nam);
 if(nam[Ø]=='\n')
  return(Ø);
 printf("street...");
 gets(str);
 if(str[Ø]=='\n')
  return(Ø);
 printf("city...");
 gets(city);
 if(city[Ø]=='\n')
  return(Ø);
 printf("state...");
 gets(state);
 if(state[Ø]=='\n')
  return(Ø);
 return(1);
}
```

Program listing 3-13. Contents of file faccess.c. This contains the file opening function.

```
#include <stdio.h>


add_data()
{
 static char mode[]="a";
 char name[20],street[20],city[20],state[2],fname[15];
 *FILE *f,*fopen();

 printf("file name...");
 scanf("%s",fname);

 if((f=fopen(fname,mode))==NULL) {
  printf("unable to open file\n");
  return(0);
 }
 while( get_record(name,street,city,state))
  fprintf(f,"%s%s%s%s",name,street,city,state);
 fclose(f);
 return(1);
 }
```

Program listing 3-14. Contents of file addat.c. This contains the functions that put new data on the end of the file.

```
#include <stdio.h>

*FILE *f,*i,*fopen();

build_index()
{
 long pos;
 char fname[15],iname[15],name[20],street[20],city[20],state[2];

 if( !(create_index(fname,iname)))
  return(0);

 do {
    pos=ftell(f);
    fscanf(f,"%s%s%s%s",name,street,city,state);
    fprintf(i,"%s%ld",name,pos);
 }
 while (!feof(f));

 fclose(f);
 fclose(i);
}

create_index(fname,iname)
char fname[15],iname[15];
{
 static char mode="r";
 int loop,ind=0;

printf("file name...");
scanf("%s",fname);

if((f=fopen(fname,mode))==NULL)
  return(0);

 iname[0]='i';
 for(loop=0;loop<=strlen(fname);loop++)
  iname[++ind]=fname[loop];

 mode="w";
 if((f=fopen(iname,mode))==NULL)
      return(0);
 return(1);
}
```

Program listing 3-15. Contents of file build.c. This contains the functions that will create the index file.

Add_data() is a straightforward function. We ask for the requisite values and then write them out to the file by using the formatted output functions. The auxiliary function get_record() helps to keep add_data() free of unnecessary complication. Build_index() reads through the main file—presumably created by add_data—to the end. Note the use of the feof() macro in the while statement. In this loop the ftell() function is executed just before each read, and this value along with the name field is put on the index file. Again we use formatted I/O functions. It is necessary to use ftell() because each of our "data records" is of variable length. For data retrieval, this number will be given to an fseek() function. Note here too we used a helper function, create_index(), to avoid complications.

3.9. Summary

In this chapter we explored the I/O functions supplied in the standard library. Of course, we must recognize that these are only a part of this library. There are a wide range of mathematical functions as well. Many implementations supply specialized libraries containing graphics routines and even data base functions. Still the core of the standard library is I/O. Once we know how to integrate these functions into our programs, it will not be difficult to extend these techniques to more specialized modules.

Perhaps the most important thing to remember from these discussions is an understanding of how I/O works. Most programming languages shield the programmer from the details of these operations, C does not. But it does supply us with a range of functions that lets us deal with the outside world at just the level necessary to solve our problem.

The flexibility and power of the standard library functions should be apparent; it is not always so to a beginner—many times it just seems confusing. This chapter should have removed that confusion.

=4=

Using Structured Data Types

Central to all useful programming is the mathematical notion of mapping. Computer programs are written to solve real-world problems. Some way must be found to convert the values and parameters of these real-world problems into a form that can be manipulated by the computer; a machine representation of these values must be found. This representation must map these values onto the simple machine word whether 8, 16, or 32 bits. The first such mapping produces the simple data types: char, int, and float (along with their modified versions such as long or double). For the most part, these data types consist of simple aggregations or subdivisions of the bare computer word. Structured data types give us another layer of representation more abstract and closer to the entity that is being modelled.

In this chapter we focus on the three main structured data types: the array, a homogeneous collection of values; the character string; and the structure, a heterogeneous collection of data of varying types. Our main goal is to make you explicitly aware of what these advanced data types are, how they are defined, and how they can be used. Attention is also given to the union, a variant form of the structure, and the enum data types.

Goals:

- To understand explicitly the mapping process that results in a computer representation of a real-world value
- To understand what a structured data type is, how it is built up from other, often simpler, data types, and how it can be used to model real-world entities
- To review arrays and how they are constructed
- To review the character string data type
- To review structures, and how they are defined and declared
- To review the union and enum data types

4.1. The Mapping Relation

The business of programming is to solve real-world problems. To do this, it is necessary to represent or model parts of this real world inside the computer:

- The assets of a firm might be represented as a series of integer values.
- The electrical current inside an electronic circuit could be a real number value.
- The holdings of a library would be stored as a group of characters.

All of these methods bring these real objects into the computer in a form that can be manipulated. Mathematicians have long been familiar with this process—mapping. We are mapping one set of objects—those from the outside world—onto another set inside the computer memory. We are setting up a correspondence between one set of entities and the other (Figure 4-1). We are actually doing more. We are making a claim. We are saying that there is a significant similarity between these two groups of objects, that the "information" content is preserved when we make this translation. We are saying that when we represent the week's sales as a series of integers, when we map the circuit current into a real number, and when we store a person's name and address as a series of characters, we can

- retrieve the data and recreate the situation from that data
- manipulate and transform these new objects and then translate them back into real-world situations

And we are saying that these transformations and manipulations make sense. This statement is really the central problem. Because these mappings and transformations are well-understood mathematical operations, the results are guaranteed to be consistent. It is up to us to make sure that they are sensible, that they represent actual real-world situations. Much computer science research and programming practice revolve around this nontrivial task.

What we need to do is take the basic units and entities offered to us by the architecture of the machine and use these as basic building blocks to store values and create representative structures. However, we must be aware that a considerable amount of transformation has already occurred before we get to these basic units. The smallest such unit that we usually consider in C is the byte; this is an 8-bit unit primarily used to store one character. On all but the very smallest machines, however, the byte must yield to the "word" as the smallest unit of access. By access we mean a single memory fetch. Only very small computers organize their main store in terms of bytes. It is sometimes useful to think of the byte as the smallest storage location for a character and the word as the smallest numerical storage unit. The size of a computer word may be the most variable quantity in all of programming; it is emphatically machine dependent. Typical word lengths vary from 16 bits to more than 60 bits. However, the most common word sizes are 16 and 32 bits. The word size has a direct effect on the various kinds of integer values—short, long, and

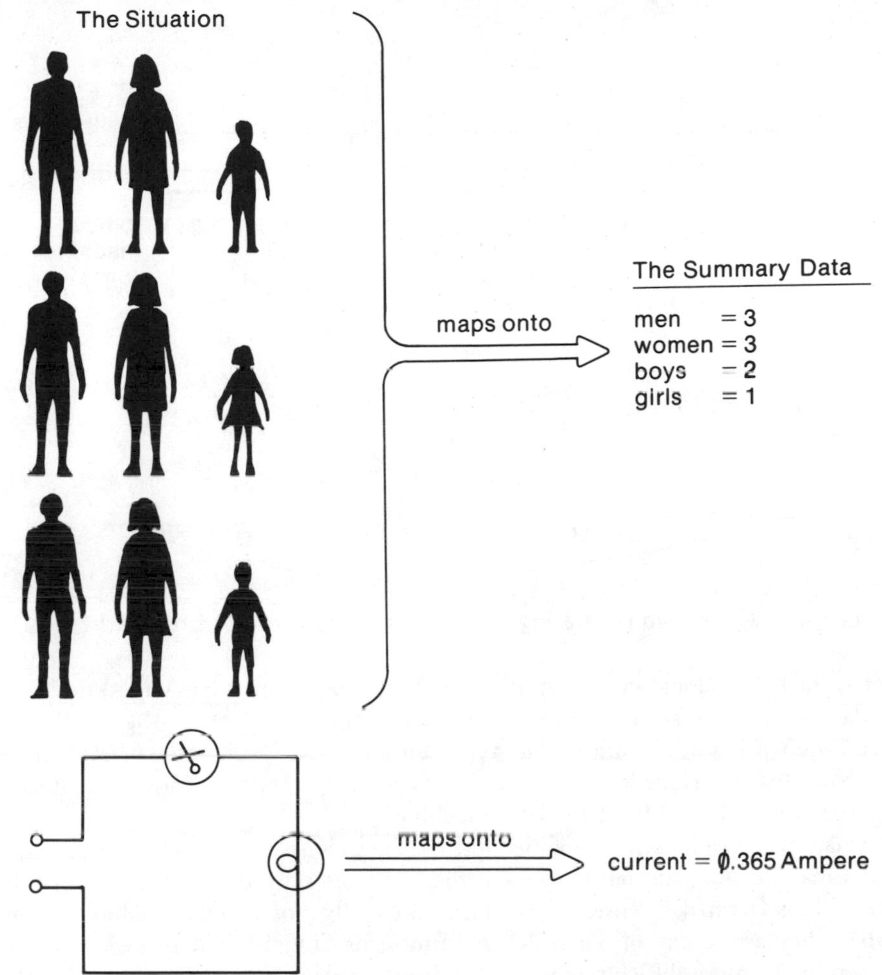

Figure 4-1. Some examples of mapping relations.

unsigned—offered by C and can be a headache for the programmer; this is one of C's more glaring defects.

Both the byte and, perhaps less obviously, the word are themselves constructs built up from a more primitive notion—the binary digit or bit. The bit is itself a mathematical representation of the electronic on-off switches that are the physical reality of a modern computer. Figure 4-2 illustrates this relationship. Although it's useful to keep this diagram in mind, we must be aware of its limitations. C gives us tools—the bit manipulation operators and bit field data type—to break through this neat hierarchy down to the bare bit level. Most high-level languages do not offer this capability.

What makes the word so significant is that it is almost always the minimum unit of memory access—one fetch cycle will bring a word into the CPU for processing—therefore, it is the basic unit of memory storage as well. As a natural consequence of

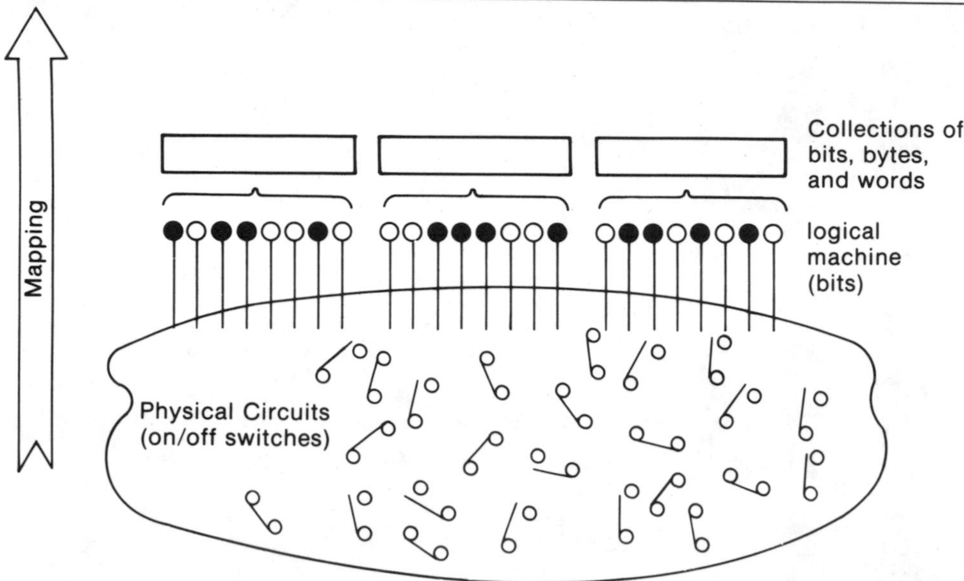

Figure 4-2. A diagram illustrating the derivative nature of words and bytes.

these two facts, C, along with most other modern progamming languages, defines its basic data types in term of the machine word. Figure 4-3 shows the relationship between the word and the simple data types for a typical 16-bit and 32-bit minicomputer. Note that we consider that basic data types are, in fact, already several layers of organization removed from the bare machine.

Int, char, and float and their modified forms—long, double, and such—exhibit only a limited capability for data representation; they support only the simplest of mapping relations. This fact makes sense. These objects are really closer to the machine architecture than they are to any of our real-world problems. This simplicity makes our task correspondingly more difficult as we try to break our problem data down into units sufficiently small to be compatible with the capacity of our building blocks. Since data storage is simple, the complexity must be exported to the program code itself, thus leading to awkward programming constructs; this problem isn't purely aesthetic. Awkward code is difficult to debug and even more difficult to maintain. Consider, for example, the input of a string of characters. Without a character string data type, each character must be entered and processed, one character at a time.

To remedy this situation, C allows the programmer to define any of a number of "structured" data types. These are aggregations or collections of other data types. Collections are precisely defined with more of an eye toward the problem set being modelled than toward the computer hardware. Their relationship to the outside world is simpler, more straightforward. The three main structured types are

- the array—storing homogenous values in contiguous memory locations
- the structure—which consists of named fields of heterogenous data types
- the character string—really a special kind of character array

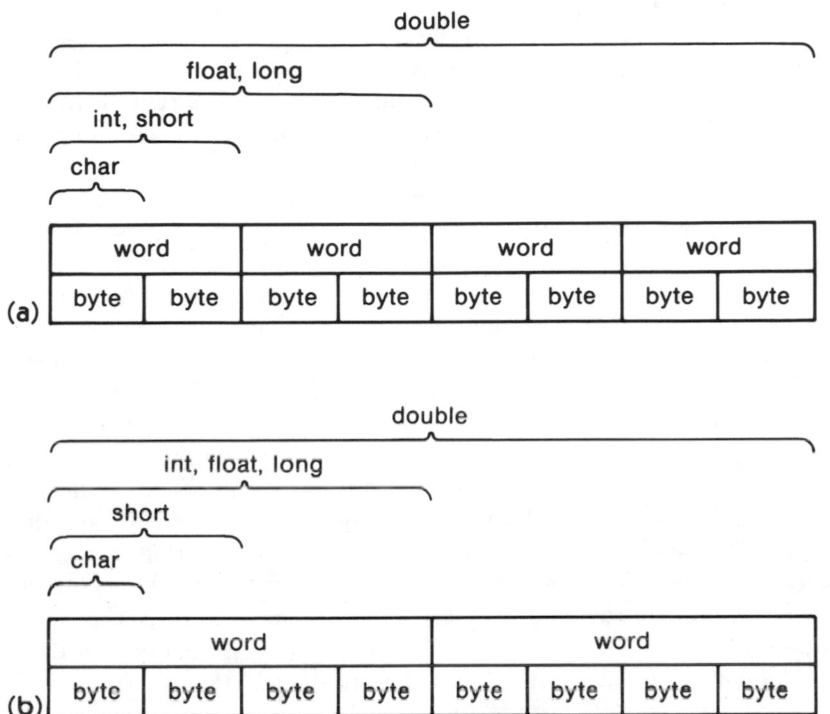

Figure 4-3. A diagram showing the mapping of simple data types onto the machine word. (a) is a typical 16 bit mapping, (b), 32 bits.

These, and the derivative types, unions; bit-fields, and enum, have a dual nature, an inside and an outside. They can be treated as a single unit, moved about, for example, as a whole, but we can always go "inside" and deal with the parts of the whole.

Another layer of structure can be created by using these structured data types as building blocks. This group consists of the "linked" data types—linked lists and trees—and other high-level constructs, chief among which we find queues and stacks. We have already used the notion of a stack in some of our examples. (These very interesting "linked" structures will be discussed in a later chapter.)

A structured data type or, indeed, any data type is a mediator between the real value that is the object of our programming and the representation of that object in a form that a program can use. The structured data type, in contrast to the simple, more basic one, trades greater complexity and overhead on the computer side of the equation for a smoother translation process on the real-world side. The structured data type is more like the object than like the collection of bits that will represent this object inside the computer.

The data type is another design element that must be used by the programmer to create a solution. Too often "data type" is considered a passive notion—just a storage strategy built into the machine and an unchangeable fact. The program is the algorithm, a kind of objective and absolute mathematical entity resident in some higher realm of being. The data types, then, are the unfortunate, dirty details that must be used to implement this pure, other-worldly algorithm. This is pure nonsense. How we store data has a great effect on the program and its implementation. First of all, the choice of a particular algorithm will be affected by the data types involved. For example, sorting a large array of values requires a high-performance sort routine, whereas a linked list, containing the same set of values, might be performed with one of the simpler sorting algorithms. More importantly, data types are not just passive constructions, but they involve the computer in actions the same as statements in a programming language. An integer is accessed differently from a real number, which is different from the way we deal with arrays or structure values. A program that uses simple data types will be very different from one that uses more complex ones.

Program Listings 4-1 and 4-2 illustrate, in a simple way, how the choice of data type can affect the algorithm. The task here is to assign a value to a particular storage location; these locations could, for example, represent weekly sales. The code in Program Listing 4-1, while not complex, is lengthy; it must contain an action clause for each of the seven separate variable locations being used. Contrast this to the function definition in Program Listing 4-2. We use an array to store these seven values. This function is dramatically simpler. The same manipulation of system entities is occurring in both cases—seven locations are set aside to store integer values. Once the proper location is chosen, that memory location is accessed and updated with the new value. But in the former case, this is done explicitly; in the latter case, the functionality is built into the data type, an array. Not only is the function code simpler but the addressing mechanism of the array is optimal; it's a faster algorithm!

```
int x0,x1,x2,x3,x4,x5,x6;

put_data(index,value)
int index,value;
{
 switch (index) {
  case 0:
   x0=value;
   break;
  case 1:
   x1=value;
   break;
  case 2:
   x2=value;
   break;
  case 3:
   x3=value;
   break;
  case 4:
   x4=value;
   break;
  case 5:
   x5=value;
   break;
  case 6:
   x6=value;
   break;
  }
 return;
}
```

Program Listing 4-1. Putting data in a particular variable.

```
int x[7];

put_data(index,value)
int index,value;
{
 if(index<=7)
  x[index]=value;
 return;
}
```

Program Listing 4-2. A simplification of the operation in Program Listing 4-1 obtained by using a structured variable.

Program Listings 4-1 and 4-2 illustrate the kind of problem that can arise when data types are treated as passive, given objects and not made an integral part of the design. The result is code that is unnecessarily complex, as we try to "shoe-horn" a complex situation into our basic storage structures (*see* Figure 4-4). We are reinventing many of the features already available in the language.

Using structured data types, where appropriate, is a complement to the other structured programming aids offered by C—separate compilation, data abstraction, and modularization. The same arguments that apply to these capabilities, apply here. Any efficiency added to the programming design process will produce better programs more rapidly.

4.2. Arrays

Probably the most commonly used structured data type is the array. Arrays in one form or another are found in every programming language, even assembly language. An array consists of a set of contiguous memory locations; thus, it has the same basic structure as memory itself. This "chunk" of memory is divided into individual members or cells. Each cell is accessed by an offset value from the first location, the index. We can move the entire array around (specifically, we can pass it whole to a function) or we can manipulate the individual locations within the array. Since each individual member is identified by this offset value, we can dynamically access each cell during program execution. But the chief advantage of the array type is that it allows us to move large blocks of data within a program (*see* Figure 4-5).

As with any data type, an array must be declared before it can be used. This declaration will also set the cell size—the number of memory locations set aside for each one—and the ultimate size of the entire array. The general form of this declaration is

```
⟨type⟩ ⟨array_name⟩ [⟨maximum_number_of_cells⟩];
```

where ⟨type⟩ is any simple or structured data type except FILE, ⟨array_name⟩ is any well-formed variable identifier, and ⟨maximum_number_of_cells⟩ is the total number of locations into which the array will be divided. The total size of the array is a function of the total number of cells, and the size of each one is dictated by their data type. Some examples of array declarations are

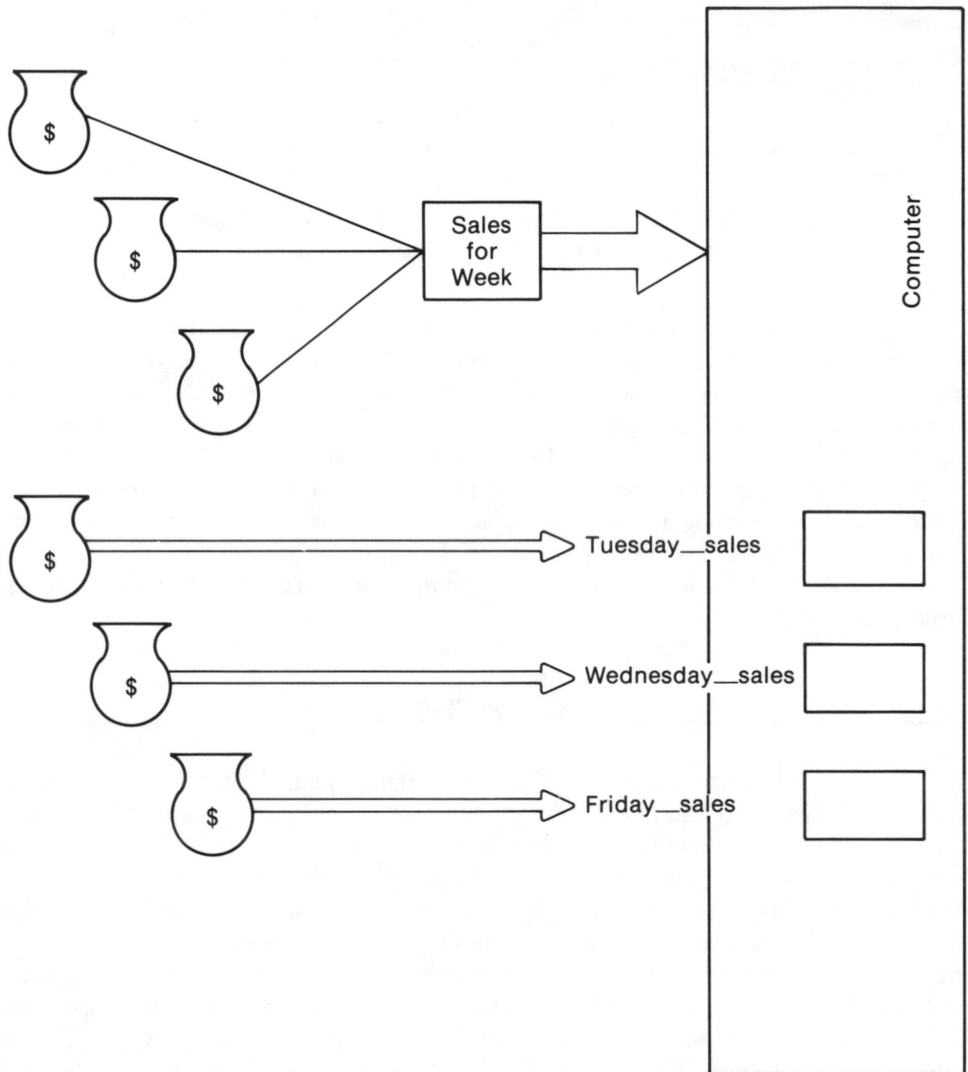

Figure 4-4. Diagram illustrating how a structured data type mediates our real-world constructs to simplify its representation in the machine.

```
int x[10];
double y[50];
```

The first statement declares an array of 10 integers; the latter statement dictates an array of 50 double-precision floating-point numbers.

Certain interesting properties of the array make it a powerful addition to our set of programming tools. Primary among these capabilities is that arrays can be passed, as a whole, to a function. What's even more important, is that it is the address of the

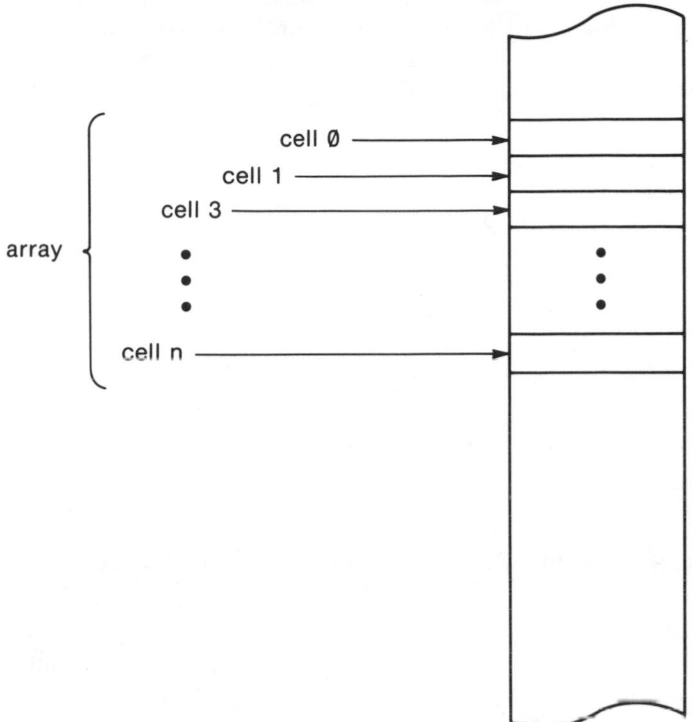

Figure 4-5. An array is a contiguous block of memory locations divided into individual cells.

array that's actually passed. As a result, changes made to members of the array in the function are reflected back in the calling function; this is not the case with ordinary parameters. We say that the relationship of array parameters to a function is "call by reference." What this means is that we can use an array as another vehicle for returning values from a function.

The array is probably one of the most well-understood structure types, but what can we do with it? What kinds of problems will it help us to solve?

Two dissimilar problem sets can use an array effectively as a representative data structure. First, there are sets of mathematical data that naturally fall within the list-like structure of an array. The processing of statistical data is a prime example, as is any situation where we are doing arithmetic analysis of a large collection of data or processing an irregularly sized collection of data sets. Program Listing 4-3 illustrates such a program. The relative frequency of a set of double-precision, floating-point numbers is being calculated; we are counting how many of these values fall into each of four predefined groups: ptile25, ptile50, ptile75, and those values greater then ptile75. We're removing some of the detail of the raw data but enhancing its information content. Applications of this technique might include a summary of test scores on an examination or, in a manufacturing plant, the number of electronic components that meet various grading criteria. The function is passed as an array, x[], with the raw data, as well as an array dist[], to contain the sorted values and the variable size, to indicate the number of occupied cells in x[]. The function loops through the raw data, and the if-else-if construction ensures that the proper cell in dist[] is incremented.

```
void freq_finder(x,dist,size)
double x[],dist[];
int size;
{
 int idx=1;

 while(++idx<=size)
  if(x[idx]>ptile25)
    dist[3]++;
  else if (x[idx]>ptile50)
    dist[2]++;
  else if (x[idx]>ptile50)
    dist[1]++
  else
    dist[0]++;
}
```

Program Listing 4-3. A function to calculate the relative frequencies of a set of data.

Several points should be noted about the function shown in Program Listing 4-3. Observe that we didn't specify the size of either x[] or dist[]. Recall that arrays are passed to a function "by reference." Only the address of the first element of the array is actually sent to the function. Any changes made to one of the elements is made to the copy back in the calling function. We don't need to specify the extent of the array because no new allocation is being done; the old array is the one being worked on.

Remember, too, that C doesn't do range checking on subscripts, so there is really no reason to cross specify. Somewhere, however, an array declaration must contain a specifier for the number of cells. Somewhere the memory space for the array must be allocated. Then, all other references to it are made through this address pointer. We'll discuss this again when we turn our attention to the subject of pointers in the next chapter.

In our current function, we have to know how many pieces of raw data we have; this is why we must pass in the parameter "size". With so few frequency categories, it may seem indulgent of us to create an array of four cells to store this information when four ordinary variables would do. But by using an array, we can easily pass this information back to the calling program; this would be difficult otherwise.

The other major use of the array data type is a result of its list-like structure. This structure mirrors the structure of memory itself. We can use this similarity to our advantage whenever we have to set up a memory buffer. This application is typically done with an array of characters if we are dealing with an I/O buffer; otherwise, an array of the appropriate data type is used. We have already used an array in this manner. Back in Chapter 2 (*see* Program Listing 2-7) we implemented a stack by using an array of floating point numbers. In a later example (*see* Program Listings 2-11 and 2-12), we defined two stacks, one number, the other character, in this way.

Program Listing 4-4 lists a function that will accept and buffer a page of character input. We are defining a page here, somewhat arbitrarily, as 60 lines of 80 characters per line which comes out to 4800 characters per page. We assign this value to the token MAXCHARS through a define macro. We also define a break input, BRK, as Ctrl-Y (octal 031) to allow us to stop input before the end of a full page is reached. The function will accept input, one character at a time, until either the cursor, mark, reaches MAXCHARS, or a BRK is entered. Each character is placed in the next position in the array pbuffer[]. If a backspace is entered, mark is decremented, thus erasing the last character entered. At the end of the input, the value of mark is returned; this value should contain the total number of characters entered. If no characters have been entered, mark will have its initial value of -1, and the conditional statement in the return will ensure that a more reasonable 0 value is sent back.

```
#define BRK '\031'
#define MAXCHARS 4800

page_in(pbuffer)
char pbuffer[MAXCHARS];
{
 char ch;
 int mark=-1;

 while ( (ch=getchar())!=BRK || mark<MAXCHARS)
    if(ch=='\b')
     mark--;
    else
     pbuffer(++mark)=ch;

 return( mark==-1 ? 0 : mark);
}
```

Program Listing 4-4. A function to buffer a page of input.

Whenever it is necessary to set aside a section of memory, the array of characters is the data structure that we use. The reasons are simple. A character is one of the smallest units of storage available to us. And many computer systems divide their memory in terms of bytes; this is true even when the unit of access is larger—the computer knows how to extract a byte. Perhaps more importantly, once we've set aside these locations in memory, we can manipulate them in many interesting ways. We can assign a pointer variable to the beginning of the array and just treat it as if it were an unstructured block of memory. Once we do, we can even change its type by using the cast operator. The details of these operations will be covered in Chapter 5. Here we should just note that the array data type has more power and flexibility than might be imagined at first glance.

4.3. Character Strings

The array of characters holds a special place in the C programmer's repertoire. As we saw in the last section, this method reserves large sections of memory for later use as a storage location or perhaps as an I/O buffer. The value of the character array goes even deeper. We can define, on top of it, a new data type that represents one of the most important of all data structures within programming, the character string.

Character strings are found at the heart of all software. As we saw in Chapter 3, almost all I/O is character oriented. A computer program starts out as a text file, a file composed of character strings. The C compiler performs a kind of text processing when it creates object code from the program's source statements. Of course, ordinary text processing programs—word processors, text formatters and the like—have become ubiquitous, not only in the workplace but also in the home. The primacy of the character string is assured.

The character string is not just a simple one-dimensional array of characters, but it is a data type in its own right and with its own characteristics. Its chief distinguishing mark is that it is dynamic. At different points in the program's execution, the character string will not only have different values but a different configuration as well; it is this feature that distinguishes it from a simple array. At one point a string variable may have the value "this is only a test" with a length of 19 characters; at another point, a string variable may have the value "John Smith" with a length of only 10. Reassigning the value will erase the previous assignment—there are no leftover characters, not like a simple array where the number of cells is static.

How do we create a character string in C? How do we manipulate a static array of characters so that it becomes a dynamic data structure? These tasks are done primarily through the string manipulation functions. Passing an array to one or more of these functions is what defines it as a character string. This underscores our point, made earlier, that the notion of a data type is not a passive one but includes the operations that can be performed on it. Within the context of these string functions, a one-dimensional array of characters becomes a character string.

The dynamic nature of a character string dictates that its length become a syntactical element. We have to be able, somehow, to know where the end of the string is for a given value. Remember, this end point changes. By convention, the last character is a special "end-of-string" marker. The symbol for this is "\0", the null character (octal 000). Any character array that ends with this particular value will be treated by the string functions as a valid character string. Figure 4-6 summarizes some of what we've been talking about here. Note that it is the position of the first end-of-string marker that determines the length of the string.

There is no special declaration for a character string; it is simply declared as an array of characters

```
char ‹string_name›[‹size›];
```

where ‹string_name› is any legal variable identifier, and ‹size› is an integer value indicating the maximum number of cells. Thus

```
char line_buf[80];
```

will create a character string that will accept a maximum of 79 characters—one position needs to be reserved for the end of line mark.

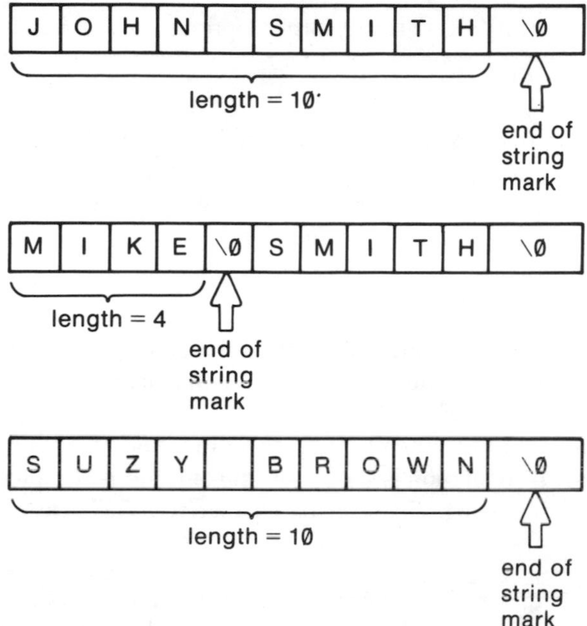

Figure 4-6. A diagram illustrating the one-to-one relationship between a real-world entity and its representative structure.

The Standard Library contains a complete and useful set of string manipulation functions. Perhaps it's best to start with string I/O. The basic string input statement is

```
gets(buff);
```

This function will fill buff with a line from stdin. The line being typed in is terminated by a newline character but this is replaced by "\0" in buff. This process is simple and unadorned line-by-line input, no formatting and no conversion. Gets() will return a pointer to its parameter, buff in our example. There is a complementary function

```
puts(buff);
```

which will send the contents of buff[] to stdout. The "\0" character will be replaced by a newline character on output. There is a cognate pair for disk file I/O

```
fgets(‹buff›,‹length›,‹file_variable›)
fputs(‹buff›,‹file_variable›)
```

where ‹buff› is a character string, ‹length› is an integer value, and ‹file_variable› points to an open file. Note a slight difference in the operation of fgets(). This function accepts a string of up to ‹length› characters. These are our unadorned string I/O statements.

Both scanf() and printf() have string format options

```
scanf("%s",buff);
```

The address-of operator, "&", need not be used as the name of the array—in this case buff—without brackets. This operator contains the address of the first member of the array. As we noted in Chapter 3, scanf() will accept characters up to the first whitespace, including, by the way, the newline character, "\n". For output

```
printf("%s\n",buff)
```

will send characters out to stdout until a "\0" character is reached. Recall, as well, that this feature is true for the entire family of formatted I/O: sscanf(), sprintf(), fscanf(), and fprintf().

Program Listing 4-5 illustrates a typical string function using some of the features we've talked about. Its operation is simple. A line of input is accepted into buf[], then the program scans this string, character by character, and checks one of three possible conditions

- A nonblank character. This is copied over to lin[], a flag value is reset to 0.
- An initial blank character. This, too, is copied to lin[] but the flag is set.
- A consecutive blank. This is not copied to the output string.

```
next_line(lin)
char lin[80];
{
 char buf[80];
 int flag=0, mark=0,point;

 while (buf(mark++!='\0')
    if( buf(mark)==' ' && flag=1)
      continue;
    else if (buf(mark)==' ' && flag=0 ) {
        flag=1;
        lin[point++]=buf[mark];
      }
    else {
       lin[point++]=buf[mark];
       flag=0;
     }

   lin[point]='\0';
   return(--point);
}
```

Program Listing 4-5. A function that will accept a line of input and squeeze out all extra blank spaces.

After buf[] has been completely scanned, the last position is assigned a null value and the length—the number of characters excluding the end marker—is returned to the calling function. The "continue" statement after the first if clause is unnecessary, it could be replaced by the null statement, but, it is tidy: It will skip directly to the next iteration of the while loop.

Since the length of a character string is an important parameter, the Standard Library supplies us with

```
strlen(⟨string_name⟩)
```

to provide this quantity. ⟨string_name⟩ is any valid character string identifier. This function, shown in Program listing 4-6, will return the number of characters in the string up to, but not including, the first null character. Strlen() is a very simple function (discussed later) but extremely useful nonetheless.

```
strlen(buf)
char buf[];
{
 int mark=-1;

 while(buf[++mark]!='\0')
    ;
 return(--mark);

}
```

Program Listing 4-6. An implementation of strlen().

Because the character string data type is not basic to C, but is rather built up and defined on top of the character array, assignments and comparisons cannot be done directly by using the operators that work for the other data types. We cannot just set one string variable equal to another, nor can we compare two strings by using the relational operators that serve for numeric and single-character values. We must again resort to functions defined in our all-powerful Standard Library. This is not as much of an inconvenience as it might at first glance seem. By separating these capabilities into separate functions, we carry only the overhead that we need. A high-level language with a built-in character string must carry this overhead in all of its programming code.

String assignment is accomplished by two cognate functions. One,

```
strcpy(⟨string1⟩,⟨string2⟩)
```

will copy ⟨string2⟩ character by character into ⟨string1⟩ up to and including the end of string mark. The companion function

```
strncpy(⟨string1⟩,⟨string2⟩,⟨length⟩)
```

will copy the first ⟨length⟩ characters from ⟨string2⟩ to ⟨string1⟩. An end-of-string mark will be affixed to the end of ⟨string1⟩. If the length of ⟨string2⟩ is less then ⟨length⟩, ⟨string1⟩ will be truncated to the actual length of ⟨string2⟩.

Another operation sometimes performed on character strings is to attach or concatenate two of them to produce a single, longer one. As with strcpy(), we have a pair of functions to accomplish this:

```
strcat(⟨string1⟩,⟨string2⟩)
```

will remove the end-of-string marker from ⟨string1⟩, attach the contents of ⟨string2⟩ to it, and place a new end-of-string mark after the last location. A copy of ⟨string2⟩ is appended to ⟨string1⟩. ⟨string2⟩, thus, maintains its integrity; only ⟨string1⟩ is altered.

The statement

```
strncat(⟨string1⟩,⟨string2⟩,⟨length⟩)
```

attaches a copy of ⟨string2⟩ of at most ⟨length⟩ characters to the end of ⟨string1⟩. Again only ⟨string1⟩ is altered. Both functions return a pointer to ⟨string1⟩.

Relational operations are handled by the functions strcmp() and strncmp(). Each function compares two character strings. The general form of these functions is

```
strcmp(⟨string1⟩,⟨string2⟩)
strncmp(⟨string1⟩,⟨string2⟩,⟨length⟩)
```

The latter function differs from the former only in that it will compare at most ⟨length⟩ characters in the two strings. The comparison will proceed character by character until a mismatch is found. Based on the collating sequence of the character set, which is almost universally ASCII, both these functions will return

1 if ⟨string1⟩ is greater than ⟨string2⟩
0 if they are equal
-1 if ⟨string2⟩ is greater

Remember, these are three-valued functions. We are so in the habit of thinking of relational operations as returning true or false that strcmp() and strncmp() can appear to be counter-intuitive.

Program Listing 4-7 illustrates the use of strcmp(). This function accesses the index file created by build_index() (discussed earlier). A name and the name of the index file are passed to it. It opens the file and reads through to the end. Each execution of fscanf() yields a name and a long integer value. The name read from the file is compared, by using strcmp(), to the name that was accepted as a parameter. If they are equal, the file is closed, and the value in loc is returned. If the entire file is searched and no match is found, the file is closed, and a value of -1 is returned. Note how we used strncmp() instead of strcmp() and that we used as a numeric parameter the length of the name sent into the function as a parameter. By doing this, we allow a match on an input of a partial name: "brow" should still find "brown". However, this capability is limited. It won't distinguish two names with the same set of initial letters—"brown" and "browne", for example. What it does do, however, is protect us from an incorrectly stored name; one with trailing blanks for example—"brown " instead of "brown".

```
long find (name,iname)
char name[],iname[];
{
 char xname[20];
 FILE *i,*fopen();
 long loc;

 if( (i=fopen(iname,"r"))==NULL
  return(0L);

 do {
   fscanf(i,"%s%d",xname,&loc);
   if(!strncmp(name,xname,strlen(name)) {
     fclose(i);
     return(loc);
    }
  }
 while (!feof(i));
 fclose(i);
 return(-1l);
```

Program Listing 4-7. Find() will access the index file created in Program Listing 3-15, returning the location of name's data in the main file.

Program Listings 4-8 and 4-9 complete our electronic address book, begun in Chapter 3. Get_dat() takes the location extracted from the index file by find() and moves to that location in the main file. The statement fseek() is used to implement this direct access operation. Program Listing 4-9 lists the main() function which ties this program together.

```
get_dat(fname,loc)
char fname[];
long loc;
{
 FILE *f,*fopen();
 char name[20],street[20],city[20],state[2];

 if( (f=fopen(fname,"r"))==NULL)
   return(0);

 fseek(f,loc,0);
 fscanf(f,"%s%s%s%s",name,street,city,state);

 printf(f,"%s\n%s\n%s\n%s",name,street,city,state);

 return(1);
}
```

Program Listing 4-8. Get_dat() will accept a pointer to a record location in the main file and will return the data found there.

```
#include <stdio.h>

main(argc,argv)
int argc;
char *argv[];
{
 char fname[15],iname[15],name[20];
 long find(),position;

 if(argc<2)  {
      printf("enter filename...");
      scanf("%s",fname);
    }
 else
      strcpy(fname,argv[1]);

 iname[0]='i';
 strcat(iname,fname);
 printf("enter name...");
 gets(name);
 if((position=find(name,iname))==0)  {
     printf("Can't open index file\n");
     exit();
   }
 else if(position==-1L)  {
      printf("name not found\n");
      exit();
    }
 if(!get_dat(fname,position))
    printf("Can't open main file\n");
}
```

Program Listing 4-9. The main function for the electronic address book.

4.4. Structures

The array is a data type made up of homogenous pieces—all character, all integer, and so on. The structure is a different kind of data type. It is an aggregation of components that may or may not be similar. It too is a powerful programming tool, but its difficult syntax causes it to suffer even more from underutilization.

Creating a particular structure is a two-stage process:

1. The structure template must be defined.
2. Variables of this type must be declared.

Only the second operation actually allocates any memory for the data structure. The general form of a structure definition is

```
struct ‹structure_name› {
  ‹type› ‹variable list›;
          :
          :
  ‹type› ‹variable list›;
 } ;
```

⟨structure_name⟩ names a new data type that can then be used to declare variables. Note the semicolon after the last brace in the definition. This is the only place in C where such punctuation is allowed, and here it is necessary to indicate the end of the definition—this is a real "gotcha." The syntax of a structure definition is also unusual:

```
struct ⟨structure_name⟩ ⟨variable list⟩;
```

will allocate one or more storage locations of appropriate size for this data type.

Program Listing 4-10 shows two examples of a structure definition and declaration. Note from Example b that the definition and declaration steps can be combined. Even the structure name is optional. If we only need a set number of variables of a particular type, we can take Example c as our model; this situation is much rarer. Of course, without a structure name we won't be able to declare any more variables of this type. Access to the individual units or "members" with the structure is either through pointers or via the dot notation; the general form of dot notation is

```
struct a_page {
 char name[30],
      street[30],
      city[20],
      st[2];
 };

 struct a_page page;
       (a)

struct phone {
   char name[30],
        area_code[3],
        exch[3],
        number[4];
  } p_page;
       (b)

struct {
   int day,
       mon,
       yr;
  } yesterday,today,tommorrow;
        (c)
```

Program Listing 4-10. Some sample structure definitions and declarations.

```
⟨variable_name⟩.⟨member_name⟩.
```

So, for example, to display the contents of the structure listed in a, we would write

```
printf("%s\n%s\n%s,%s\n",page.name,page.street,
                         page.city,page.st);
```

It is important to remember that the variables inside the structure, the members, have data types of their own; and these data types govern the behavior of the variables in a program. The somewhat complicated syntax of a structure access makes it easy to forget this. A particularly good source of this kind of error is the use of scanf() with a structure member. This input function requires the address of the input variable, usually supplied by using the address—of operator, "&". In the case of an array, particularly a character string, the name itself is a constant containing this address. With a structure, it is easy to become confused about where to apply this operator.

Consider Example c. Suppose we wish to fill this structure.

```
scanf("%d%d%d",&today.day,&today.mon,&today.yr)
```

would do it. The members are associated with the structure and each of their addresses is in relation to that of the structure as a whole. Indeed, since a number of variables can be of a given structure type, how else could we have it? How else could we distinguish yesterday.day from today.day, if we didn't make this connection? The case of a character string embedded in a structure is handled analogously.

```
scanf("%s%s%s%s",&p_page.name,&p_page.area_code,
                 &p_page.exch,&p_page.number);
```

will accept input into these various fields. The use of pointers with the structure data type greatly simplifies this kind of access, as we shall see.

The structure, which is the most powerful of all our data types, has few restrictions on it. It allows us to create arbitrary data structures through a combination of any of the existing simple, or even structured, data types. Structures may even be nested in other structures. This is the main tool we can use to model the complex entities that we find in the real world. Let's look at an example.

Program Listing 4-11 gives a structure definition that might serve for a typical employee record. In it we can store the name, address, and phone number, as well as job information, for an individual employee. In an application such a structure would serve as a buffer between the user interface and a disk file. Each logical unit, name, address, and so on, is defined as a separate structure; then, these structures are combined in the main structure, emprec. This method is primarily a matter of style. In this kind of application, it is doubtful that these individual structures would be used outside of the main structure, so it's not flexibility that we're concerned with.

What it does do, and at no cost in terms of performance, is to simplify the definition set. It's easier for us to keep track of the members; thus, fewer mistakes are likely to occur. Program Listing 4-12 offers a contrast; all members defined in one monolithic structure definition. Access to the members of nested structures is a logical extention of the dot notation

```
<variable_name>.<member_name>.<member_name>.
```

If we declare a variable record

```
struct emprec record;
```

we can print out the last name, job title, and salary members by using

```
printf("%s-%s-%d\n",record.name.last,record.job.title,
                                     record.job.salary);
```

```
struct nm {
  char last[30],
       first[30],
       mid[30];
};
struct adr {
  char street[30],
       city[30],
       state[2],
       zip[5];
};
struct phn {
  char area[3],
       exch[3],
       number[4];
};
struct jb {
  char title[10];
  int code,
      years,
      salary;
 };
struct emprec {
  struct nm name;
  struct adr address;
  struct phn phone;
  struct jb job;
 };
```

Program Listing 4-11. Structure definitions for an employee record.

```
struct emprec {
  char last[30],
       first[30],
       mid[30],
       street[30],
       city[30],
       state[2],
       zip[5],
       area[3],
       exch[3],
       number[4],
       title[10];
   int code,
       year,
       salary;
 };
```

Program Listing 4-12. A monolithic definition of the employee record structure. There is no provision in C for automatically printing the value of a structure.

The example in Program Listing 4-11 is a good illustration of how we can use the structured data type to create a model. We have a real-world entity, the employee. This entity is defined by certain values: a name, address, and phone number; a job; and some kind of pay for that job. The structure data type allows us to create a representation that allows us to map these conglomerations of values into the computer. It's not that we couldn't deal with these quantities before, it's that, by defining a structure, we gather them together into one location, a location that we can then move around with one command instead of the several it would take to move its discrete components. On a practical level, this means that there is less chance of forgetting a particular value, having a key variable masked by a local one, or any of the hundreds of mysterious problems that can befall values within the workings of a computer system.

A structure bears a much more direct relationship to the entity it's modelling than to the actual representation done inside the memory of the computer (*see* Figure 4-7). Each real-world abstraction has a corresponding abstraction in the data structure-this is particularly evident in our example since the members of the structure are themselves structures. How these are rendered into machine-readable form is hidden by the mechanics of C. The structure mechanism is built-in. Those details are handled automatically. All of our creative energies go into discovering these entities in our problem world. Creating their representation in our computational world should not be another problem.

Data processing examples, such as our emprec structure, provide good illustrations of the value and the mechanism of structure definitions—the "how-to". But we must avoid thinking of the data type solely in this context. If we do, we'll miss some interesting and very useful constructions.

Complex numbers are needed in a number of important problems in engineering and physical science. For example, the impedance of an electrical circuit is a complex quantity. Yet this data type is rarely implemented as a basic built-in one in most

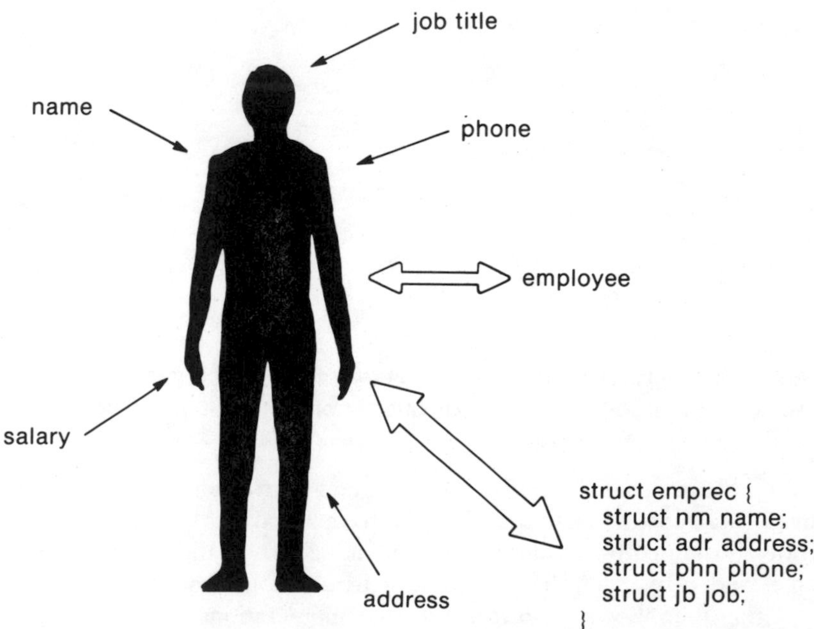

Figure 4-7. A diagram illustrating the one-to-one relationship between a real-world entity and its representative structure.

high-level languages, and C is no exception. However, using a structure definition, we can create such a data type and then, using our definition, we can develop support functions that will perform the basic mathematical operations. Recall the form of a complex number

a + bi

where a is the real component and b is the imaginary one. The i—or j in electrical engineering—is a marker to indicate the status of the quantity b; both coefficients are real quantities. Examples might include

2.345 + 3.3 i
6.6 + 0.4 i

Now note the structure definition in Program Listing 4-13. Here, too, we have a division into two discrete quantities. There is that one-to-one correspondence we talked about earlier. The two functions in this example, add_cmpl() and sub_cmpl(), illustrate how we can create functions that will implement the arithmetic operations defined for these numbers.

```
typedef struct {
  double real,imag;
 } complex;

complex add_cmpl(x,y)
complex x,y;
{
 complex z;

 z.real=x.real+y.real;
 z.imag=x.imag+y.imag;

 return(z);
}
complex sub_cmpl(x,y)
complex x,y;
{
 complex z;

 z.real=x.real-y.real;
 z.imag=x.imag-y.imag;

 return(z);
}
```

Program Listing 4-13. A definition of a complex data type and some functions defining operations on them.

Also in Program Listing 4-13, we used a typedef statement in conjunction with the structure definition. The typedef statement, you'll recall, can be used to give a new name to an existing data type; it might be more correct to say "another name" since the old one remains in force. For example

```
typedef float real;
```

will allow us to make floating-point declarations with the word "real." Since a structure definition creates a new data type, it, too, can be renamed by using this statement. That's precisely what we've done here. Note that since we're defining a new data type with the name "complex," we didn't bother to name the structure. The FILE data type, defined in stdio.h, is created in this way. What we've gained is a clearer perception of the data connections. The word "complex" tells us just exactly what we're trying to do.

For another example, reconsider the character string data type. Recall that a character string is a dynamic data type; its size grows and shrinks during the execution of a program. The typical way to handle this in C is, as we have seen, to put a special end-of-string marker as the last in an array of characters. Another approach to the implementation of a character string is to use an array of characters and to keep track of the current length of the string, the number of character positions filled. Program Listing 4-14 illustrates some of the code necessary for such an implementation. Again, we use the typedef statement since it is a situation similar to our last example. The structure consists of a character array, to hold the value of the string, and an integer, length, to hold the number of characters currently in the string. Strcat() and strcmp() have been rewritten in light of this new data type as examples of how it could be used to implement string-processing functions.

```
typedef struct {
  char s[256];
  int length;
 } string;

string strcat(a,b)
string a,b;
{
 int loop,loopØ=Ø;
 if((a.length+b.length)>256)
  return(NULL);
 for(loop=a.length+1;loop<(a.length+b.length);loop++)
   a.s[loop]=b.s[loopØ++];
 a.length=loop;
 return(a);
}

string strcmp(a,b)
string a,b;
{
 int loop;
 if(a.length==b.length) {
   for(loop=Ø;loop<=a.length;loop++) {
     if(a.s[loop]<b.s[loop])
       return(-1);
     if(a.s[loop]>b.s[loop])
       return(1);
   }
   return(Ø);
  }
 return(a.length<b.length ?-1:1);
}
```

Program Listing 4-14. A module defining an implementation of a character string data type.

Our last example can be generalized. Whenever we need to set up a character buffer, instead of using a simple character array, it is frequently advantageous to use a structure definition that includes not only the necessary array but also other interesting information. The length of the current value is a common choice, perhaps the port identification for an I/O buffer. The point is that we're able to associate more data with the buffer by using a structure definition than by using a simple character array.

4.5. Combining Structured Data Types

Our two main structured data types are frequently found linked together in C. We have already seen that arrays can be included within a structure definition; indeed, it is a common occurrence. It is also not uncommon for a designer to create an array of structures.

In using an array to custom design a new data type, we are usually interested in creating a class of objects in our program, for example, two buffers, three I/O buffers, 25 lines. Single structure definitions, such as our earlier one for "complex," are relatively rare in practice. The best way to create multiples of a data type is to declare an array of that type. The most obvious advantage for creating these multiple occurrences is the automatic indexing and identification of the the data structure provided. A particular buffer or a particular line can be picked programmatically. An example is found in Program Listing 4-15.

```
struct in_buf {
   char ch;
   int flag;
  }message [1024];

struct m_form {
   char ch;
   int messno;
};

rebuild (packet)
struct m_form packet;
{
 if(packet.messno<0 || packet.messno>1023)
   return(-1);
 if(message[packet.mesno].flag)
   return(0);
 message[packet.mesno].ch=packet.ch;
 message[packet.mesno].flag=1;
 return(1);
}
```

Program Listing 4-15. A function to rebuild a message from individual character packets.

One very reliable way for one computer to send a message to another is for the first one to break the message into individual pieces. Each piece is then sent off to make its own way to the target system. In a modern communication network, this could be quite a circuitous trip. Even then all the pieces of the message may not arrive at the destination in the proper order. One way around this problem is simply to number each such "packet" and use this number to reconstruct the message once all the pieces have arrived. Program Listing 4-15 illustrates a very simple implementation of such a procedure.

The keys to this example are the two structure definitions. The first one associates a flag with each character in the message and creates a buffer by defining an array large enough for 1024 characters—the magical "1 K". The second structure defines the packet format as it comes from the interface function; it contains the character and an integer indicating the position of that character within the message. When a message arrives, it is placed in the appropriate cell, and the flag for that cell is set. Note that the function rebuild() returns 1 on a successful assignment and -1 if the packet has an illegal position number. The function also takes cognizance of the situation where a character arrives more than once. In a modern network, this doesn't automatically mean trouble, but it is something for the rest of the program to monitor.

Just as we can have an array of structures in C, we can also have an array of arrays. Thus,

```
double matrix[10][5];
```

will define an object, matrix, that has 10 cells. Each cell, in turn, has 5 cells of double-precision, floating-point numbers associated with it. This is the way C implements multidimensional arrays. Dimensions of three or more are simply logical extensions of this format. Except for specialized applications, these higher order arrays are seldom seen. The important point is that unlike most modern high-level languages, in C the multidimensional array is not a composite data type but is built up from the simple array.

Program Listing 4-16 illustrates the definition of a matrix data type and an input function appropriate to it. Again we've used the typedef statement to create this new data type. We've tried to squeeze as much of the power of a built-in data type as possible. By using a two-dimensional array embedded in a structure, we can, to a limited extent, simulate a dynamically allocated matrix—a maximum of 256 x 256 may be too generous for all but the largest computers. Maxrow and maxcol identify that part of the matrix currently in use. Input() is a straightforward input function. Note that the scanf() return value is used to signal the end of data gathering both for a particular goal and for the entire function. Scanf() returns zero if no data conversions were made—just the situation if a single carriage return is entered.

```
typedef struct {
  int maxrow,maxcol,
      m[256][256];
 }matrix;

matrix input()
{
 matrix z;
 int loop0,loop1,ch;

 for(loop0=0;loop0<255;loop++)
  for(loop1=0;loop1<=255;loop1++) {
   if((scanf("%d",&ch))==0)
     if(loop1==0) {
      z.maxrow=--loop0;
      z.maxcol=--loop1;
      return(z);
     }
     else
       break;
    else
       z.m[loop0][loop1]=ch;
   }
 z.maxrow=z.maxcol=255;
 return(z);
}
```

Program Listing 4-16. A definition of a matrix data type and a function for entering data into it.

4.6. Initializing Structures and Arrays

Both structures and arrays can be initialized, but some restrictions exist that do not apply to simple variables. Structures or arrays whose storage class is automatic—those local to a function—cannot be intialized at the time of their declaration. If their storage class is static, such initialization is possible. Finally, all such variables externally defined are set to a default value of zero at declaration time unless some other value is specified. This situation is summarized in Program Listing 4-17. Formal parameters to a function cannot be initialized.

To initialize an array, we only have to enclose the values in brackets. Thus,

```
static xarray[5] = {10,20,30,40,50};
```

will set each member of xarray equal to a value. It isn't even necessary to supply a value for each location.

The statement

```
static yarray[5] = {10,20};
```

will put 10 in yarray[0], 20 in yarray[1], and 0 in the remaining three locations. In fact, it isn't even necessary to indicate how many locations are being declared.

```
struct time {
  int day,
      mon,
      year;
};

int xarray[23]                          external storage class set to zero
struct time today;                      unless another value is supplied.

funky(x,y)
int x[];                                formal parameter--may not be
struct time y;                          initialized.
{
 int z[23];                             automatic storage class--may not
 struct time tomorrow;                  be initialized.

 static w[23];                          static storage class--may be initialized
 static struct time yesterday;          at designer's descretion.
        :
        :
}
```

Program Listing 4-17. A chart describing the various kinds of structured variables and whether or not they can be initialized.

The statement

```
static warray[] = {10,20,30,40,50};
```

will create and initialize an array with five cells.

Character strings enjoy a special status in C. They can be initialized in two different ways: just like any array:

```
static char str[] = {"h", "e", "l", "l", "o", "\0"};
```

or by a character string constant:

```
static char str0[] = "hello";
```

Note that in the latter case, the end-of-string mark need not be explicitly included. Structures are initialized in the same way:

```
struct tim {
  int day,mon,year;
} time={2,20,85};
```

will set each member of tim. Here, too, if only a partial list of values is supplied, the remainder of the members will be set to zero.

Compound, structured data types, arrays of arrays and arrays of structures, can also be initialized. The format of this initialization is a logical extension of that of the simpler forms:

```
int carray[3][5]={  {1,2,3,4,5},
                    {6,7,8,9,10},
                    {11,12,13,14,15}  };
```

will initialize a two-dimensional array. The value list for each row is bracketed, and the entire declaration is also set off this way. A structure array is initialized in the same fashion:

```
static struct time[5]=  {  {1,2,85},
                           {1,4,85},
                           {1,6,85},
                           {2,5,85}  };
```

will set the member values for the five tim structures. Here as well, if insufficient values are supplied, the rest will default to zero.

4.7. The Union and Enum Data Types

To finish this chapter, we will look at two infrequently used data types. One looks backwards towards a programming environment that existed at the time C was first formulated, and the other looks forward to more modern programming construction.

The union data type is a variation on the structure; it allows us to use the same piece of memory to store variables of different types. As with the structure, allocating space for a union variable is a two-stage process: definition, then declaration. The general form of this definition is

```
union <name> {
  <type> <member_name>;
            :
            :
  <type> <member_name>;
};
```

and of its declaration

```
union <name> <variable_list>
```

The declaration can be done immediately following the defintion just as with the structure. For example

```
union all_num {
   int m;
   double r;
  }numeric;
```

will define and declare a variable that can be either real or integer. Access is also the same as with a structure data type; we use the dot notation. In a union, the member name used indicates the type of the variable:

- numeric.m is an integer.
- numeric.r is a double-precision real number.

Several points must be noted. The same memory location is used for each data type so enough space is allocated by the system to hold the largest of the member types. It can only be one kind of data type at a time, and no conversion is done. That is, we cannot assign a value to one member and get a type converted value back from another—what we'll get is garbage. We have the type-cast operator for this sort of conversion.

The union looks back to a time when memory was more of a scarce resource than it is on today's systems. It still finds use in situations where, for one reason or another, the same memory location must be reused. If this condition is not obtained, the union should be avoided. It will tend to produce code that is both inefficient in its use of resources and unnecessarily complex.

The enum data type is similar to the user-defined or enumerated type found in such languages as Pascal. This allows the programmer to specify a set of values that are linked together as a data type. Again, like the structure and the union, this requires both a definition and a declaration. The general form of this definition is

```
enum ⟨name⟩ = {⟨value list⟩};
```

and the general form of the declaration is,

```
enum ⟨name⟩ ⟨variable list⟩
```

Program Listing 4-18 lists a simple function that illustrates a use for the enum data type. We declare a data type, days, to consist of the days of the week. Then we create an array of structures that will store the sales and the name of the salesperson for each day. The index of the array is our newly defined enum data type. To print out the values for each day, the function loops through the days of the week from sun to sat inclusive. What we have gained is a more logical looking program. The sales are associated with the days of the week, not the numbers 0–6, but aside from this, there is no real difference. Note that the values of the loop are mon, tue, and so on, and not their character string equivalents.

```
enum days={sun,mon,tue,wed,thu,fri,sat};

enum days week;

struct sales {
  char name[30];
  int amount;
 } s_report[week];

weekly_out()
{
 enum days week;

 for(week=sun;week<=sat;week++)
   printf("%s\ntotal sales:%d\n",s_report[week].name,s_report[name].amount);
}
```

Program Listing 4-18. Illustrating the enum data type in action.

The function in Program Listing 4-18 works because the enum data type is really an integer type. Each value in the definition is associated with an integer value starting with 0 and going up by one. We can alter this sequence:

```
enum days={sun=65,mon,tue,wed,thu,fri,sat};
```

will associate "sun" with 65 and all the other days of the week will take values starting with this initial one. There is no predecessor or successor function as in Pascal. The enum data type is, for the present, restricted to this minor role.

4.8. Summary

In this chapter we have explored C's structured data types. These included primarily the array, the structure, and the character string. Most of these data types are found in other programming languages as well; the ubiquitous array is even used in assembly language programming. We have explored new ways to use these objects to increase our problem-solving power. Thus,

- We have used the array as a general way to allocate memory.
- We have used the structure data type to create new mathematical objects.
- We have explored the character string data type and its access functions.

Of course, our explanations have extended to multidimensional arrays and arrays of structures. Some discussion was reserved for the exotic enum and union data types.

The lesson to be learned from this chapter is that these data structures are both powerful and flexible, and that they can be pressed into service to extend the language.

5

Pointers

Indirect addressing is used more in C than in any other high-level language. In this it betrays itself as a replacement for assembly language programming and justifies its sometime description as a "mid-level" language. The pointer is the medium for indirection in C. However, the pointer does not only allow low-level access; it also makes possible a new level of abstraction—linked data structures. These, in turn, simplify the implementation of sophisticated sorting and searching algorithms.

This chapter will show you how both low-level and high-level access can be achieved and will explore some of the example problems. Through a close study of key examples, you will gain not only a practical knowledge of pointers and indirect access, but you will develop an appreciation of why pointers are used in C instead of more traditional access methods.

Pointers are used extensively with the structured data types and with functions. A subsidiary goal of this chapter is to demonstrate the mechanism and the advantage of such access. You can gain an understanding of this often obscure part of the C syntax when you finish this chapter.

Goals:

- To understand the concepts of direct and indirect memory access
- To understand the notion of a pointer variable and how it is implemented
- To review the indirection and address-of operators
- To explore pointer arithmetic
- To understand the relationship between pointers, arrays, structures, and functions
- To explore the linked data structure

5.1 Pointers and Memory

The main memory or core of a computer system is one of its key subsystems. Every piece of data that comes to the CPU must first go into memory, and every result from a CPU operation is deposited there. It is in memory that our fancy data structures are created and have their existence. Once they are processed in the central processing unit (CPU), they lose their structure to become a series of binary numbers, and once they leave memory for the outside world, they are reduced to mere streams of characters. Although we tend to take it for granted and treat it as a necessary but uninteresting part of the computer system, the main memory is the focus of much of our design work.

We have discussed the structure of memory before but perhaps without realizing its full significance. Its architecture is relatively straightforward, a linear list of fixed-size storage locations. The size of each location—really the number of bits—is a significant factor, and it can vary from a low of 8 bits (one byte) to a high of 64 bits. The usual working range is 16 or 32 bits, but as the price of memory drops, this could change drastically and quickly. The basic unit of memory, this storage location, is known as the word. It is the basic unit of memory access as well. One memory fetch cycle will bring one word into a CPU register for processing. The situation is somewhat complicated because some machines allow individual bytes to be addressed, and all systems allow these bytes to be extracted from the word. Usually we can ignore these problems and trust the hardware and its associated software (or firmware) to take care of dealing with the machine on this level; it's good to know what's going on behind the black box.

Memory, then, consists of a linear list of words. Each word is uniquely identified by its position in this list (*see* Figure 5-1). This position is called its address. The address has even more significance; it can be used to directly access a particular memory location. We order the hardware to fetch location 1020 or location 1050 or any other part of memory we need.

The size of this list is a significant system parameter. While a program is running, memory is being shared by both the running program and its data and by the operating system along with its tables, and such. The operating system software is fixed, so the total amount of memory dictates the maximum size available to the program. All of this is complicated since, on most large systems, some sort of virtual memory scheme is implemented.

Virtual memory is really a system of memory management that allows the designer to write programs that require more memory locations than are available in the system. Figure 5-2 illustrates virtual memory's operation. A program is decomposed into small units or modules. These modules are loaded into memory as the instructions or data storage locations they contain are needed. This decomposition is done by the operating system, not the programmer. Virtual memory is almost a universal feature among large systems but is absent on most small, single-user systems. Some C implementations for these smaller systems supply tools that allow the

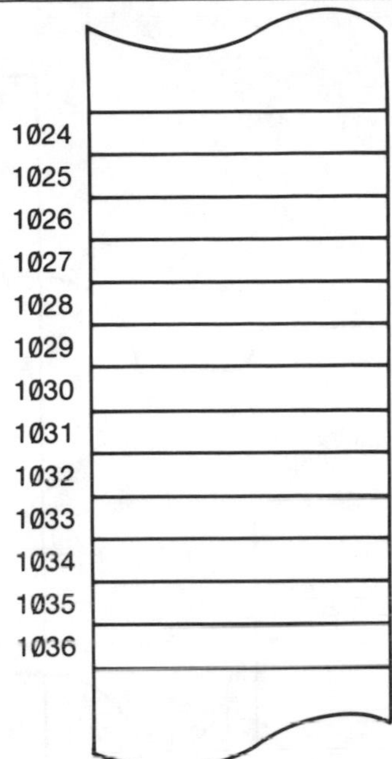

Figure 5-1. Memory is a linear list of basic storage locations or words.

programmer to divide a program into modules and then overlay memory with these modules as execution of the program proceeds.

It is within the realm of memory that the C pointer and its related operations function. A pointer is nothing more than the address of a memory location, and the manipulation of pointers involves transformations on these addresses.

There are two forms of memory addressing: direct and indirect. Direct addressing is the form most often used. Most high-level languages only have this capability. In this form of access, a variable name is associated with a particular memory location. Whenever a statement within the program uses that variable, either to get the value or to change it, the request is translated into a direct reference to the associated memory location. Figure 5-3 is a symbolic illustration of this operation. The variable, num, is associated with memory location 2048. Any read access of num will return the value stored in location 2048, and any write access will change this location.

Look closely at the address. It's nothing more than an integer value, just a number. Indirect access trades on this fact.

- a direct access to retrieve the value stored in the variable's associated memory location
- a direct access using this retrieved value as an address

This, too, is illustrated in Figure 5-3. We access num and that sends us to memory 2048. At this location, we pick up the value 2071 stored there. Then we do an access to location 2071.

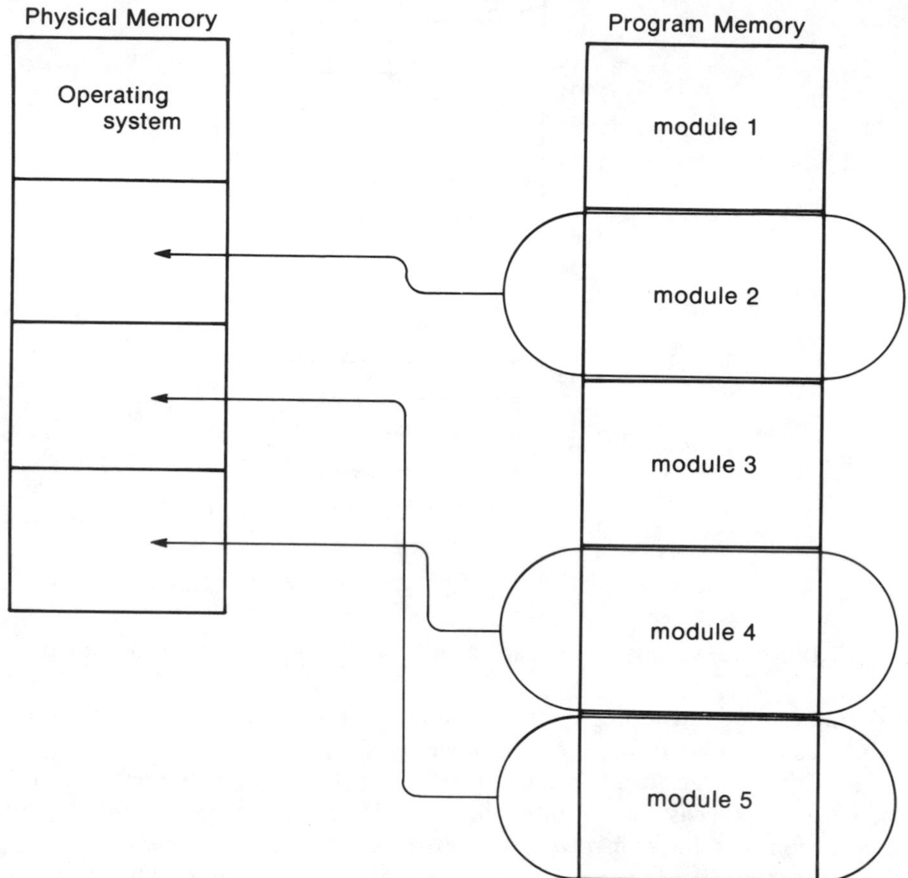

Figure 5-2. Illustrating virtual memory management.

The capability to do indirect memory access has long been a feature of assemblers. Indeed, most have many kinds or modes of indirect memory reference available. Assemblers are specific to a machine or family of machines. Also in writing assembly language programs the programmer has to deal with the intricacies of memory management including virtual memory. C has made indirect access into a portable high-level function, where these problems are eliminated. There is only one mode of indirect addressing instead of many. C restricts these address manipulating functions to a well-behaved subset. The truth is a bit more complicated. On a small system without virtual memory, you do a lot. On a medium- to large-size multiuser, multiprogramming system, several layers of protection bar you from effectively going crazy.

The use of pointers in C programming is not just another way to produce dense and opaque code that not even the creating programmer understands after a few weeks. Nor is it useful as a necessary tool to circumvent machine limitations, which is, in contrast, a big motivation with assembly language programmers; if this were

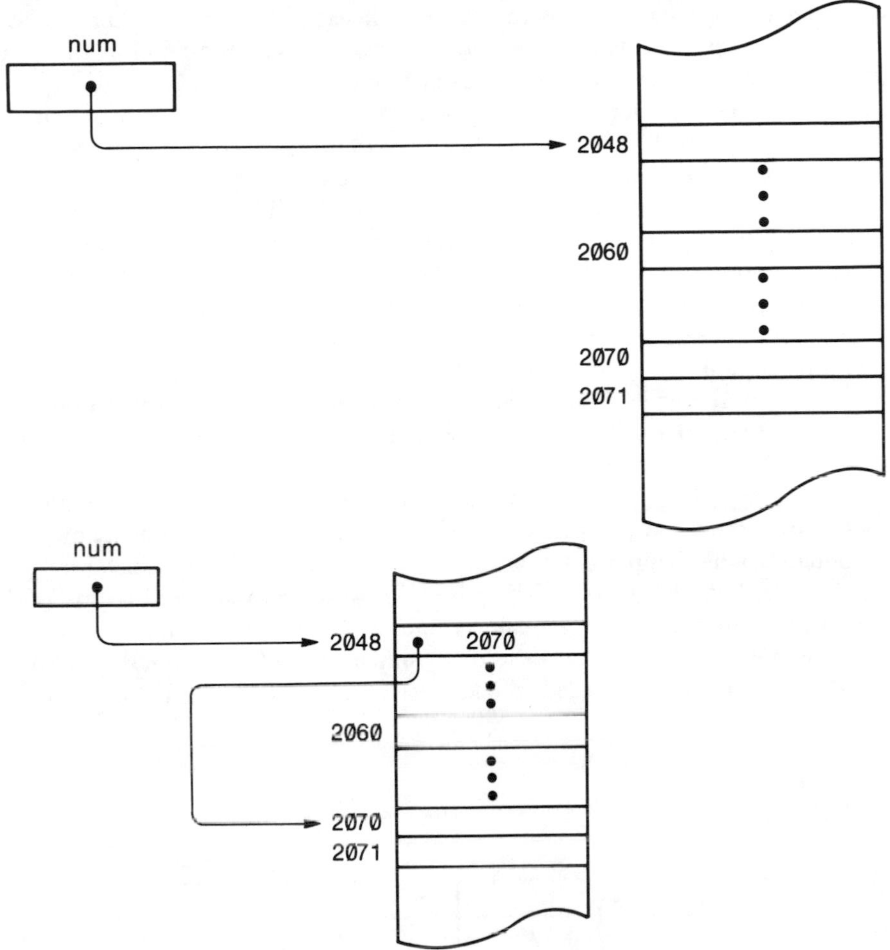

Figure 5-3. Direct vs. indirect memory access.

the only value of pointers, they would have long since disappeared from C programs. The normal constructions of variables, arrays, and structures aren't quite up to the task of implementing our algorithms in an efficient manner. Rather, the use of pointers allows us to expand our programming capabilities and to create not only new data types but new kinds of data structures, and it allows us to create another channel of communication between functions.

Just as the use of structured variables allowed us to create high-level data structures that facilitated the representation of real-world entities and situations, the use of pointers coupled with these high-level data types, allows us to create even higher-level, more abstract data manipulation schemes. The chief feature of these new data structures is their dynamic nature. They grow and shrink during program execution rather than maintain a static size from program load to program termination. Unlike the character string data type where dynamic allocation was only simulated, with pointers, we can set up truly dynamic structures whose only limitation is that of the overall computer system on which they are running.

The dynamic data structures that we will be particularly interested in are the linked list and the stack. Figure 5-4 illustrates these two data structures in brief outline. The linked list is a very flexible data type made up of nodes. Each node contains data and the address of its successor node. The stack, of course, we have implemented before by using a simple array. Using pointers we can simulate a true dynamic stack; this example will highlight some of the differences of this class of data structure and will serve as an interesting contrast to the earlier implementation.

The utility of pointers is not restricted to creating new kinds of data structures. It also allows us to implement a different kind of connection between functions. The connection between the calling function and the called function can be either by externally declared variables common to both routines or by formal parameters passed from the calling function. When a value is passed to a function through parameter assignment, only a copy is passed over. The original variable maintains its value no matter what happens to it in the called functions. We say the variables are passed "by value" to the function. There is a third possibility for setting this kind of connection. Commonly known as "call by reference", it can be implemented easily by using the pointer operators. Instead of passing a copy of the value that resides in the variable, the function call sends the address of the variable (*see* Figure 5-5). This

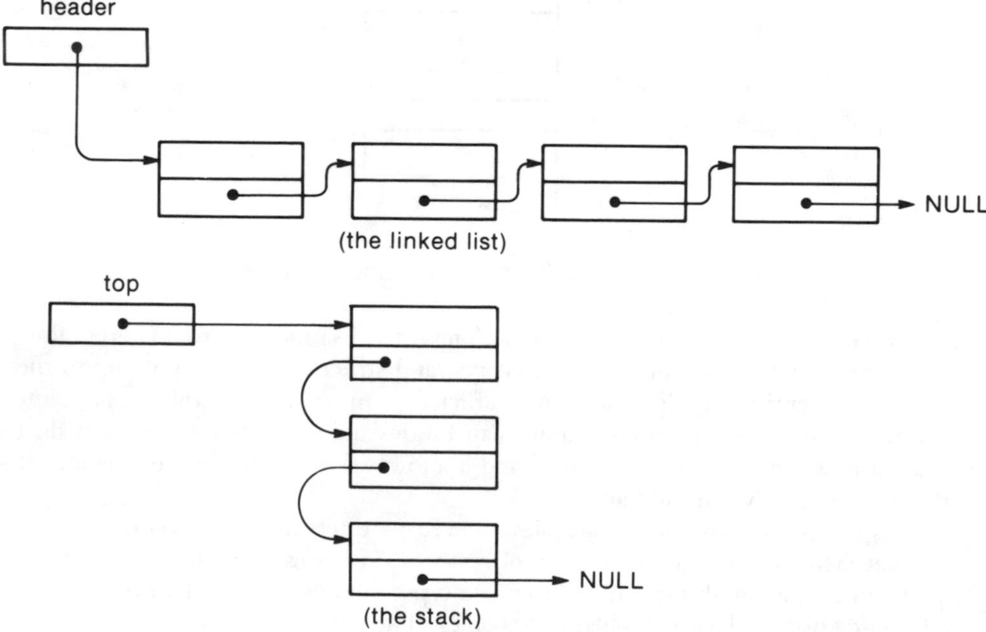

Figure 5-4. Interesting dynamic data structures.

means that any changes made to the formal parameter are actually being made to the original variable location.

The pointer mechanism also allows us to pass functions to other functions. We can set up a pointer to a function and pass that address to another function that can call, in turn, the function just passed to it. One easy-to-understand application of this would be a sort routine that would order its data either in ascending or descending order depending on which comparison function was passed to it. This capability is not unique to C— Lisp has it in a more highly refined form—but it is certainly not a common programming capability.

Although the indexing mechanisms of C are quite efficient, pointers are often used in C to access the members of an array. This is particularly true in the case of character strings and arrays of structures. Pointers are used almost exclusively with these two data types. The motivation is convenience and clarity. In the case of character strings, stepping through by address pointer seems more natural than using an index value. For one thing, it effectively hides the static allocation upon which the

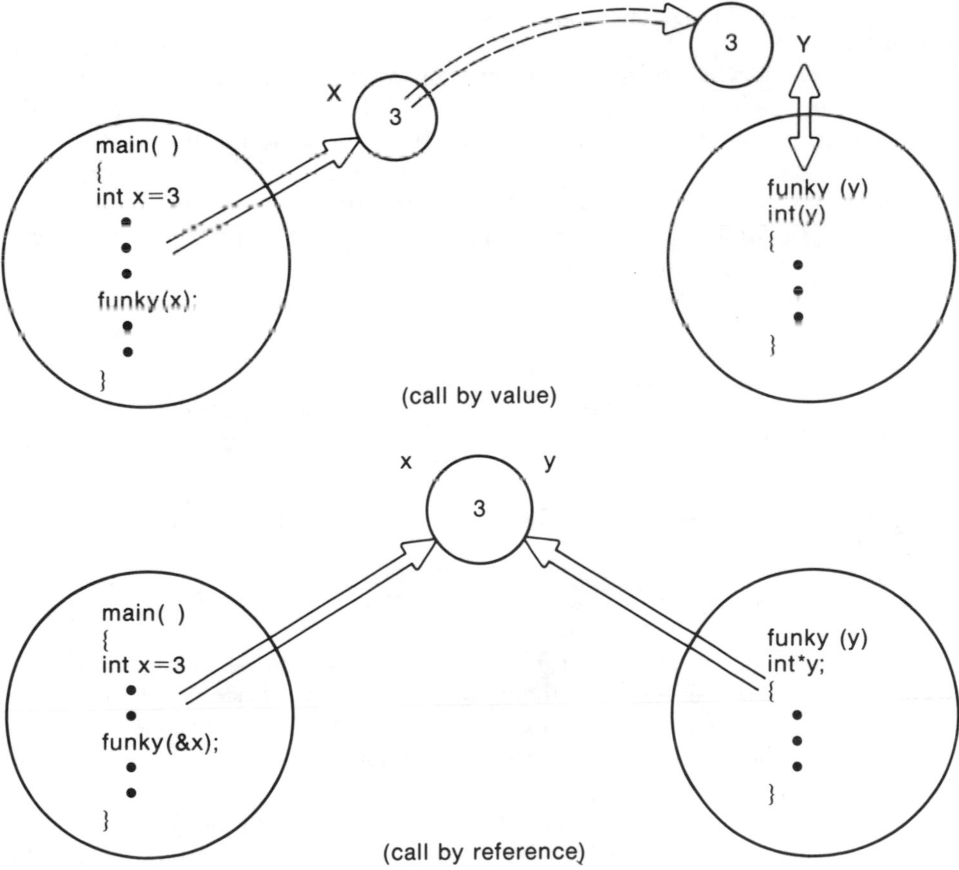

Figure 5-5. Comparing 'call by value' to 'call by reference'.

dynamic character string is defined. In the case of arrays of structures, the pointer notation for accessing the members of the structure are much simpler if we use the pointer "arrow" notation than if we stick to the dot notation.

As we can see, it is profitable for us to explore the pointer and its various manipulations. Although C pointers have a reputation for being obtuse, we shall see that once mastered, their syntax is logical and very powerful.

5.2. Declaring a Pointer, Address-Of, and Indirection

So far we've established that a pointer is a variable that contains the address of another location, but how do we declare a pointer variable. How do we assign values to it? Perhaps most importantly, what kind of values do we assign to it?

The first step in answering these questions is to clarify to what kind of object a pointer variable is pointing. We talked in the last section about addresses of individual memory addresses. We formed our definition in terms of these basic units. All of this is true as far as it goes, but, unfortunately, it is oversimplified to the point of being misleading. In some cases, on some machines, this word-by-word organization is literally true—if the computer has a 16-bit word and if an "int" data type is being pointed to. Pointer variables are always associated with a specific kind of object, either simple or structured. The specific object is set by a declaration statement:

```
int *i_ptr;
```

will set up a pointer variable to an integer type, and

```
char *c_ptr;
double *d_tpr;
```

will designate a character and a double-precision, real-number pointer, respectively. Generally,

```
⟨type⟩ *⟨variable_name⟩;
```

will create a pointer variable named ⟨variable_name⟩ pointing to a data object of ⟨type⟩. It is the asterisk prefacing the variable name as a preface that indicates that the variable is a pointer. As a matter of style, pointer variable names should be chosen to somehow indicate their special status since in the body of the program nothing else indicates their status.

The declaration of a nonpointer variable, whether simple or structured, allocates space for that variable when the module it is in becomes active. Remember some classes of structured variables also require a definition. A pointer declaration is an exception. It allocates no space but sets up the proper overhead for subsequent operations on itself. Actually, it creates an entry in the system table that keeps track of variables, but no other space is allocated. Recall that a pointer variable was previously "associated" with a data object. A pointer is, itself, always an integer type no matter what it's pointing to. This makes sense. The pointer contains addresses—large integer values—not the objects themselves. We really cannot exploit this fact, or at least we shouldn't; but, it's important to recognize this situation now so that we don't become confused later on when we start to manipulate these pointer variables.

Because we recognize that a pointer is an integer value, even if it's not an ordinary integer, why not have a general purpose "pointer" type? Why do we have to declare a pointer as a "pointer to" a particular data type? What does this 'association' with a data object mean? Two kinds of activities are governed by this declaration:

- maintaining type integrity
- keeping track of data object size

Values can be stored in a storage location by using a pointer variable; thus, the normal rules of type class and mixed expressions need to apply. Somewhere this information must be supplied. Also, the size of the data object must be noted to allow manipulation of the pointer. C is one of the few high-level languages that allows arithmetic operations to be performed on pointer values; therefore, this information is vital.

Now that we've declared a pointer variable, how do we assign values to it? This is not a simple question to answer; there are many ways and not all of them desirable. The simplest assignment is by using the address-of operator, "&". We've already seen this used in the scanf() function. When a program executes

```
scanf("%d",&x);
```

the address of the variable, x, is being sent to the function. We can use this operator to make a direct assignment to a pointer variable. Consider the following situation:

```
int x,*i_ptr;
i_ptr=&x;
```

Here we've declared an integer variable, x, and a pointer to an integer, i_ptr. The second statement assigns the address of x to the variable i_ptr. We are not limited to simple variables. Program Listing 5-1 summarizes the more common possiblities for these statements. Note that there is no asterisk in front of the array name in the assignment statement. An array name contains the address of the first element of the array.

```
struct tod {
 int hour,
     min,
     sec;
 } time, *t_ptr;

int i,*i_ptr;

long x, *l_ptr;

char ch, *c_ptr;

float y,*f_ptr;

double z,*d_ptr;

int a[3],*a_ptr;

t_ptr=&time;

i_ptr=&i;

l_ptr=&x;

c_ptr=&ch;

f_ptr=&y;

d_ptr=&z;

a_ptr=a;
```

Program Listing 5-1. Summarizing some of the possible uses of pointers and the address-of operator.

The absence of an asterisk or any other kind of mark before the pointer variable name should be noted. From its point of view, this is a normal, direct assignment. But what's being assigned is not the contents of the variable on the right but its address. This may seem like restating the obvious, but it can get confusing when we start to use the pointer variable to assign values to a storage location, the inverse of what we're doing now.

The complement to the address-of operator is the indirection operator, "*". When applied to a pointer variable, this operator instructs the computer to take the value stored in that variable as an address and access the indicated location. Figure 5-6 contains a fragment of code that illustrates a simple example using this operator. We declare an integer variable, x, and a pointer to an integer, ptr. We assign to ptr the address of x. At this point, both x and ptr refer to the same location in memory. Using the indirection operator, we assign to the location whose address is in ptr, the value 2; this of course puts this value in location x. When we print out x, we get the value 2.

A common use of pointers in a C program is to effect a "call-by-reference" scheme for function parameters. By sending the address of a variable to a function, any assignments or changes made to that variable will be reflected back in the calling function, thus giving us a way to pass more than one value out of a function. Program Listing 5-2 illustrates a function that depends on "call by reference" to return the desired values. The purpose of this function is to return three summary values

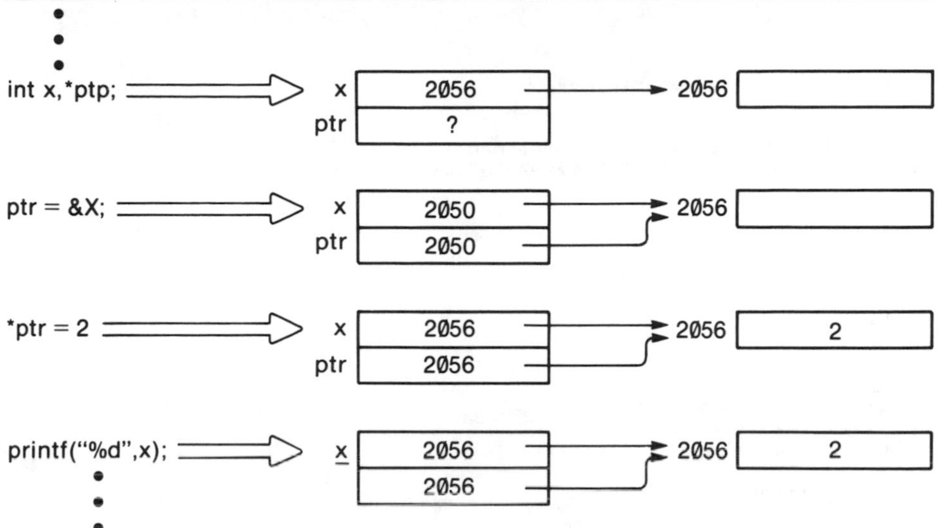

Figure 5-6. Illustrating a simple application of the indirection operator.

for a particular set of data: the minimum, maximum, and mean values. The data set enters the function via the array, a, with "size" elements. The array is scanned, and the appropriate calculations are performed. Values are returned through the pointer variables mean, min, and max. Note the use of the indirection operators. Program Listing 5-3 contains the other two functions that go into making up the program. The variables mean, min, and max are declared as ordinary variables but their addresses are passed to mean_minmax(). This program illustrates a common but still relatively simple use of pointers. The important thing to remember is the symmetrical way the two operators, * and &, interact. Mean_minmax() expects to receive the address of a variable; thus, it uses the indirection operator to get at the values. The main() function, in turn, passes to the function the addresses of the variables where it expects to find the results; it, of course, uses the address-of operator.

```
mean_minmax (a,size,mean,min,max)
int a[],size,*mean,*min,*max;
{
 int loop,total=1;

 min=max=a[Ø];

 for(loop=1;loop<size;loop++) {
   total+=a[loop];
   *max=(*max<a[loop]) ? a[loop] : *max;
   *min=(*min>a[loop]) ? a[loop] : *min;
  }

 *mean=total/size;
}
```

Program Listing 5-2. A function that accepts an array of integers and the number of cells in that array and returns the mean, maximum, and minimum of the numbers in the array.

```
main()
{
 int a[50],size,mean,min,max;

 size=get_array(a);
 mean_minmax(a,size,&mean,&min,&max);
 printf("mean=%d\nmin=%d\nmax=%d\n",mean,min,max);
}

get_array(x)
int x[];
{
 int idx=-1;
 char ch[80];

 do {
  gets(ch);
  if (strcmp("stop",ch)!=0)
    x[++idx]=atoi(ch);
 while(strcmp("stop",ch)!=0);

 return(++idx);
}
```

Program Listing 5-3. The rest of the program that utilizes mean_minmax().

Does it make sense to assign a value to a pointer variable directly without using the address-of operator? In two easily identifiable cases, there is no question. We can certainly assign the vaules of one pointer variable to another as long as they both point to the same data type. Thus, in Program Listing 5-4, the code fragment in a will produce results identical to those produced by the fragment in b. It's important to realize that the pointer to pointer transfer is a simple variable interchange. Functioning on this level, pointer variables are no different than any other kind of variable. It is only by using the two operators, & and *, that the special power of these pointers is accessed.

```
        :
        :
int x=2, *ptr0;

ptr0=&x;

printf("%d",*ptr0);
        :
                              (a)
        :
        :
int x=2, *ptr0, *ptr1;

ptr1=&x;

ptro=prt1;

printf("%d",*ptr0);
        :
                              (b)
```

Program Listing 5-4. Illustrating how pointers can be assigned to each other.

There is one other value that can safely be assigned directly to a pointer variable. This is a special address to indicate a null position. It is defined in the Standard Library as "NULL," usually it is zero. This value is useful whenever it's necessary to access a pointer variable before a value may have been assigned to it. By assigning a NULL, we can indicate to the function that we haven't yet given a legitimate value to the variable. It's a kind of place holder.

Whether or not it makes sense to assign integer values to a pointer variable depends very much on the operating system environment. On small, single-user systems without virtual memory, we can get away with it. The addresses of all the variable locations are stable for the entire duration of the program's execution. On a larger system, particularly one with some form of virtual memory—which is to say every such system—this address stability is absent. Unless our program was small, it would be divided into more than one module. Each of these modules would be in and out of memory several times during the program's run and would probably not be in the same physical location each time. Under these circumstances, absolute values for an address variable would have no meaning.

Any attempt at assigning an absolute value to a pointer variable will lead, at best, to program code that is specific to one machine. This is antithetical to C's basic goal of absolute portability. If we stick with the address-of operator, the indirection operator, and the special NULL value, we will be able to write portable programs and still get the power of indirect addressing.

5.3. Using Pointers

One of the things that distinguishes C from other high-level languages that support pointer operations is that C has a respectable set of operations that can be performed on these objects. This set even includes some arithmetic operations. Because so much can be done with them, pointers are an important part of C programming. Not all arithmetic operations are allowed, only those that make sense. Specifically, addition and subtraction, in their many forms, are allowed, but multiplication and division are not. When we consider what pointers are and how we use them, these restrictions are reasonable. Pointer operations are, by their nature, integer operations. We access a location with a pointer value. We may want to access the next location or the one three locations back. These are well-defined operations. With multiplication and division, exactly the opposite is true. One or two situations may make sense—dividing by two to get the middle element during a binary search—but the great majority of situations will yield a nonsensical answer.

The two most common operations on pointers are increment and decrement. We can take a pointer variable and move it to the next address in the sequence or we can move it to the previous location. Thus, in

```
int k, *i_ptr;
i_ptr=&k;
i_ptr++;
```

the pointer is first given the address of the variable k. Using the increment operator increases the value of i_ptr by one. It now points at the storage location that is next over from k. The statement

```
i_ptr--;
```

will decrement the pointer value, and the pointer will now be positioned back at the address value for k. Any value expression that adds or subtracts one from the pointer variable would yield the same results. For example, an increment could also be accomplished by the expression

```
i_ptr=i_ptr-1;
```

But, in fact, only the increment and decrement operators are ever found in this context.

The increment and decrement operators must be scaled for the data type. Each type takes up a different number of memory locations. To go to the next location might mean just the next memory cell while to increment a floating-point pointer might mean skipping over four such locations; this is, of course, implementation dependent. Figure 5-7 illustrates this for a typical 16-bit system. This scaling factor is what is set up by the declaration statement; this is the "association" that a pointer variable has with the data type to which it points.

Increment and decrement are not the only allowable operations on a pointer. We can also add and subtract any integer value. Again, although any legal integer expression will work, it's best to use the operator assignment form for the sake of clarity. Thus,

```
i_ptr+=2;
```

will move the pointer two integer locations forward, and

```
i_ptr-=2;
```

will return it to the original location by moving it backward two. This movement could be controlled programmatically by using a variable in place of the integer expression.

Two pointers associated with the same data type can be subtracted. This may seem like the strangest operation of all; but, in fact, it is a very useful one. What do we get if we subtract two pointer values? We get the total number of storage locations between them scaled for that particular data type.

```
int *i_ptr0,*i_ptr1;
        :
        :
        :
printf("%d\n",i_ptr1-i_ptr0);
```

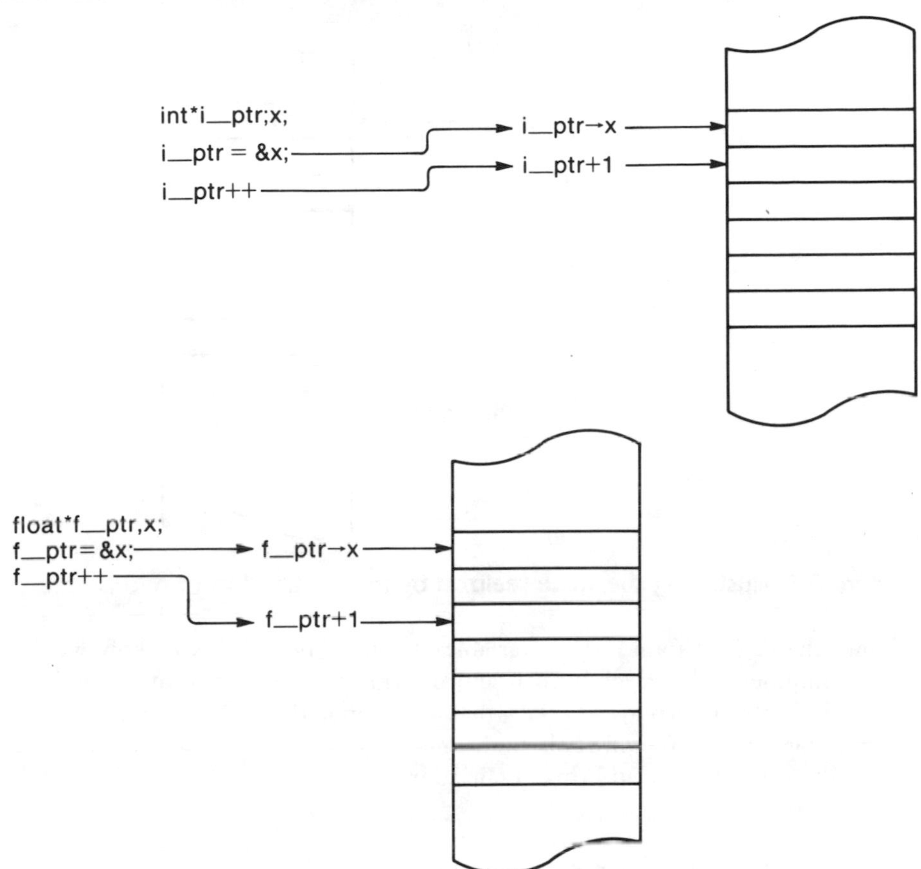

Figure 5-7. Illustrating how the increment operation is scaled for the data type.

will give us the number of integers that can be stored in the contiguous memory area between the location i_ptr0 and i_ptr1; this is illustrated graphically in Figure 5-8. Care must be taken that the linear order is maintained, and that the pointer with the smaller value is subtracted from that with the larger. If we invert this order, unpredictable results will occur. Remember, the subtraction of two pointers always yields a nonaddress value. Addition of pointers is not permitted.

The usefulness of these pointer expressions presupposes a block of contiguous memory. A caution must be sounded here. Consistent with C's overall approach to error checking and reporting, no test will be made that this situation is true. All such concerns must be explicitly dealt with by the programmer.

Program Listing 5-5 illustrates an application of pointer variables to implement a very simple binary search routine. The assumption of this function is that the pointer variables, begin and end, delimit a contiguous set of integer values sorted in ascending order. Operation proceeds by continually shrinking the search domain by

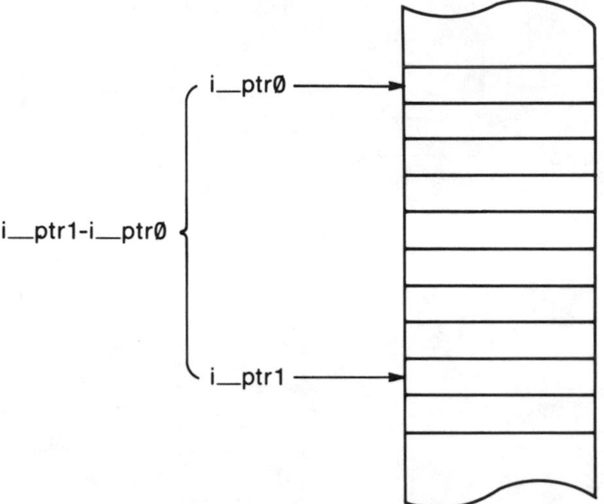

Figure 5-8. Illustrating the value realized by the subtraction of two pointers.

half until the value is found or the variables go out of bounds. Note how we divide the total number of locations by half and use this as an offset from the address in begin; this is a way around the fact that we cannot divide a pointer value. The difference between two numbers is an integer value. Dividing by 2 will still yield an integer. We can certainly add this to our address value.

```
table_find(value,begin,end)
int value, *begin,*end;
{
 int *middle;

 do {
   middle=begin + ((end-begin)/2);
   if(value==*middle)
     return(1);
   if(value<*middle)
     end=middle;
   else
     begin=middle;
  }
 while (begin<=end);

 return(Ø);

}
```

Program Listing 5-5. A function that will do a binary search on a contiguous section of memory

The application of the indirection operator and that of the increment/decrement operator are usually just as clear with pointer variables as with ordinary ones. When these operators are used together, however, there can be confusion as to how they're applied. The problem stems from the fact that decrement, increment, and indirection all have the same level of precedence. There is a further complication; usually, operators on the same level are evaluated left to right, this particular group—which includes most of the unary operators—is evaluated right to left. The left-to-right rule is so ingrained in us, that we cannot trust our intuition to yield the correct answer.

There are three specific instances where the application of the increment—or decrement since they are absolutely equivalent in this regard—and the indirection operator might produce results that are seemingly ambiguous. If we want to increment the value pointed to by a pointer, ptr, we must use the indirection operator first, then the increment operator.

```
++*p;
```

will accomplish this task. Suppose we wish to take the value pointed at by p and then increment that value. Here our intuition will fail us.

```
*p++;
```

will not do the job. Since the two operators are on the same level, they will be evaluated right to left. This means that the increment will be applied first, then the indirection operator will work on this new value. The result of this combined operation will be to access the value at the next location. p will be incremented, and the indirection operator will be applied to this new address.

```
(*p)++;
```

will accomplish our original goal. This will take the value pointed to by p first, and then increment. Finally, if we want to increment the address in a pointer and then take the value at that new address, we must use

```
*++p;
```

This construction may seem awkward, but it will do the job. What we have said here about the increment operator is just as true of the decrement operator. The same situations arise in exactly the same way. These four situations are summarized in Figure 5-9.

Pointer values can participate in relational expressions. It certainly makes sense to say that two pointer variables are equal; it means that they contain the same address. Of course, inequality is also sensible, they do not contain the same address. What may not be as obvious is that it is reasonable to to talk about "greater" and "less than" in this context. Recall that memory is a linearly organized list; it has an order to it. Also, from a practical standpoint, whenever we use pointers, they usually refer to a contiguous block of memory, and, for ease of programming, one of ascending memory locations. It is quite useful to be able to compare addresses. Program Listing 5-6 lists a function that will guarantee that ptr0 always has the lower address.

```
++*p   ==> takes the value pointed to by p and increments it.

           equivalent to:  *p=*p+1;

*p++   ==> takes the value pointed to by p then increments p.

           equivalent to:  *p;

                           p++;

(*p)++ ==> takes the value pointed to by p and increments it.

           equivalent to:  x=*p;

                           x++;

*++p   ==> increments p, then takes the value pointed to by p.

           equivalent to:  p++;

                           *p;
```

Figure 5-9. Illustrating four tricky situations that can arise when increment/decrement and indirection operators are used together.

```
swap_ptr(ptrØ,ptr1)
int *ptrØ,*ptr1;
{
 int *ptr;

 if(ptrØ>ptr1) {
   ptr=ptrØ;
   ptrØ=ptr1;
   ptr1=ptr;
 }

}
```

Program Listing 5-6. A function to swap pointer addresses.

5.4. Using Pointers with Structured Data Types

Pointers have a special relationship to the array data type in C. Not only are the two nearly interchangeable, but for many designers, pointers are the preferred way to access this data type. One advantage to using pointers is that access is direct and usually faster than array indexing and gives the programmer absolute control over all the details of this operation. This is particularly true if we're dealing with multidimensional arrays—the indexing is more complex for this type of array. The trade-off here is the greater complexity involved in dealing with pointers versus speed, but, as we shall shortly see, much of this complexity is illusory. It's a good trade-off.

Recall that we can pass the name of an array to a function. For example,

```
int a[50];
funky(a);
```

will send the array, a, over to the function funky(). Note further, that the array is passed by reference. The actual locations are sent to the function not just a copy of the array. The mechanism for this parameter passing will show us how we can use a pointer to access an array. The name of the array contains the address of the first member of the array—the zero location. From this point, we can use the increment or decrement operators to move up or down the array as we please. The pointer will automatically be scaled to move from cell location to cell location.

Two important provisions must be kept in mind. The data type of the pointer and the array must agree. Only an integer pointer can access an integer array, a float pointer, an array of floats, and so on. Also, an array name is not a pointer variable. It contains the address of the array, but it cannot itself be manipulated; this is a common source of confusion to the programmer new to pointers.

Program Listing 5-7a shows a function that will accept an array of integers and a position in that array and will return the value at that position. The array is assigned not to an array variable but to an integer pointer. Using the value "pos" to control the loop, we increment the pointer variable and then, using the indirection operator, we return the value at that position. Program Listing 5-7b shows a second version of this function considerably shortened, more efficient, and more like the code we would find in actual programs.

```
index (a,pos)
int *a,pos;
{
 int loop;

 for(loop=Ø;loop<=pos;loop++
   a++;

 return(*a);

}
```

(a)

```
index(a,pos)
int *a,pos;
{

 return(*(a+=pos));

}
```

(b)

Program Listing 5-7. Two versions of a function to accept an array and a position in that array and return the value at that position.

Character strings are most frequently accessed by pointers and not by indexing. Incrementing and decrementing pointers are more obvious ways of dealing with this data structure. Consider Program Listing 5-8. This figure shows a function that implements a string concatenation algorithm. Two character strings are passed as pointers to the function. This function attaches a copy of the second string to the end of the first and returns the length of the new string through the function name. The body of the function consists of two "while" loops. The first loop moves the pointer to the end of the first string, incrementing a counter variable idx. The second loop goes to the end of the second string copying its values cell by cell to an extension of the first. Again the counter variable is incremented; this value is returned as the length of the new character string.

```
s_cat(sØ,s1)
char *sØ,*s1;
{
 int idx=Ø;

 while(*++sØ!='\Ø')
   idx++;

 while ((*sØ++=*s1++)!='\Ø')
   idx++;

 return(idx);

}
```

Program Listing 5-8. A function to concatenate character strings.

Contrast the function in Program Listing 5-8 with that in Program Listing 5-9; here the same function has been done by using array indexing instead of pointer arithmetic. The two functions are very similar. The first while loop takes us to the end of the first character string. The second loop takes us to the end of the second string and assigns each member of the second string to a cell in the second loop. In this case, the index idx is returned as the length of the new longer string. Note that idx must be decremented before being returned as the length. By the time the end of string2 is found, the idx has already overshot this value.

```
s_catØ(sØ,s1)
char sØ[],s1[];
{
 int idx=Ø,idxØ=Ø;

 while(sØ[++idx]!='\Ø')
     ;

 while((sØ[idx++]=s1[idxØ++])!='\Ø')
     ;

 return(--idx);

}
```

Program Listing 5-9. The concatenation function done with array indexing instead of pointers.

What recommends the pointer version of this function over the array version? We can almost always rewrite a pointer function in nonpointer terms, particularly one that deals with character strings. Frequently, the pointer version is shorter and more to the point. This example was chosen for the similarity of the two implementations because, even here, there is an additional performance cost to the array implementation. Each time we specify a position in an array, a calculation must be done to find the offset from the zero location. Each access must start from the beginning. With the pointer implementation, we have a kind of cursor that is being moved along through the data structure. Each move is relative to the last one. The bottom line is, as one would expect, that there is less overhead with indirect addressing than with using the indexing mechanisms native to C.

Program Listing 5-8 illustrates a common problem when using pointers and arrays—particularly character strings. Pointer declarations allocate no memory. If this function is to work properly, somewhere in the program the locations in memory that these pointers will access must have been allocated. One common way to do this is through an array declaration; this will set aside specific memory locations. In the case of s_cat(), character string s0, must be declared large enough to contain the extra characters. If these are not set aside at the beginning of the program's execution, there's no way that we can have them available later during its run.

The idea that all pointer values must eventually refer back to an actual declaration is sometimes unclear to a programmer just starting to work with pointers, and it often leads to unnecessarily complicated, even confused software designs. C is still a language that allocates storage space in memory statically, not dynamically. If we wish to simulate dynamic allocation, we must allocate enough space initially so that we never run out during the program's execution, which means we're either very lucky or we waste a lot of space. There are ways to get true dynamic allocation of memory resources but they involve an intimate connection with the operating system and are not available on every computer. We'll defer discussion of these to a later chapter. Pointers might seem magical in operation but they can't move across variable locations that aren't there or, rather, they can but with disastrous results. The compiler will give no warning of pointers overrunning the allocated space. The system will happily let your pointer access values beyond the allocated space whether it be data or code. Of course the worst case is the one where disaster doesn't strike, where reasonable but incorrect values are used.

An array declaration is the preferred way to set aside blocks of memory space for data storage. The most basic such declaration is an array of characters. A byte, one character, is the smallest division of storage in C. Once the space is allocated, access can be through pointer variables. In fact, we can even change the data type through a judicious combination of pointers and the cast operator. Thus,

```
char space[50];
double *ptr;
ptr=(double*) space;
```

will allow us to take a block of characters and use it to store floating-point numbers. For example

```
*ptr=2.356;
printf("%f\n");
```

will be legal operations.

To complement our discussion about pointers to array, let's talk about an array of pointers. This array consists of an array of which each cell is a pointer to some other location. Arrays of pointers are frequently used with character strings. A typical application would be a table look-up function. An example is listed in Program Listing 5-10. Here we have an external array ops[] initialized with a number of character strings representing various arithmetic, relational, and boolean operators plus a special end-of-the-table marker, EOTB. The function, is_op() accepts a character string argument and returns a boolean value of:

1 if the character string is on the list
0 if it is not

The algorithm is simple. We loop through the array and compare each string found with the parameter value. If we find a match, we return a 1. If we reach the EOTB mark, we return 0.

The choice of an array of pointers is a good one for this function. We have an array of character strings. Each one may vary in length; this would complicate access if we were going to compare character by character. By switching to pointer access, we

```
#define EOTB "\Ø"

char *ops[]= { "+",
               "-",
               "/",
               "*",
               "**",
               "mod",
               "and",
               "or",
               EOTB };

is_op(op)
char *op;
{
 int idx=-1;

 do {
   if(!strcmp(op,ops[++idx])
    return(1);
  }
 while(strcmp(EOTB,ops[idx]);

 return(Ø);

}
```

Program Listing 5-10. A table look-up function.

have simplified the code. Note too that with a two-dimensional character array, much of the space would have been wasted.

Finally, we must mention the use of pointers with the structure data type. Here the pointer variable offers a superior way to access the member of a structure. Instead of the dot notation, we use an arrow. Program Listing 5-11 illustrates the use of this new notation. If we have a pointer variable associated with a structure, we can extract the individual member locations by connecting the pointer to the member name with an arrow (illustrated in Program Listing 5-11). The members of a union data type can be handled in the same way.

```
struct time  {
  int day,
      mon,
      year,
      hour,
      min;
  } *s_ptr,tim;

funky()
{
  s_ptr=&tim;

      :
      :

  printf("%d/%d/%d\n",s_ptr->mon,s_ptr->day,s_ptr->year):

  printf("%d:%d\n",s_ptr->hour,s_ptr->min);
      :
```

Program Listing 5-11. Illustrating the use of the arrow notation with structures and pointers.

5.5. Linked Data Structures

The power available in the C pointer allows us to create even more abstract and useful data structures than those we discussed in Chapter 4. Actually, these data structures are built up by using the structure definition and declarations of pointers to those structures. These are the linked data structures.

The most common linked structure is the linked list. There are several variant forms of this data structure but the base notion is contained in the singly linked list; this consists of a node that contains both a data part and a pointer to the next such node in the list. It was a singly linked list illustrated back in Figure 5-4. There are three points to note:

- A linked list always has a head, a variable that is not a node but points to the first node.
- A linked list always has a special flag marking the last node in the list.
- A singly linked list always has a direction. One can only move through the list in one way.

This last point is important; it seems to be a point often confused. *You cannot move backwards in a singly linked list.* Figure 5-10 diagrams these points.

The linked list performs some of the same tasks as the array, but it possesses some unique characteristics which allow it to do much more. First, however, let us consider some of the similarities. Like the array, the linked list stores values in a particular order. Like the array, the linked list is used to store data that is repetitive—copies of the same kind of data. Here the similarities end. The linked list is not necessarily stored in contiguous locations in memory. Since each node contains the address of its successor, nodes can be stored anywhere a memory location is available—this makes it enormously valuable for systems programs, especially those that manage memory. If an array contains sorted values, inserting a new value and maintaining that order can be a costly operation. Wherever that value is to go, everything below must be moved down to make room for it; it's even possible that the entire array, each member, might have to be moved. Inserting a new node into a list is a simple matter of copying pointer values and finding free memory locations. The linked list is the ideal way to handle sorted data that changes frequently.

The implementation of a linked list involves, first, a structure definition of a peculiar kind.

```
struct node {
  int data;
  struct node *next;
 };
```

defines a linked list node. For demonstration purposes our datum is a single integer, but any variable or set of variables could replace it in a real-life example. It is the last declaration in the structure that sets this apart as a linked list node; the variable, next, is a pointer to a structure of its own type. Of course, this is only a definition. No memory has been allocated yet.

The first declaration produces the "head" variable. Recall that this is not a node but a pointer to the first node on the list; this is the anchor from which we begin searching through the list:

```
struct node *head;
```

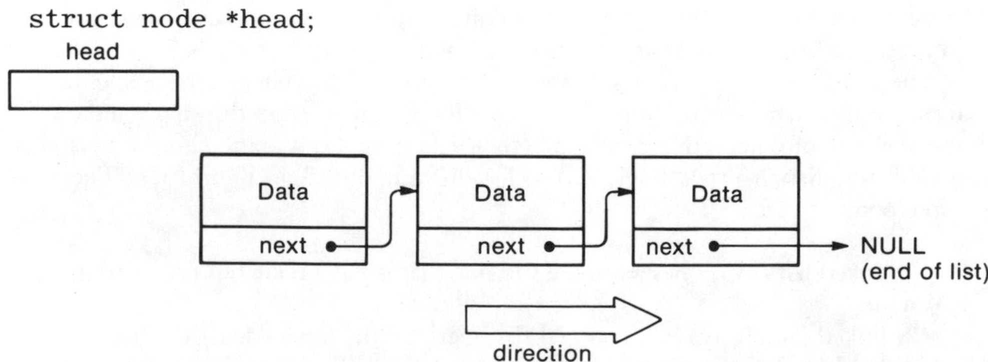

Figure 5-10. Illustrating directionality in a singly linked list.

will accomplish this task, although, in fact, we would probably do it in combination with the definition. We still have the problem of allocating individual node variables and linking them together. One possibility is to create a large array of this structure type. Every time a new node is needed, the next unused member of this array would be returned. There is nothing wrong with this approach. We could hide the array in its own file and even maintain a list of nodes that had been used but were now available for reuse. The only drawback is that, as with the character string data type, we're only simulating a true dynamic data structure.

As an alternative to doing our own memory management, the Standard Library offers us several functions that interact with the operating system to allocate and deallocate memory locations.

```
malloc(⟨size⟩);
```

will return a pointer to a free area of ⟨size⟩ bytes. Bytes were chosen because, as we mentioned earlier, they represent a kind of basic unit of memory measurement. Program Listing 5-12 illustrates a function that will return a pointer to a new location of type node. We use malloc() to allocate enough memory from the operating system to store the new node. We use the sizeof operator to indicate precisely how many bytes we need. Malloc() allocates and returns a pointer to a set of byte locations, but we need memory configured to store structures of type node. We use a type-cast operator to coerce the value returned from malloc() into the proper format for our structure type. Once we've created the node, we initialize its variables— data to 0 and next to the NULL value—and send it on its way through the return statement.

```
struct node {
  int data;
  struct node *next;
 };

struct node *new_node()
{
 struct node *ptr;

 ptr=(struct node *) malloc(sizeof)(struct node));

 ptr->data=0;
 ptr->next=NULL;

 return(ptr);
```

Program Listing 5-12. Illustrating a function that will create a new node for the linked list.

The three major operations that we can perform on a linked list are

- move through the list
- add a node to the list
- delete a node from the list

Moving or "navigating" through the list is a simple matter of following the pointer chain starting at the first node—the one whose address is in head—and following the chain of pointers to the end. It is usually convenient to create a temporary pointer variable to move through the list. It's important that the value in head not be changed; once this value is gone, we've lost the entire list and in a particularly unpleasant way. We can't get at the data and we can't reuse the memory. Linked data structures have a fragile existence tenuously maintained by the pointer links.

Figure 5-11 illustrates the insertion procedure. If a new node is to be inserted at the end of the list, we simply navigate to the last node and set its pointer equal to the new node's address. If we wish to insert a node anywhere else in the list, we must use the two-part procedure:

1. We move to the node in front of which we wish to insert our new one. We copy this node's pointer value into the pointer variable of the new node (*see* b in the figure). At this point we have two nodes pointing to one of the other nodes on the list;
2. We put the address of the new node into the pointer field of the node that will come before it in the list (*see* c in the figure).

These individual tasks must be performed in this order. If we do the second operation first, putting the address of the new node in the pointer field of its predecessor, we will lose the rest of the list. Once we lose the address of the next node, there's no

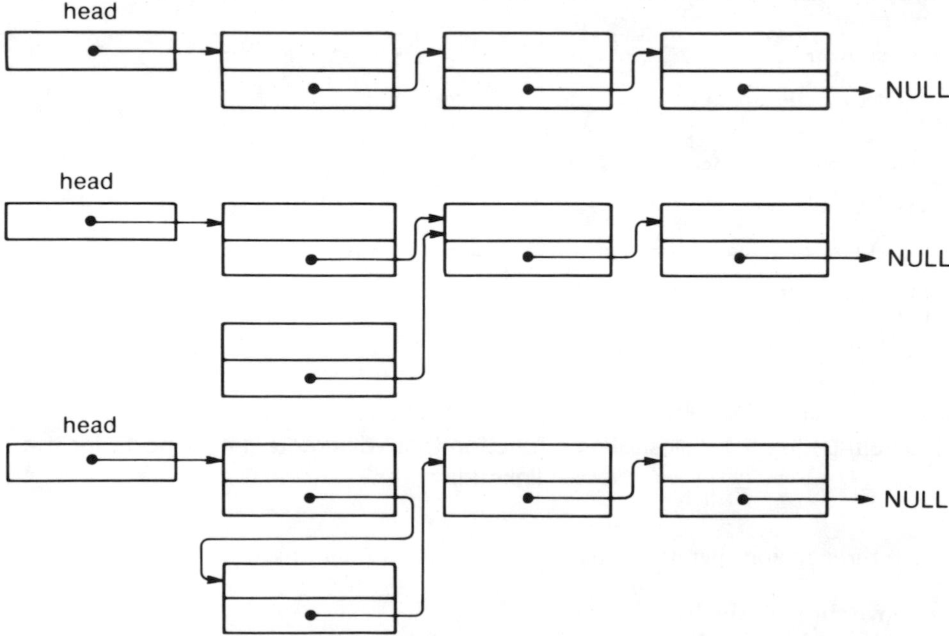

Figure 5-11. Inserting a node in a linked list.

way to recapture it. We must be sure that this value has been placed in the new node pointer before it's been erased from the old node.

There is a similar procedure for deleting a node from a list. If the last node is to be deleted, we simply move to the next to last node, copy its pointer field into a temporary pointer variable and set it to NULL. The temporary variable can be used to reclaim the space. If we wish to delete a node in the middle of the list, we must use the set of procedures illustrated in Figure 5-12. Again we have a two-stage process:

1. Move to the node that is to be deleted and copy its address into a temporary pointer variable (*see* b in Figure 5-12).
2. Copy this node's pointer field into the pointer field of its predecessor (*see* c in Figure 5-12).

The value in temp may be returned to the operating system so that the now unused memory location can be salvaged. As with the insertion, the order of operations is important; but, here the result of changing the node is less drastic, merely the reuse of that particular memory location. The rest of the list remains intact minus, of course, the deleted node.

Program Listings 5-13 through 5-16 show a program that will do a minimum of manipulation on a singly linked list. Specifically, we will be able to

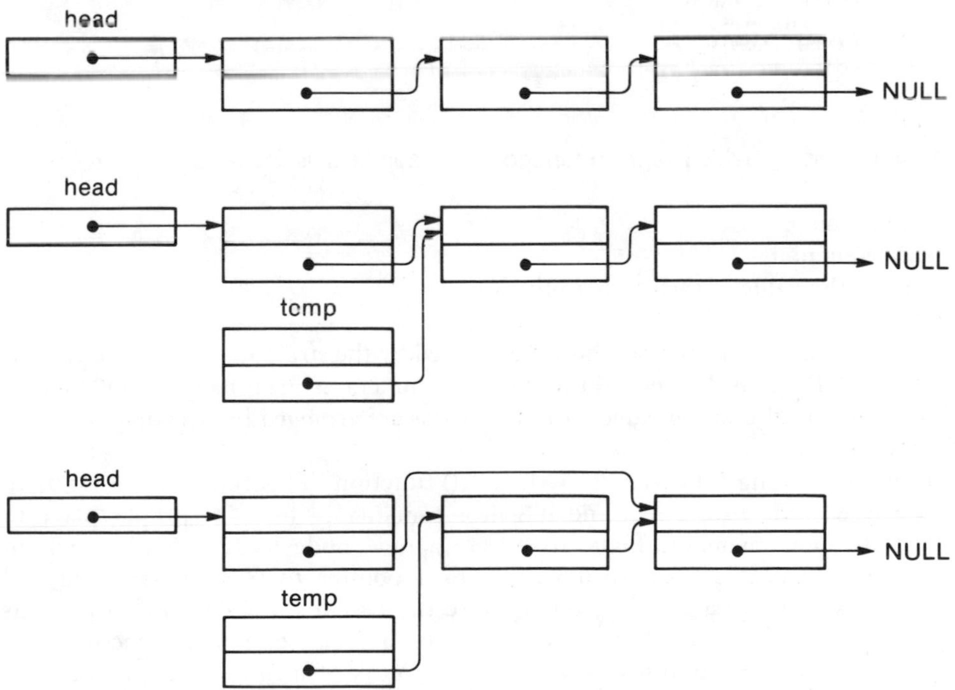

Figure 5-12. Deleting a node from a linked list.

```
struct node {
  int data;
  struct node *next;
 } *head=NULL;

main()
{
 int ch;

 while((ch=menu())!='s')
  switch(ch)  {
    case 'a':
      add_node();
      break;
    case 'd':
      delete_node();
      break;
    case 'p':
      print_nodes();
      break;
  }

}

menu()
{
 int ch;

 printf("a(dd a node)\n");
 printf("d(elete a node)\n");
 printf("p(rint nodes)\n");
 printf("s(top)\n");
 printf("enter function...");
 scanf("%d",&ch);
 return(ch);
}
```

Program Listing 5-13. The main function of the linked list manipulation program.

- add a node
- delete a node
- print the value of each node in the list

The format of each member of this list is defined by the structure, node. The value is an integer. Program Listing 5-13 lists the two functions main() and menu(). These allow access to the various functions. The nodes are arranged in ascending order by their value.

Program Listing 5-14 lists the add_node() function. This function allows us to add a new node to the list, and it will automatically find the proper place to insert the new member. First, we create a new node location with a call to malloc(). We coerce the return value into a pointer to type struct node and assign this value to a variable, temp. Note the use of the sizeof operator. This operator returns the number of bytes used by a variable or data structure. We use it here to indicate to malloc() how big a chunk of memory we require. The next step is to initialize the value and pointer field of the new node. We prompt for the integer value and set the pointer to NULL. This action will simplify our task if the node happens to go at the end of the list. A special case is made if head points to NULL, an empty list; we simply set head to point to the new node. Otherwise we must scan each node and compare it to the value of the new node. We'll either find a node that has a larger value or we'll reach the end of the list. When we find this node, we put its address in the pointer field of our new node. Now we have a dilemma. We need to put the new node's address in the pointer field of the predecessor node, but we can't go backwards in the list. Remember, a singly linked address has only one direction. What we use is a holding variable, last, that contains a pointer to this node.

```
extern struct node *head;

add_node()
{
 struct node *cursor,*temp,*last;

 last=head;
 temp=(struct node *) malloc(sizeof(struct node));

 printf("enter data--->");
 scanf("%d",&temp->data);
 temp->next=NULL;

 if((cursor=head)==NULL) {
   head=temp;
   return;
  }

 last=cursor;
 while(cursor->next!=NULL)  {
   if(cursor->data>temp->data)   {
     temp->next=last->next;
     last->next=temp;
     return;
    }
   last=cursor++;
  }
 cursor->next=temp;

}
```

Program Listing 5-14. This function will add a node to the list maintaining the ascending order of the nodes.

Program Listing 5-15 shows the delete_node() function. This function allows us to remove a node from the list. The node to be removed is identified by its value which is taken from the keyboard. Here, too, we must have a variable to hold the last node we accessed so that we can adjust its pointer field. In this function we scan the list until we find the proper node. At this point we place the address of this node in a pointer variable, temp, and copy its pointer field to the pointer field of its successor. Temp is then passed to the function free(). Note how it was coerced into character pointer format. Free() is a function in the Standard Library that will return memory locations to the operating system.

```
extern struct node *head;

delete_node()
{
 struct node *cursor,*temp,*last;
 int value;
 last=cursor=head;

 printf("enter value of node...");
 scanf("%d",&value);
 printf("deleting %d...\n",value);

 cursor=head;

 last=cursor;
 while(cursor->next!=NULL)  {
   if(cursor->data==value) {
     temp=cursor;
     last->next=cursor->next;
     free( (char *) temp);
     return;
    }
   last=cursor++;
  }
printf("node not found\n");

}
```

Program Listing 5-15. This function will delete a node from the list and return its memory locations to the operating system.

Print_nodes() is listed in Program Listing 5-16. This function displays the values at each node. We create a cursor variable and step through the linked list until the last node is reached.

```
extern struct node *head;

print_nodes()
{
 struct node *cursor;

 cursor=head;

 while (cursor->next!=NULL)  {
   printf("node value=%d\n",cursor->data);
   cursor++;
  }
}
```

Program Listing 5-16. This function will display the values of each node.

We have been dealing with the simplest of the family of linked lists. Figure 5-13 lists two additional types that are commonly found in software systems. The doubly linked list is unidirectional; it allows movement both forward and backward. The circular list is commonly used for well-behaved buffering systems—those where data arrives at a constant rate and there is no worry of overwriting any storage locations.

Let's close out this section with a new implementation of the stack data structure. Instead of storing values in an array, we create nodes and link them by pointers.

Figure 5-14 illustrates push() and pop() schematically. We are actually implementing a stack by using a linked list.

Program Listing 5-17 shows the function code for this implementation. The structure definition for stack sets up the format for the stack structure. The pointer variable, top, is declared as static to hide it from the rest of the program. Unlike our earlier example of a linked list, this one points backward toward a predecessor node.

```
struct stack  {
  int value;
  struct stack *last;
 };

static struct stack *top=NULL;

push(x)
int x;
{
 struct stack *temp;
 temp=(struct stack *) malloc(sizeof(struct stack));
 temp->value=x;
 temp->last=top;
 top=temp;
}

pop()
{
 struct stack *temp;
 int x;

 if(top==NULL)
  return;

 temp=top;
 x=top->value;
 top=top->last;

 free( (char *) temp);

 return(x);

}
```

Program Listing 5-17. A stack implementation that uses true dynamic allocation of memory.

To push a value onto the stack, we create a new node, intialize it with the value in question, and assign its address to a temporary variable. We assign the new node's pointer field to top and only then change top so that it points to the new node. Popping a value is just as simple. First we check for an empty stack. If this is the case, we return, otherwise we copy the address stored in top onto a temporary variable. We assign the pointer field from this top node to top, and by moving it down to the next node, we send the address of the former top node to free() for reclamation. The value is returned through the function pop().

Admittedly this implementation of the stack is not as neat and consise as our earlier one. The advantage that this implementation has, however, is a formidable one. Unlike that earlier one, it is truly dynamic, only acquiring space when it needs it and returning space with which it is finished.

5.6. Pointers to Functions

C will allow us to set up a pointer to a function as well as to an ordinary variable. Once we've created such a pointer, we can then manipulate functions as freely as variables. The most common use for this construction, however, is to pass functions to other functions as parameters; this itself is quite a useful capability.

The general form of a function pointer declaration is

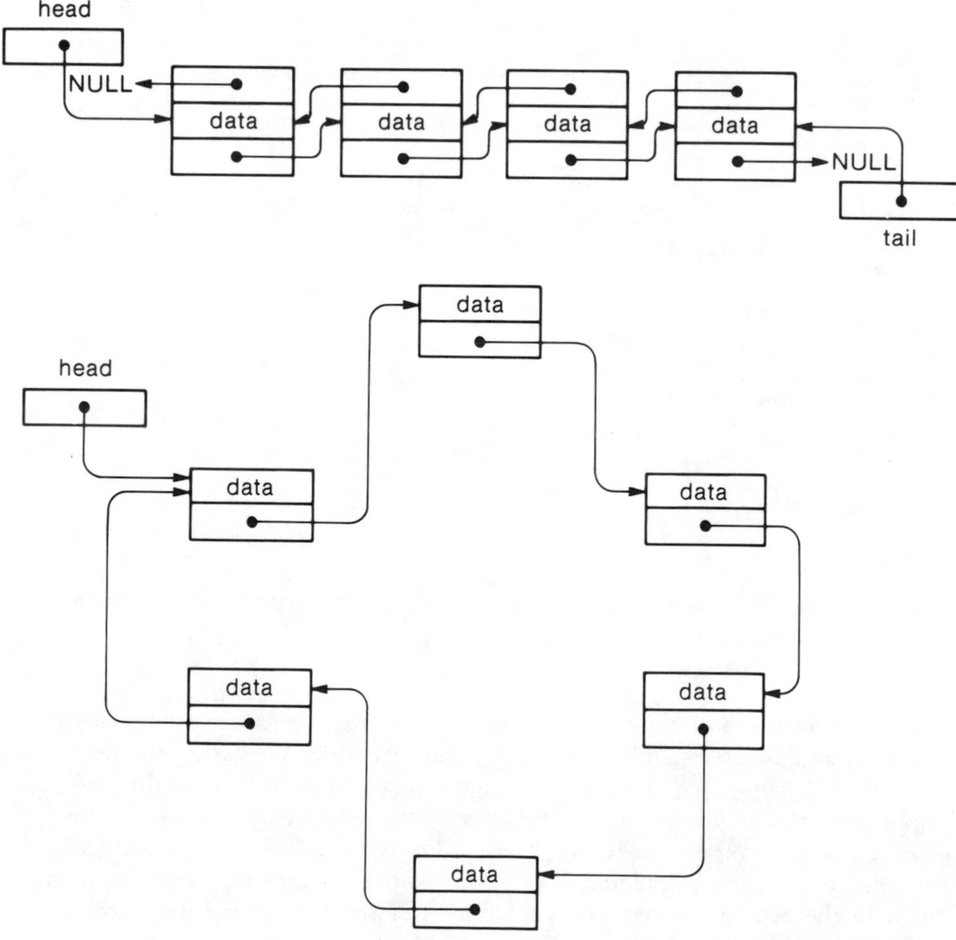

Figure 5-13. Illustrating two varieties of linked lists.

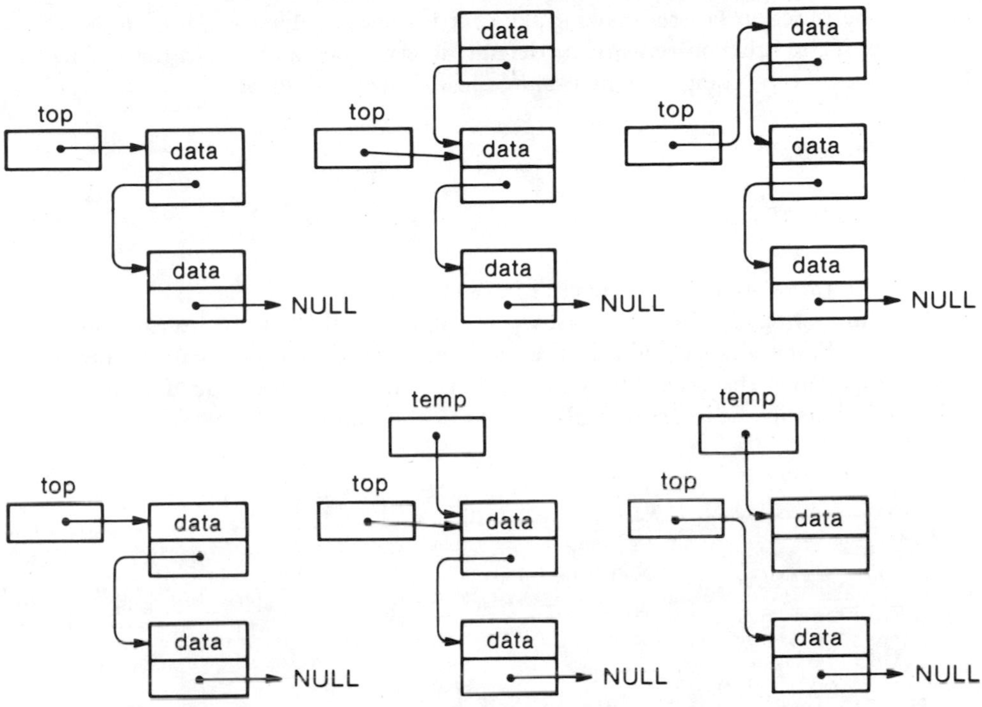

Figure 5-14. Illustrating stack operations.

```
⟨type⟩ (*⟨variable_name⟩)();
```

where ⟨type⟩ is the data type that the function will return and ⟨variable_name⟩ is a legal variable identifier. For example

```
int (*f)();
```

indicates that f will be pointing to a function returning an integer value, and

```
double (*x)();
```

declares x to contain a pointer to a function that will return a double-precision, floating-point number.

In calling a function that is passed another function as a parameter, we simply use the latter function's name. Thus, if func0() is a function, then we can pass func0() to another function, func1() with the calling sequence

```
func1(func0);
```

We use only the function name here. We do not include the parentheses usually associated with a function. However, to pass a function like this, we must explicitly declare the function before invoking the called function. This declaration is necessary even if the function returns the default, integer type and would not ordinarily be declared. To be complete, the example just shown should be

```
int func0();
     :
func1(func0);
```

If func1() returns an integer, it doesn't have to be explicitly declared.

Program Listings 5-18 and 5-19 list a program that will allow the user to enter two numbers defining a range and a choice criterion. It will then return all the numbers within that range that meet the stated requirements. The user can display all the prime numbers in the interval or all the odd or even ones.

```
main()
{
 int begin,end,ch,
     is_prime(), is_even(), is_odd();

 printf("begin..");
 scanf("%d",&begin);
 printf("end....");
 scanf("%d",&end);
 printf("find\n");
 printf("...p(rimes)\n");
 printf("...e(vens)\n");
 printf("...o(dds)\n");
 printf("in the interval %d to %d\n",begin,end);
 printf("===>");
 scanf("%c",ch);

 switch(ch)  {
   case 'p':
     all_nums(begin,end,is_prime);
     break;
   case 'e':
     all_nums(begin,end,is_even);
     break;
   case 'o':
     all_nums(begin,end,is_odd);
  }

}

all_nums(a,b,f)
int a,b,(*f)();
{
 int loop;

 for(loop=a;loop<=b;loop++)
  if((*f)(loop))
   printf("%d",loop);

}
```

Program Listing 5-18. The main and looping functions for the print-all-the-numbers-that-are program.

```
is_even(x)
int x;
{

 return( (x%2) ? Ø : 1 );

}

is_odd(x)
int x;
{

 return(!is_even(x));

}

is_prime(x)
int x;
{
 int loop

 for(loop=2;loop<x;loop++)
   if( (x%loop)==Ø)
    return(Ø);
 return(1)

}
```

Program Listing 5-19. The boolean functions to our print-all-etc. program.

Program Listing 5-18 contains main() and all_num(). The former prompts the user for the interval and the selection criteria. On the basis of this input, it calls all_num() passing it the end points which define the interval and the function that will do the appropriate selection. Note that we explicitly declared three functions even though they are all of type int. All_num() loops through the interval. For each number, it invokes a testing function and either prints it out to the screen or ignores it, depending on the returned value.

Program Listing 5-19 lists the testing functions. All three are straightforward and easy to understand. The function is_prime() does a series of sample divisions on the number passed to it; if it is ever evenly divisible by one of these numbers, it has failed to be a prime, and zero is returned; otherwise, the value 1 is sent back. The function is_even() simply tests the number by doing a division by 2 on the number. If it is even, this expression will be 0, and the conditional expresssion will return 1. Otherwise it will return 0. Finally, is_odd() returns the opposite of is_even().

5.7. Pointers and the Register Storage Class

The register storage class is a controversial element of the C syntax. Briefly, we can declare variables to be "register" variables; this alters not their data type but the way they are stored. In this it functions like the static declaration. Thus,

```
register x;
```

will declare x to be an integer of class register. What this means is that the compiler is requested to place these values in faster CPU registers rather than ordinary memory locations. However, so few of these registers are available to the programmer, that rarely more than one or two of these requests are honored. Furthermore, there are restrictions on the data types that can be used with this storage class. Integers can always be stored, but whether or not other data types can be accomodated is hardware dependent. The register storage class buys you very little.

Since a pointer is a kind of integer, it, too, can be stored in a register; but, this relationship is complicated by further restrictions on the register storage class. Specfically, we cannot use the address-of operator on a register. It makes no sense to ask for the address of an object that doesn't reside in memory. We can, however, store a pointer in a register:

```
register *ptr;
```

will accomplish this for us. Later on we can place a value into this variable

```
ptr=&x;
```

as long as x is a regularly declared integer and, not, itself, a register variable.

It's not clear that any real advantage is gained by putting pointer values into registers. It's attractive because of the speed of access of these objects over ordinary memory. But on the negative side, we must be careful of the restrictions—particularly those that affect portablility—and we have no guarantee that the compiler will even comply with our request. Still, we must be aware of this construction because we will see it used from time to time.

5.8. Summary

In this chapter we have covered a lot of the most difficult material in C. The proper use of pointers is what really defines the mature C programmer from the novice. Pointers are used extensively in C more than in any other programming language except possibly assembly language. To write powerful programs we must learn to use them well.

We have covered the gamut of pointer usage. We have the utility of pointers for stepping through arrays and especially character strings. We have seen how the natural alliance between pointers and the structure data type simplifies access to these structures, and we have seen how pointers to functions allow us to pass them to other functions, thus simplifying many formerly complex tasks.

Using pointers and structures, we were able to create an entirely new and powerful set of data structures, the linked structures. These have significantly extended the range and power of C. We have covered a lot of material but all of it is bread-and-butter programming activity.

6

Calling the Operating System

Although the standard I/O library offers a complete range of service functions particularly in the area of input/output, there inevitably comes a time when the problem at hand demands a more intimate interaction with the computer. This kind of interaction is accomplished by service requests placed with the operating system—more commonly known as system calls. In C, this kind of thing is accomplished in a straightforward and elegant way. However, for most programmers this area remains mysterious. This chapter should clear up this mystery and introduce the reader to the range of possibilities this facility offers.

This chapter will focus on system calls that interact with the file management subsystem of the operating system. This is not as restrictive as might first appear since modern technique collapses all I/O into file I/O. We also discuss error handling in a system context as contrasted to error handling that is local to a program.

Goals:
- To understand the trade-offs involved with using operating system calls instead of the standard library
- To review the distinction between disk files and device files
- To explore system error-handling techniques

6.1. Dealing with the Operating System

The operating system and how to engage it in useful dialogue are still great mysteries even to seasoned programmers. Once it was considered the dangerous province of the systems programmer, not to be trespassed on by the merely mortal programmer tilling in less magical programming vineyards. Even today, the operating system of even a small computer appears complicated, confusing, and often inconsistent in its operation. This is due to the relative youth of the discipline of computer science and its state of accelerating development. Improvements are constantly made, features added and others changed. To have three new versions of an operating system within a single year is not unusual. Of course, no two operating systems use the same terminology. This situation is changing. With the widespread introduction of microcomputers, standardized operating systems— systems that work on many different kinds of computer—have become popular. The rise of Unix as a de facto standard that spans all sizes of computer systems has only accelerated this process.

Within this chapter, we will be discussing system calls from the perspective of a Unix environment. This doesn't mean that the chapter will be useless for an individual doing C programming under some other operating system. Many of these modern systems take Unix as a model and, thus, are similar to it. Also, the system calls we will be concentrating on, file I/O, are often added to non-Unix implementations of C, for the sake of "portability." Unix will offer us a common ground since most individuals with an interest in C will have at least a passing acquaintance with this operating system—certainly enough of an acquaintance to make sense of our discussion here.

Although a computer's operating system is frequently described as a master executive program controlling the overall operation of the system, from the perspective of the programmer it functions more in the nature of a mediator to the actual hardware. These two views are not mutally exclusive, but the latter is more appropriate to our current discussion. The computer's hardware does things. It sends streams of characters to the outside world, it accepts such streams from that outside world, it stores characters on disk, and it engages in a thousand other such activites. Other necessary tasks that might not be so obvious include:

- loading programs and data into memory
- scheduling processes on multi-programming systems
- keeping track of individual users on multi-user systems

In addition, the whole issue of file security opens up an entirely different realm of activity. All of these tasks are complex sequences of operations that require nontrivial programs of their own to accomplish. All such programs together are the operating system.

We can see, then, that from the programmer's point of view, the operating system simplifies and rationalizes access to the system's resources. If we want to communicate to the outside world, the operating system will take our message and see that it either gets where we want it to go or tells us why it didn't get there. If we want to create a file on one of the disk drives, it relieves us of the onerous chore of finding empty space on the disk, calculating sector addresses, and updating tables. It also catches us before we can do something dangerous to the computer system's integrity or if we try to violate the security of someone's file. In a nutshell, the operating system offers a series of services. This is the way it is organized: as a set of system functions, sometimes called "entry-points," that request specific actions or values from the hardware system. In Unix, the format of these system calls is the same as that of any C function. This is partially a result of the intimate connection between C and this particular operating system, but it's also a fact that this is the way most modern operating systems are designed. However, there are a few systems that use more esoteric and less obvious means of access.

We will be primarily concerned with the file management subsystem: opening and closing files, creating and deleting them, and read/write access. For most programs that are not explicitly systems oriented—and even for some that are—this is the most heavily used part of the operating system. Thus, it is also one where it might be desirable or even necessary to customize an interface. It must be pointed out, however, that this area is well represented by functions in the Standard Library; it's always possible that a proposed customization or optimization has already been done and packaged for us.

For what reason would we wish to forego the Standard Library functions and go to the lowest level possible on the machine? What's the trade-off? Performance is one possible answer. All the functions supplied with C have to be general purpose ones to a greater or lesser extent. These functions have to be able to deal with a variety of situations and deal with them adequately. The particular application that we're using it for may be only one of many it can handle. Thus, there is probably extra code, extra overhead, that is imported into our program but never used. For example, scanf() can accept integers, floats, and other numeric types as well as characters and character strings. This function contains statements to handle all these types of conversions, yet our application program may only require integer conversion. A function might do extensive error checking including checking for conditions that can never arise in our application. Ultimately, we are at the mercy of the individual who designed the function. The performance is a function over which we have no control.

Another motivation for going directly to the systems level arises when we must interface a new device to the computer. Each peripheral device has an operating environment that includes operational parameters and special command sequences. To create I/O functions that deal with this environment, we need to distill I/O procedures down to their most basic form. Not only for physical devices but also for logical ones, devices that utilize existing computer resources to create new kinds of objects. Message systems—electronic mail—even a full-blown computer network would be examples of such logical objects.

The advantages of the existing, Standard Library functions is portability. These functions are the same and act the same over many different hardware systems, implementations of C, and, even, under non-Unix implementations. Programs or functions that make direct system calls may or may not share such portability. Certainly in transporting a program from Unix to another operating system, these system calls would not hold and would have to be rewritten. Even from Unix to Unix transportation is easier if the Standard Library is used. Having said this much, we shouldn't dwell on the difficulties. Even if a rewrite is necessary, we are talking about a small amount of actual code. It doesn't take much to tip the scales in favor of using direct system calls, and C, especially C under Unix, makes such calls so matter of fact that we will find ourselves continually tempted to customize our functions.

6.2. Accessing System Commands

Our first access to the operating system is not really a system call at all but, rather, a function in the Standard Library:

```
system(⟨command⟩);
```

where ⟨command⟩ is any valid command name that can be executed from the shell. Such commands include

- date—to retrieve the date and time
- ls—to list out a directory
- cat—to display the contents of a file
- dc—a desk calculator emulator

This function may be used to utilize system commands within a program—for example, displaying the system date on the screen—or to allow temporary access to a program during the execution of another program. The calling function is suspended and waits until the program or command passed to system() is executed. At that point the original program resumes.

Program Listing 6-1 illustrates a very simple menu function that utilizes system(). First, a list of choices is printed, and the user is prompted for a particular choice. A switch statement takes this input and picks the appropriate piece of code to be executed. If it is one of the presumed functions, add(), remove(), or update(), an appropriate integer value is returned. If the user wishes a directory listing or the use of a desk calculator, system() is called with the appropriate string parameter. Note that these system calls are handled within the menu function; and the ordinary function calls are sent to the calling function for execution. An input of "S" causes an execution of the exit() function and the termination of the program.

System() is only for the kind of light-duty interaction between programs that we find in our example. Any more intimate connection of programs will require more sophisticated techniques. With system() we don't even have interaction between caller and called program. We can send values to the program called in system(), but we can't get any value, any result, back. Although control is returned to the original program, that original program is blind to anything that might have occurred while it was asleep.

```
menu()
{
 int ch;
 for(; ;)  {
   printf("\n A(dd)\n");
   printf("R(emove)\n");
   printf("U(pdate)\n");
   printf("D(irectory)\n");
   printf("C(alculate)\n");
   printf("S(top)\n");
   printf("function...");
   scanf("%c",&ch);
   switch(ch)  {
     case 'A':
      return(1);
      break;
     case 'R':
      return(2);
      break;
     case 'U':
      return(3);
      break;
     case 'D':
      system("ls");
      break;
     case 'C':
      system("dc");
      break;
     case 'S':
      exit();
   }

}
```

Program Listing 6-1. Illustrating the use of the system function.

6.3. The File Management Subsytem

Every operating system must make some provision for dealing with files. It must be able to name them, keep track of them, and send them to appropriate places. We are being purposely vague and general here. Our model of a file is that of a collection of bytes resident on a disk drive. In Unix, however, and most modern operating systems, the file system has been expanded to include any data object that has an existence external to the main computer components—memory and the CPU—yet interacts with it. Terminals, printers, and all peripheral devices are files. On some advanced, network systems, entire computers are considered to be files. The advantages of this perspective are a unification of the I/O subsystems of the computer, thus making it consistent across all object types and more reliable and easier to maintain.

To access a file, whether disk or device, we have to have certain key values about the object in a place where they are readily available; most important among these are

- where a file is located
- how big it is

- what kinds of access have been authorized to us

All this information is maintained by the operating system in various places. Before access is requested, these data are stored in a data base about files called the directory system. At any given time, some of this directory is in memory and some is stored on disk. After access is requested, these values are copied into a data structure resident in memory sometimes known as the file control block (fcb). Unix maintains a table of these fcbs.

When we use the functions in the Standard Library, we take these fcbs and create an additional data structure that also contains buffer locations that hold the values as they move between memory and disk. This is the FILE declaration that we discussed in Chapter 3. In doing direct system calls, we deal directly with the file system, any buffering will have to be explicitly done by us.

To keep the record straight, even the direct system calls are several layers removed from the raw input and output found deep in the machine. Some buffering is done even at this level to aid the efficient operation of the machine, and it is entirely transparent to the user. We look right through it and see direct input/output operations.

Files are identified through the fcb data structure; this, in turn, is identified to the individual function or program via the file descriptor. Unlike the file pointer in the Standard Library functions, the file descriptor is a simple integer value that will be used to identify the file for the duration of he program execution. When a file is closed, its fcb is removed, and any necessary update information, such as last date accessed, is written out to the directory entry for that file. Every time a C program starts executing files 0, 1, and 2 are automatically opened and assigned to the user's terminal, either display screen or keyboard. These are stdin, stdout, and stderr; they can be redirected if necessary.

It's not really necessary for us to know the details of the file control data structure or how the connection between a function and a file is made even if we wish to use the direct I/O system calls, but it is useful to have a general notion of what transpires in this heady realm in order to explain those sometimes seemingly inexplicable problems that come up from time to time.

6.4. Making the Connection: open(), creat(), and close()

Before we can access a file, two things must be true

1. The file must exist, at least in the directory.
2. We must announce to the operating system that we are interested in connecting to it.

The first condition is accomplished by the creat() system call, the latter by open(). Although these bear a similarity to the functions we find in the Standard Library, a closer scrutiny will reveal the system calls as more primitive functionalities. One very important point: Each of these calls performs only one of the tasks necessary to access a file. Open() will only attach a file to a program. If that file does not exist, creat() must be called first. Fopen() will automatically take care of this for you. The only way fopen() will fail is by trying to open a nonexistent file for reading. System calls are building blocks; it is actually a mark of good design that they each accomplish so little.

The logical first step is to create a new file:

```
creat(⟨file_name⟩,⟨mode_value⟩);
```

will accomplish this. ⟨file_name⟩ is a locally legal file name, and ⟨mode_value⟩ sets the security level of the file. Common mode values include

777 total access to everyone,
700 access only to the file's creator,
755 total access to the creater, read and execute access to everyone else.

If it's successful, creat() will return a file descriptor. An unsuccessful attempt will yield the value -1. If creat() is passed the name of an existing file, it will truncate that file but not change the security values. Creat() opens the file for writing.

To attach an existing file, we must use:

```
open(⟨file_name⟩,⟨access_mode⟩),
```

This call operates only on an existing file even for write access. ⟨file_name⟩ is a legal file name on the system, and ⟨access_mode⟩ is a code indicating the type of access being sought. This access can take one of three values:

0 read only access
1 write only access
2 read and write access

A file descriptor is returned of -1 if an error has precluded the opening of the file in question.

There are two ways to sever the connection between a program and a file. Any graceful exit from a program back to the operating system will automatically close all open files. However, it is sometimes wise or even necessary to detach a file during the execution of a program. There is an upper limit on the number of files a program may have open at once, and, in general, a file should be closed as soon as the program is finished with it.

```
close(⟨file_descriptor)
```

will sever the file indicated by ⟨file_descriptor⟩ from the program. A returned value of 0 indicates that the file was successfully closed, but -1 is returned if an illegal file descriptor was used.

Program Listing 6-2 illustrates a function that will open a file in one of three modes and return a file descriptor. These three modes are

r read only
w write only
r/w read and write

We have a filter of if statements that pick out these three possible situations. If the mode is read only, we simply execute an open() call, with the proper mode set. Error reporting is automatic; open() will return a -1 if the file is nonexistent. With a read there is no way to correct for an error. If the mode is "w", we use the creat() call; this will not only create a new file but will open it for writing. The drawback here is that if there is an existing file with the same name, it will be destroyed. Finally, if the mode requested is "r/w" (read and write), we have a slightly more complex situation. First we try an open() call, if this works, we return the resultant file descriptor. If it doesn't work, we create a new file, but we cannot simply use the file descriptor produced by our call to creat(). This system call opens a file for write access. It is necessary to close the file and then use a call to open() to reopen it with proper mode set—read and write. If none of these situations is found, a -9 is returned to indicate a total failure.

One difficulty with using the creat() call to open a file for write access is that it will destroy any existing file of that name. Program Listing 6-3 lists safe_attach(), a more robust version of our earlier function, attach(). The difference lies in the write and read/write sections. Here we test first to see if a file by that name exists, if it does not, then we create it. If the file does exist, we open a generic file, noname, and return a value of two (2) to indicate that this was done. Our test is a trial open() call.

```
attach(file,mode)
char *file,*mode;
{
 int f;

 if(!strcmp("r",mode))
   return(open(file,Ø));

 if(!strcmp("w",mode))
   return(creat(file,755);

 if(!strcmp("r/w",mode))
  if((f=open(file,1))==-1)   {
    f=creat(file,755);
    close(f);
    return(open(file,2));
   }

  return(-9);

}
```

Program Listing 6-2. A function to open a given file in one of three possible modes.

```
safe_attach(file,mode,des)
char *file,*mode;
int *des;
{
  if(!strcmp("r",mode))  {
    *des=open(file,0);
    return((*des==-1 ? 0 : 1));
   }

  if(!strcmp("w",mode))
    if((*des=open(file,1))==-1)  {
      *des=creat(file,755);
      return(1);
    }
    else  {
      close(*des);
      *des=creat("noname",755);
      return(2);
     }

  if(!strcmp("r/w",mode))
    if((*des=open(file,1))==-1)  {
        *des=creat(file,755);
        close(*des);
        *des=open(file,2);
        return(1);
     }
    else  {
      *des=creat("noname",755);
      close(*des);
      *des=open(file,2);
      return(2);
    }

   return(-9);

}
```

Program Listing 6-3. A more robust version of attach.

There is a great similarity between a system call and an ordinary function call; this is one of the things that makes C, and especially C with Unix, a powerful systems programming language. However, we should also note the differences. Our earlier point about the simplicity of the system calls has been underscored by our two examples. Consider how much more complex they are than if they had been written with the Standard Library. The reason is simple. With these system calls, we have to explicitly concern ourselves with every detail of the interaction including the anticipation of every possible situation and problem. Still our reconciliation is that we also have control over almost all the parameters of our transaction.

6.5. Accessing the Values: Read() and Write()

Once we have opened a file for write or read/write access, we can put values on it with the write() system call. This has the form

```
write(⟨file_descriptor⟩,⟨buffer_name⟩,⟨number_bytes⟩)
```

where ⟨file_descriptor⟩ is an integer created by a previous call to open() or to creat(), ⟨buffer_name⟩ is a pointer to a set of contiguous character locations, and ⟨number_bytes⟩ is an integer indicating the locations from the buffer area that are to be transferred. In the face of a disastrous failure, write() returns a value of -1. Under ordinary circumstances, the value returned is the number of bytes actually transferred. Afer a normal write() operation, the number returned should be the same as ⟨number_bytes⟩. If these numbers are not equal, then something has gone awry.

Notice that as with the open() and the creat(), all the details of this transaction with the operating system must be handled explicitly. There are no defaults, and there is no elegant way to write to the file "whatever is necessary." We have to specify precisely what we're sending, where it's going, and how much of it is going there. We mustn't get too carried away with this notion of basic I/O. We are still not on the level of the hardware; we still have the mediation of the operating system between us and the "ground level." In fact, some buffering is still occurring. Anytime data are being sent to a disk drive, it has to be buffered for the sake of efficiency. Writing or reading a disk, character by character, would be an absurd waste of time. At very least a sector must be collected before any access operation can be performed.

Figure 6-1 illustrates the relationship between the system calls, the operating system, and the actual hardware. The position of some comparable Standard Library functions is offered as a contrast. The operating system must buffer not only the disk drive but, for similar reasons, the terminal I/O. Most terminal devices are "smart" units that transmit to the computer, not character by character, but one line at a time. Some provision must be made to accept this line before any processing can be done on it. And there is a class of peripheral, most notably the line printer, which are shared by the entire system. Such sharing is usually accomplished by creating "copies" of these devices on disk—a kind of "virtual" or imaginary device—by writing out to a disk file the data that would normally go directly to it. Software in the operating system then copies these disk files to the actual device one at a time; this is called "spooling". The point is that in each of these cases buffering is going on. The Standard Library functions add another layer on top of this one in the form of the FILE structure. The system calls are, in contrast, direct access and affect those parts of the operating system responsible for these devices.

Taking output from the file requires the read call

```
read(⟨file_descriptor⟩,⟨buffer_name⟩,⟨number_bytes⟩)
```

Here the parameters are the same as for the write() call. The read() call also requires a contiguous area of bytes to serve as a buffer. A disastrous error will cause read() to return -1, an end-of-file mark (eof) will yield a zero value, and a successful read() operation will return the number of bytes transferred from the file. If fewer bytes are read than were requested, this does not necessarily indicate an error condition.

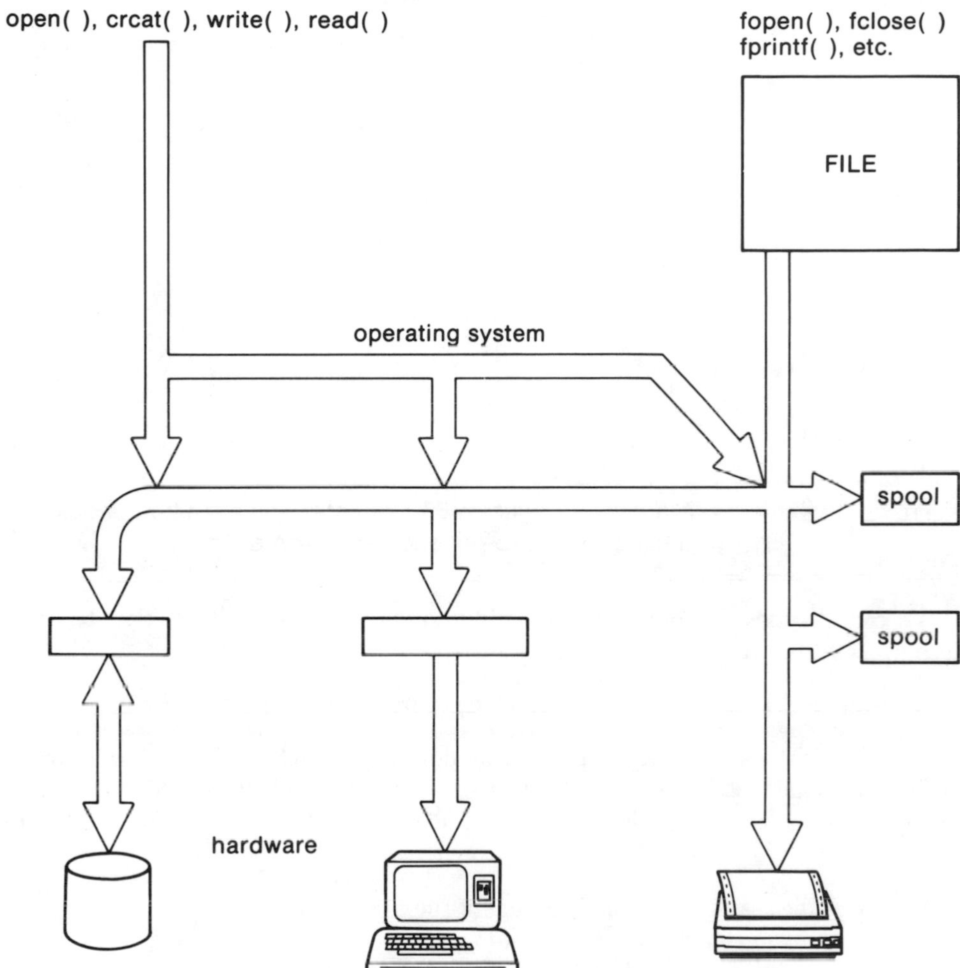

Figure 6-1. Illustrating the relationship of system calls and Standard Library functions to the operating system and hardware.

Program Listing 6-4 illustrates two very simple functions that use the read() and write() call. Get_line() returns the most information. It accepts as parameters, the file descriptor integer and the address of a buffer of byte locations. It does a read() call asking for 80 characters to be stored in the buffer. If the call fails, 0 is returned. If an end-of-file condition is detected, a value of 1 is sent back to the calling program. In all other cases, 2 is returned. Put_line() also takes a file descriptor and a buffer pointer as arguments. It, in turn, calls write() and gives it 80 characters from the buffer. If exactly 80 characters are accepted by the file, the value 1 is returned to indicate success. Otherwise, zero is returned. Note again, how explicit we must be about the details of each interaction.

```
get_line(f,line)
int f;
char *line;
{
 int n;

 if((n=read(f,line,80))==-1)
   return(0);
 else if (n==0)
   return(1);
 else
   return(2);
}

put_line(f,line)
int f;
char *line;
{
 if((80-write(f,line,80))==0)
   return(1);

 return(0);

}
```

Program Listing 6-4. A function to get an 80 character line from a previously opened file and one to put such a line on a file.

We can also position ourselves in a file prior to doing a read() or a write(). To accomplish this, we use

```
lseek(⟨file_descriptor⟩,⟨number_bytes⟩,⟨from⟩)
```

where ⟨file_descriptor⟩ identifies the file, ⟨number_bytes⟩ tells us how many bytes to move—conveniently, a file is just a large array of bytes—and ⟨from⟩ indicates where the origin of the counting will be. This last quantity will have one of the following values:

0 moves the cursor from the begining of the file
1 moves the cursor from the current location
2 moves the cursor ⟨number_bytes⟩ from the end of the file

The position in the file is returned or a value of -1 if there is an error condition. It's important to note that ⟨number_bytes⟩ is a long integer value as is that returned by the system call itself.

Figure 6-2 and Program Listings 6-5 through 6-10 define a program that will access a file containing bibliographic information through the use of two indices:

1. A primary index always resident in memory.
2. A secondary index keyed to the first letter of the search argument.

The basic algorithm is simple

1. We enter a book title.
2. The first letter of the title is used as an index into a table of file names; this file is loaded into memory.

3. A linear search is performed on this secondary index, and a file offset is retrieved.
4. The resulting offset is used to access the complete information from the file.

This algorithm is schematically illustrated in Figure 6-2a. In Figure 6-2b, the layout for these three data structures is shown. The primary index holds the system names of the secondary indices. The secondary index files consist of a record made up of the title of a book and an integer value that indicates the position in the main file of that title's information record.

Program Listing 6-5 shows declarations for these data structures. It's a good idea to keep these two sets of objects distinct in our minds. The data structures are defined by the problem and are independent, to a degree, from the declarations that

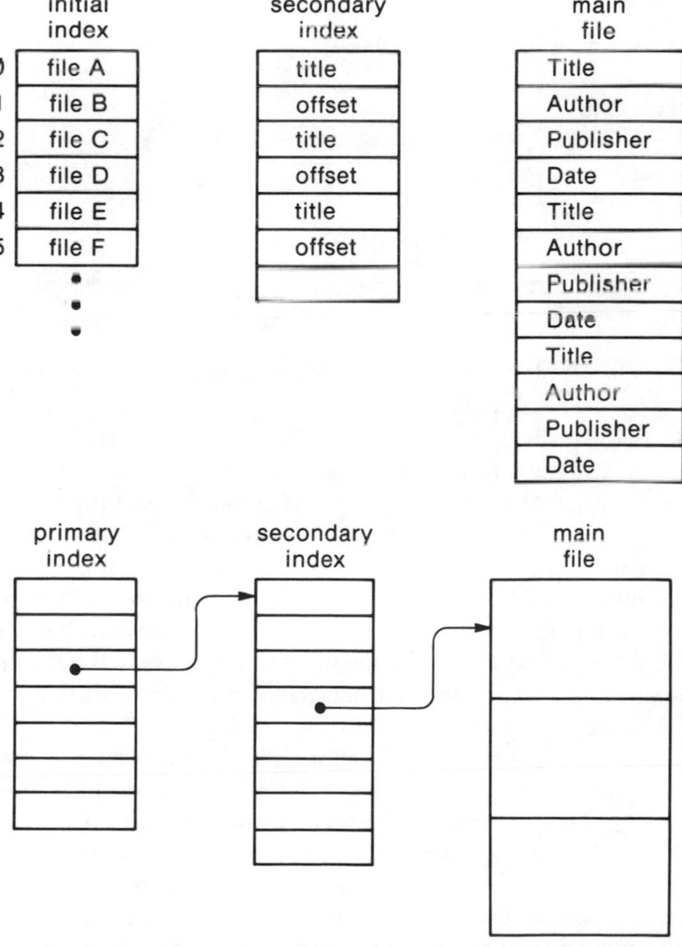

Figure 6-2. File layouts for the indexed file access system.

implement them. There are a number of different ways we can design our solution even given the restraint of a set of data structures and an algorithm. For example, we are implementing the primary index as an array of pointers, permanently installed in memory, but our algorithm would be implemented just as correctly if we stored these values on disk instead—although it wouldn't be as fast.

```
char *p_index[]={ "filea","fileb","filec","filed","filee","filef",
                  "fileg","fileh","filei","filej","filek","filel",
                  "filem","filen","fileo","filep","fileq","filer",
                  "files","filet","fileu","filev","filew","filex",
                  "filey","filez" };

          (a) Primary index buffer declaration.

struct t_index  {
  char title[80];
  long offset;
};

          (b) main file buffer definition.

struct m_file  {
  char title[80],
       author[30],
       publisher[30],
       date[8];
 };

          (c) main file buffer definition.
```

Program Listing 6-5. Data structures needed by the indexed file access program.

Why use two levels of indexing? Why not create one large index file instead of 26 small ones? The main argument against a single, large index revolves around the issue of performance. The search time through the index is the main factor influencing the access time to the information in the main file; it is also one of the few factors that we have direct control over. A large file is going to take longer to search, and it almost certainly will have to be maintained in sorted form—this will add an additional, if only periodic, time penalty. If we break the index into smaller units, some of which can always reside in memory, the search time will be optimized and we may not even have to keep them sorted. Another problem will be solved by using short indices. When we add items to our file, the insertion will be simpler if we are dealing with short data structures—particularly if they are unsorted—than if we are inserting in the middle of a massive one.

Program Listing 6-6 lists the main function. This is just a straightforward question and response design. The user is queried for the title of a book and that is accepted as a character string. This string is passed, in turn, to the function search along with a structure variable that will hold the resulting data retrieved from the main file. If search() cannot find the title, an error message, "title not found", is printed; otherwise, the record is sent to the function, display(). This function (*see* Program Listing 6-7) will print out the information from the main file onto the user's screen. Main() will prompt us for a new title until "stop" is entered.

```
#include <stdio.h>
#include "dstruct.h"
#define TRUE 1

main()
{
 char title[80];
 struct m_file record;

 while (TRUE) {
   printf("enter title...");
   scanf("%s",title);
   if(!strcmp("stop",title))
     exit();
   if(search(&record,title))
     display (&record);
   else
     printf("title not found\n");
  }

}
```

Program Listing 6-6. The main function of the library search program.

```
display(record)
struct m_file *record;
{

 printf("******************************************\n");
 printf("%s\n%s\n",record->title,record->author);
 printf("%s\n%s\n",record->publisher,record->date);
 printf("******************************************\n");

}
```

Program Listing 6-7. The display function for the search program.

In Program Listing 6-8, we have a listing of search(), the heart of our program. This function accepts title, the search argument, and record, which will hold the data gleaned from the main file. Record is called by reference so that we can send this data back to the main function. We open the appropriate index file by using the first character in title as an offset into the p_index[] table. Note that we've mapped "A" onto 0, "B" onto 1, and so forth. We create a temporary location, s_index, to hold 10 records from the index file. The body of this function is the do loop. Within this loop, we first load our secondary index buffer, s_index with a call to load(). Then we loop through the 10 locations and compare the search argument, title, to the key value, s_index->title. (Note: there is no conflict of variable names here.) If we find a match, a call to the function load_main() will place the information from the main file into the structure variable record.

```
search(record, title)
struct m_file *record;
char *title;
{
 struct t_index *s_index;
 int loop,flag,fd;

 fd=open(p_index[*title-'A']);
 s_index=(struct t_index *) malloc(10*sizeof(struct t_index));

 do  {
    flag=load(s_index,fd);
    for(loop=0;loop<10;loop++)
       if(!strcmp(s_index->title,title)) {
          record=load_main(s_index->offset);
          close(fd);
          return(1);
       }
    }
 while(flag!=EOF);

 close(fd);
 return(0);

}
```

Program Listing 6-8. The search function will fill the main file buffer and return a signal indicating the success or failure of the search.

We must give load_main() the offset value that we retrieved from our secondary index file. Then we close this secondary index file and return the value 1 to the main function. Note the use of the variable flag. Load() will return EOF if it reaches the end of the file; this is also our condition for ending the loop, so we must retain this value until the end of the loop. The do loop will only be exited normally if the search argument is not found in the index file. In this case, we close the secondary index file and return a zero to the main function. Note we chose a do loop instead of a while loop because even if load() has reached the end of the file, there still may be records in the memory buffer that have to be compared to the search argument.

```
load(inx,fd)
struct t_index *inx;
int fd;
{
 int loop,flag;
 char buff[80];

 for(loop=0;loop<10;loop++)   {
    flag=read(fd,buff,80);
    strcpy(buff,inx->title);
    flag=read(fd,buff,8);
    inx->offset=atol(buff);
  }

 return(flag);

}
```

Program Listing 6-9. The load function fills the secondary index buffer.

Program Listing 6-9 lists the function load(). This will load 10 records from the opened file into the index buffer and pass it back to search(). This function has a straightforward design but two things should be noted. The read() system call requires that we specify explicitly the number of bytes to be transferred by the transaction. We must specify all of the bytes allocated to the field even if the actual values are shorter. In this case, the field must be filled with some filler value—perhaps an ASCII null—so that each record in the file is exactly the same size. Note further, that system I/O calls provide us with no conversion. The file is just a long string of bytes. If we must interpret a string of digits as a number, we must explicitly convert it. In load(), the first field, title, is 80 bytes long and the second field, offset, is eight digits maximum converted to a long integer.

Load_main() is listed in Program Listing 6-10. Its type is the structure m_file. We use the system call lseek() with the offset value imported from search() to position the file pointer after we open it, then we do a read. Again we must read all of the allocated bytes even if the actual value is less. Our task is simpler here because no further conversion is necessary—each field is a character string. We close the file and return the values we've just read through the function name.

```
struct m_file load_main(offset)
long offset;
{
 struct m_file buff,*ptr;
 int fd;

 ptr=&buff;

 fd=open("main",0);
 lseek(fd,offset,0);
 read(fd,ptr->title,80);
 read(fd,ptr->author,30);
 read(fd,ptr->publisher,30);
 read(fd,ptr->date,8);

 close(fd);

 return(buff);

}
```

Program Listing 6-10. The loadmain function returns the next record in the file.

To round out this section, we have the system call

```
unlink(⟨file_name⟩);
```

This call will remove ⟨file_name⟩ from the current directory, and it allows us to erase files programmatically. But there are certain qualifications. If we pass unlink() the name of an open file, its destruction will not occur until after it has been closed. In any case, the file will only be removed from the system if we have removed the last link. If we have removed one of many such links, the file will remain on the system but unavailable to us, at least through the current directory.

6.6. Error Checking

The system calls that we've been discussing all have error return values. Often a -1 will be returned to indicate that something went amiss. The system is prepared to give us more specific information about these errors. This information is contained in an integer value, errno, which is global to the entire program—actually to any program. Each possible error recognized by the system is assigned an integer value. This value is placed into errno whenever an error condition occurs. These message assignments are changeable and could be different in different systems—mostly in terms of additional errors rather than reassignment of existing ones. Some common errors and the error numbers include

1 This indicates an attempt to access a file in a way not permitted.
2 This is set when an attempted access is to a nonexistent file or directory.
5 A physical error has occurred in the I/O subsystem.
9 A file descriptor points to an unopened file, or an attempt was made to access a file in a mode for which it was not opened.

When a system call produces an error, a peek at errno can help identify the particular error. Caution must be exercised about any access to this variable. It is not reset after an error condition is registered, even if operations following it are correct and successful. The error reported in errno is the last one caught by the system.

In addition to errno, the system maintains two other global variables relating to error reporting.

- sys_list is a table of error messages linked to the error numbers.
- sys_nerr is the current number of error conditions recognized by the system.

These variables, like errno, are available within the program. Indeed, errno indexes the sys_list table and can be used to extract these "official" error messages.

We also have available to us a Standard Library function that will send error messages out to the stderr file.

```
perror(〈id_string〉)
```

will put the character string 〈id_string〉 and the error message associated with the last error recognized by the system onto the stderr file. 〈id_string〉 can be the program or function name or some other character string that will identify the location of the error.

Functions in the Standard Library may also put values in errno. These, too, can be accessed and can generate error messages. However, without knowing the internal structure of the function, the error reported may be misleading.

6.7. Summary

In this chapter we have taken a brief look at directly interacting with the operating system. We compared its advantages:

- speed of execution
- the simplicity of its operations

to its disadvantages. The very simplicity of each system call means that to do some useful work, we must combine these system calls in explicit ways leaving nothing to default. Whether or not a Standard Library function or a system call would be more appropriate in a given situation is a matter of judgement and circumstance.

We have been most concerned in this chapter with disk file access; this is reasonable, since most forays into the system involve attempts to maximize this type of I/O. However, some attention has been given to other system interfaces. For example, system() allows us to call a command from within a program. Errno stores error conditions discovered during the execution of a program.

We have centered our attention on the Unix operating system because it is most frequently associated with C. But many of the direct system calls we have discussed are also available on other implementations, particularly those that deal with direct access to the file subsystem.

We have not discussed every possible direct interface into the operating system, but we've seen how it can be done. What's more, we've seen how easily this kind of programing can be done in C.

—7—

Bit Manipulation

Another important area where C differs substantially from other high-level languages is in its ability to go into an individual machine word and directly manipulate the bits. While not the stuff of every program, this ability is the building block of some useful and interesting algorithms and data structures—arithmetic algorithms and bit maps to name just two. This chapter will introduce you to these bit manipulating techniques. We focus first on the bit operators: (complement)~, (and) &, (or) |, (exlusive or) ^, and (shifting) >>, <<. These operators directly affect the word and can be used for masking, retrieving, and powers-of-two arithmetic operations—operations similar to their assembly language counterparts. The other focus is on a structure unique to C, the bit field structure; this structure is a variant form where the members do not represent individual variables within the greater whole but represent individual collections of bits within a machine word. This is a powerful data type that allows a facile and straightforward way to set and read bits. It is particularly useful for bit maps and masking operations.

Goals:

- To understand what the bit manipulation operators do to the underlying hardware elements
- To review the bit manipulation operators and the bit field data type
- To understand the kinds of algorithms and data structures that can be implemented with these facilities

7.1. Twiddling the Bits

If C really is a "mid-level" language then its programming is a replacement for assembly language programming. One of the strongest arguments for this is the access that it gives the programmer to the hardware itself. C is one of a very few languages that allows us to get inside a computer word. Using the built-in bit-manipulation functions, we can perform a number of extremely low-level actions on the bits themselves. These actions are usually restricted to assembly language. C runs the gamut from the very high-level, linked data structures—the linked list—to the individual bit in the machine. This wide range makes C a uniquely powerful tool for doing software development; with it, we can quickly produce software that has a high degree of integration with the hardware. Even applications software can directly access the machine level and its resources. This is why C is the preferred programming language under Unix.

Long conditioned to think of a word or perhaps a byte as the minimum unit of storage, it may not be immediately clear what we can or even should do to the bits themselves. One very important class of problems where bit-level access becomes important is in dealing with hardware control and status words. One way the computer system can communicate with us is by reserving locations within the memory address space and placing values in these locations to indicate the presence or absence of certain important conditions. In Figure 7-1, we have a simplified example of a status word that might be associated with an I/O port. Within the word, bit locations are associated with specific conditions: Bit 1 indicates a "clear to send" condition, bit 3 tells us whether or not a character has been received at the port, and bit 6 indicates that the port is ready for another output character. To extract this information from the status word, we need to rely on the bit-manipulating capacity of C.

Status and control words are not restricted to the physical I/O system but are found throughout the computer system. Any time we have a set of conditions that occur together or close together and are either on or off, a status word is appropriate. Similarly, if we need to indicate the on/off status of a set of conditions, we would use these operators to create a control word.

The motivation for the use of status/control words underlies all bitwise structures: economy of memory resources. On/off or boolean questions require only one, two-state object—the bit—to indicate an answer. Within the context of a program, such boolean questions usually occur in clusters. Even common sense argues that we should combine them into a single word; it's a matter of conserving resources. This motivation underlies some of the other situations where bitwise operations are found. In data communications, for example, we sometimes need to squeeze the representation of values into smaller locations to improve performance and increase the speed of transmission.

Other contexts in which we operate directly on the bits in a word are not primarily an attempt at conservation. There is a broad class of situations that involve mapping two or more values onto a single word where the motivation is one of performance.

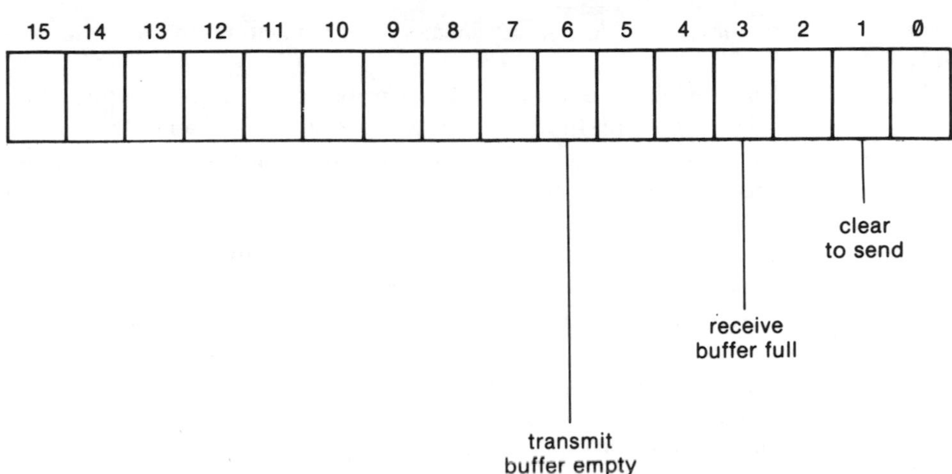

Figure 7-1. A typical example of a status word.

We may wish, for example, to divide our memory space into one or more discrete modules or banks and specify a particular address as a bank and an offset from the beginning of that bank. We can accomplish this in a single word or address through bit manipulation (*see* Figure 7-2a).

Another example in which mapping occurs is that of a computer network. One way to send messages through such a network is to package each character—or more commonly, a group of characters—with the address of the node to which it's being sent. Figure 7-2b shows, in greatly simplified form, how we can accomplish this

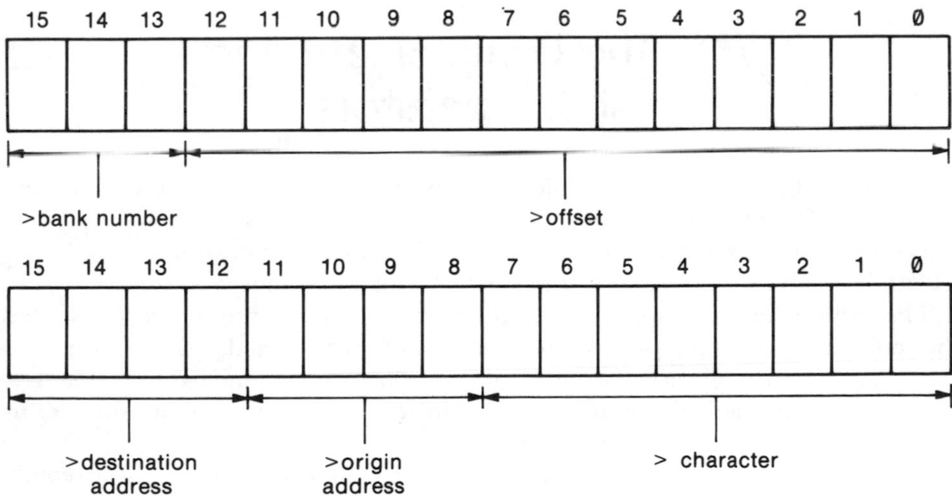

Figure 7-2. Two examples of bit packing where conservation of memory is not an issue

mapping. In both these examples, saving memory space is either an absent or secondary motivation.

The bit map, another very common structure maps resource usage information onto a bitwise boolean structure. In Figure 7-3, we see a simplified example of such a map. Here we have a sequence of 16 buffers allocated in memory. Each of these buffers is associated with one of the bits in our bit map. A 1 in the bit location indicates that the buffer is in use, a 0 indicates that it is available. Bit maps are commonly used by systems programs. A bit map could be set up to keep track of the status of memory locations for example. Any context in which we have a set of fixed resources where usage changes frequently is a good candidate for such a data structure.

There are two categories of bitwise operations:

1. bit manipulation functions
2. the bit field data type

Bit manipulation functions represent a subset of the kinds of operations available to assembly language programmers. Thus, we have complement, shift, and the bitwise logical operators. Bit field data types are unique to C. They allow us to give names to the bits or collections of bits within the word.

We have been concentrating on bitwise operation on the computer word. Bit manipulation functions will work on any integer data type, long, short, char as well as integer. Our examples so far have assumed a 16-bit word representing an integer data object. In fact, our examples will work for any of the allowable types. Using bit manipulation techniques on float and double type, however, is undefined. In most instances, the unsigned integer is probably the best choice.

7.2. The Complement and Shift Operators

The first bitwise operator we'll deal with is also the simplest. The complement operator, "~", works on each bit in the data object it's applied to by switching that bit's value to its opposite: a 1 becomes a 0, a 0, 1. This is illustrated in Figure 7-4 by a truth table and some examples of its operation on 16-bit integer values.

The truth table is an explanatory device we've borrowed from logic; it describes the result for each of the possible combinations of operator and operand values. In the case of the complement operator, there are only two combinations, 0 and 1. Actually the bit manipulation operators are logical ones so it shouldn't surprise us that we can use things like truth tables.

Shifting the bits in a word is another common operation familiar to assembly language programmers. Many shift operations are restricted to one bit at a time. C defines two general purpose, bit-shifting operations that allow us to specify not only the direction of the shift, but the numbers of positions as well:

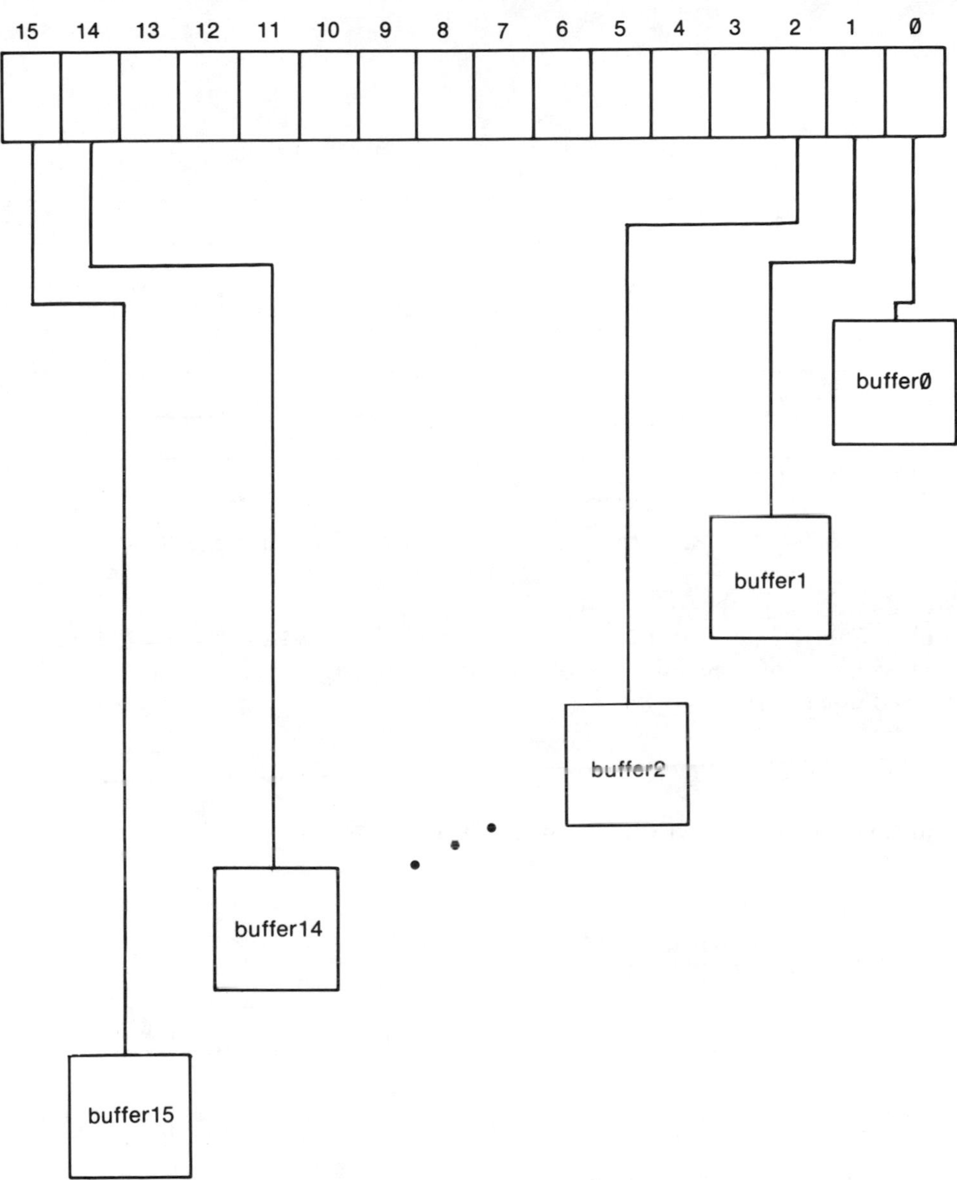

Figure 7-3. An example of a simple bit map.

```
‹variable› ‹‹ ‹positions›
```

will shift the bits in an integer value, ‹variable›, ‹positions› places to the left. Vacated bit positions on the right side of the word will be filled with zeros. Thus,

```
x ‹‹ 5
```

X	~X
0	1
1	0

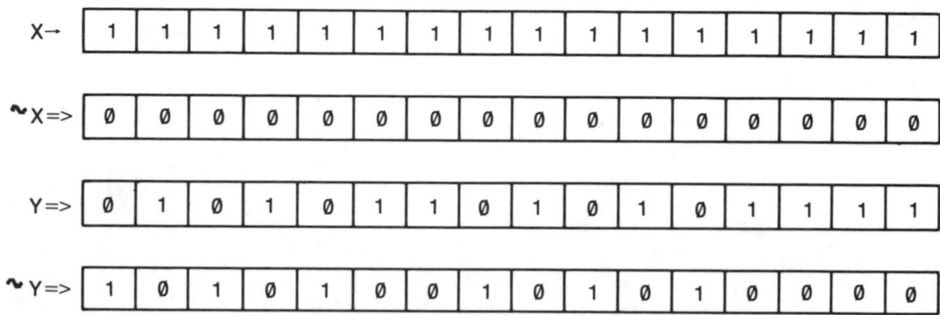

Figure 7-4. Illustrating the truth table and operation of the complement operator.

will shift the bits in variable x 5 positions to the left. Figure 7-5 provides a graphical representation of some examples of the left-shift operation. Right shifts are accomplished in a similar way:

```
<variable> >> <positions>
```

will shift the bits in ⟨variable⟩, ⟨positions⟩ places to the right. For example,

```
Y >> 4
```

will cause a right shift of four bit positions.

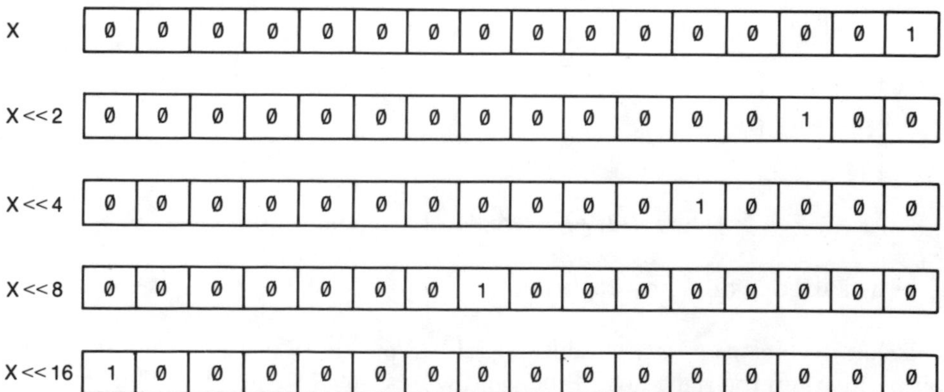

Figure 7-5. Illustrating the left shift operation.

There is an ambiguity with the right-shift operator. When the bits are moved to the right, what value is put in the vacated positions at the left of the word? The answer to this question depends on which of the integer data types this operator is being applied to and the hardware implementation of the underlying machine code. If the right shift is applied to an unsigned value, then the operator will fill the vacated spaces with zeros. Figure 7-6 illustrates this operation. However, if we right shift a signed value, then it may or may not zero fill the vacated positions on the left. Some machines implement "sign extension" for this kind of shift. This means that whatever was in the sign bit will be pulled over to fill the bit positions left open during the move. If there was a zero in the sign position, zeros will fill the vacated position and it will be no different than with nonsign-extended machines. If, however, there is a 1 in the sign bit, ones will be drawn across into each empty bit position. Figure 7-7 illustrates this. The simplest solution to this problem is to stick to unsigned data types. Otherwise we'll have to mull through our system documentation to discover whether or not sign extension is in force.

There is a mathematical component to the shift operation. Shifting the bits within a word one position left, multiplies the value by 2. Shifting right, divides by 2. Multiple shifts will multiply or divide by a power of 2—two positions 4, 3 positions 8, and so on. Although we'll rarely find ourselves implementing arithmetic algorithms this way, it's important to recognize this fact because it may turn up in other situations involving shifts.

7.3. The And, Or, and Exclusive Or Operators

C defines three bitwise logical operators. Unlike the complement and shift operations, these are binary relations. They relate the individual bits in two words rather

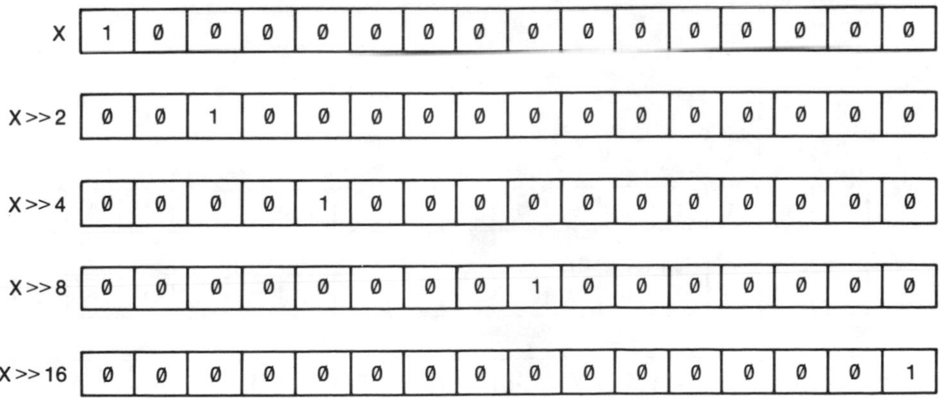

Figure 7-6. Illustrating right shift implemented as a logical operation (no sign extension)

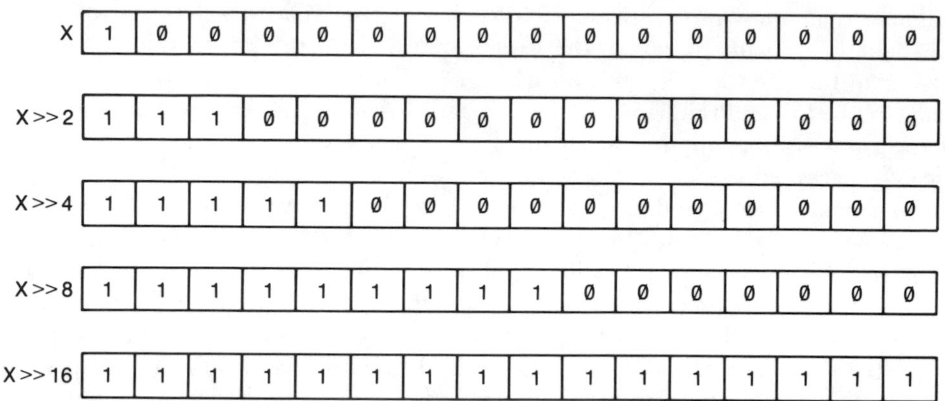

Figure 7-7. Illustrating right shifting implemented with sign extension.

than operate on one single one. Figure 7-8 lists the truth table for the bitwise "and" operator, "&". Since two values or operands are associated with this operator, the truth table is longer than that of the complement. The & operator will yield a 1 only if both of its operands are 1, otherwise it results in 0. Note the example also included in Figure 7-8.

We have to be careful not to confuse this operation with that of binary addition. Here there is no carry. Each bit position is compared only to the corresponding bit position in the other operand. The result is either one or zero and has no effect on the comparisons being performed on any of the other bit positions. Note the similarity of the "&" to the boolean operator "&&"; this can be the source of some difficulty.

Complementary to "&" is the "or" operator, "|". This too is a binary relation. It will return 1 if either operand or both are 1. Zero will be returned only if both operands are zero. Figure 7-9 illustrates the truth table of the | operator as well as an example. Note here too a possible confusion with its boolean counterpart, "||".

X	Y	X & Y
1	1	1
1	0	0
0	1	0
0	0	0

X	1	0	1	1	1	0	1	0	1	1	0	1	0	1	0	1
Y	1	1	1	0	0	0	1	1	0	0	0	1	1	1	0	1
X & Y	1	0	1	0	0	0	1	0	0	0	0	1	0	1	0	1

Figure 7-8. Illustrating the truth table and operation of the bitwise and operator.

Finally, C's repertoire of bit manipulation operators includes the "exclusive or" operator, "^". The truth table for this is shown in Figure 7-10. The result of this operation is 1 if either operand is 1 and zero if both operands are zero or both are 1—the exclusive or is more in tune with our ordinary language notions of or. This figure also contains an example of exclusive or.

Frequently we will find it necessary to set the bits in a data object to some initial value. We can use an appropriate combination of the operators we've just discussed. The drawback to this technique is that it robs us, whenever we're using bit manipulation, of the clean, well-structured initialization that we've come to expect with C. However, we can set the bits of, say, an integer, just by assigning it a value:

```
unsigned x=1;
```

will set the first bit position to 1 and all the other positions to 0. It becomes more confusing, however, when we need to set more of the positions in a word. There is an easy solution. By using the octal or hexadecimal number system for our initial specification, we can more easily match the bit positions in the word to a number. With both these number systems, there is an easy translation from a binary value to one in a more tractable form. Box 1 summarizes the relevant facts for octal numbers, and Box 2 summarizes facts for hexadecimal numbers.

Each octal digit translates into three binary digits, and each hexadecimal one translates into 4 bits. The "quick and dirty" way to calculate an initial value or a particular bit pattern is:

1. Write down the binary representation.
2. Break it up into groups of 3 (octal) or 4 (hexadecimal) binary digits.
3. Convert each of these groups to the appropriate digit.

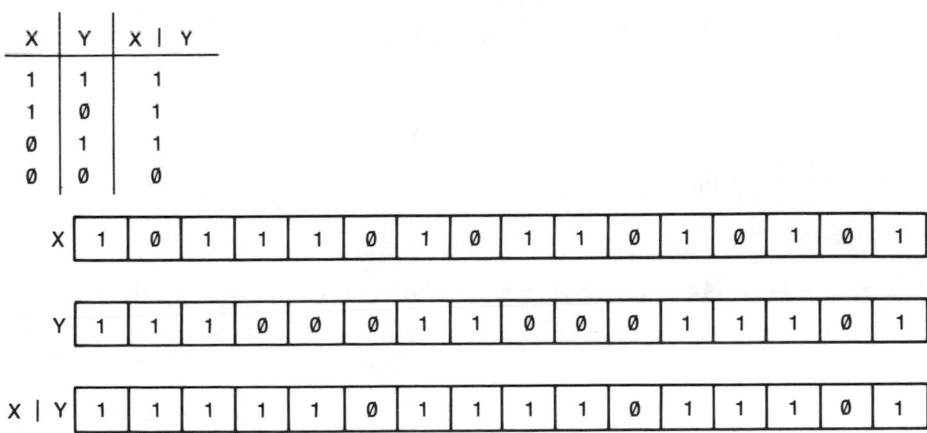

Figure 7-9. Illustrating the truth table and operation of the bitwise or operator.

X	Y	X ^ Y
1	1	0
1	0	1
0	1	1
0	0	0

X	1	0	1	1	1	0	1	0	1	1	0	1	0	1	0	1
Y	1	1	1	0	0	1	0	1	0	0	0	1	1	1	0	1
X ^ Y	0	1	0	1	1	0	0	1	1	1	0	0	1	0	0	0

Figure 7-10. Illustrating the truth table and operation of the bitwise exclusive or operator.

These procedures are summarized with examples in Box 3 (for octal) and Box 4 (for hexadecimal). Which number system is used for this is solely a matter of taste. Hexadecimal would seem to be ideal for word sizes which are multiples of 4 (16 and 32 bits) but octal notation is traditionally used with minicomputers and minicomputer derived systems.

Box 1. Some interesting facts about octal numbers.

Base: 8

Digits: 0-7

Conversion to/from binary:

--0	001	010	100	101	111
0	1	2	4	5	7

Decimal evaluation:

012457 =

(0 x 85) + (1 x 84) + (2 x 83) + (4 x 82) + (5 x 81) + (7 x 80)

Box 2. Some basic facts about hexadecimal numbers.

Base: 16

Digits: 0-9, A-F

Conversion to/from binary:

```
1010   1111   0101   0000
  |      |      |      |
  |      |      |      |
  |      |      |      |
  A      F      5      0
```

Decimal evaluation:

AF50 =

(10 x 163) + (15 x 162) + (5 x 161) + (0 x 160)

Box 3. Translating a set of bit positions (octal).

Problem: initialize x so that bit positions 1, 3, and 5 are set.

Create a binary representation:

0000000000101010

Break it up into groups of 3:

```
--0   000   000   000   101   010
```

Translate each group into an octal number:

```
--0   000   000   000   101   010
 |     |     |     |     |     |
 |     |     |     |     |     |
 0     0     0     0     5     2
```

The declaration is

unsigned x = 000052;

Box 4. Converting set of bit positions into a hexadecimal number.

Problem: initialize x so that bit positions 1, 3, and 5 are set.

Create a binary representation:

0000000000101010

Break it up into groups of 4:

0000 0000 0010 1010

Translate each group into an octal number:

```
0000  0000  0010  1010
  |     |     |     |
  |     |     |     |
  0     0     2     9
```

The declaration is

unsigned x=0X0029;

7.4. Using the Bit Manipulation Functions

It is difficult to come up with good, general purpose examples that use these bit manipulating functions. They usually come in handy when we're working at a very low level, close to the machine hardware. These kinds of programs and functions are the least portable and the most specialized of any that we write. Here we can only suggest possible uses, not give code that can actually be copied and run.

Although C has a right- and left-shift operator, it doesn't have a rotate operation. This is an operation commonly found in assembly language. Its operation is simple: it's a left shift by one, and the bit value in the last position—the most significant bit—is put in the last position—the least significant bit. Figure 7-11b illustrates this. Figure 7-11a lists a function that will accomplish this task. The function accepts an unsigned integer as an argument and will return that integer with its bits rotated one position.

The operation of rotate is straightforward. We declare a temporary variable, hold, and a mask variable of the appropriate data type. Mask is initialized to the hexadecimal value 8000. Referring back to our earlier discussion of conversion between binary and hexadecimal, we see that this value results in a bit pattern of

```
1000000000000000
```

```
unsigned rotate(X)
unsigned X;
{
 unsigned mask=0X8000,hold;
 hold=(X & mask) >> 16;
 return ( (X << 1) | hold);
}
```

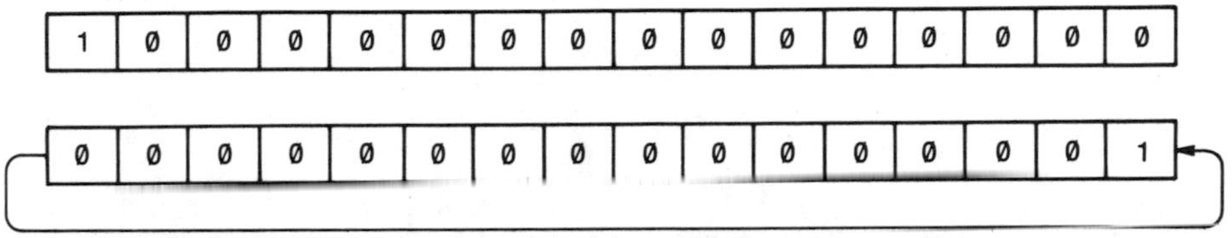

1	0	0	0	0	0	0	0	0	0	0	0	0	0	0	0
0	0	0	0	0	0	0	0	0	0	0	0	0	0	0	1

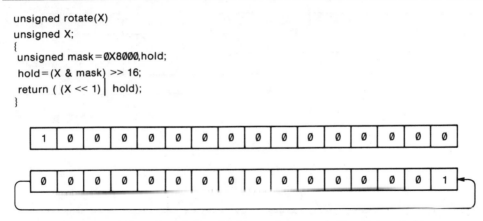

Figure 7-11. A function that will do a rotate operation on an integer.

The first step in the process is to "and" this mask value with the parameter x; this step gives us the value in the left position and 0 everywhere else. By doing a right shift of 16 places, we move this value down to the rightmost position; the resultant value is stored in hold. We do a left shift by 1 on the original parameter and "or" in hold, and we have rotated the value. We can "or" in hold because the rightmost bit positions in x will always be a zero after a shift; thus, a 1 in hold will yield a 1 in the return value but a 0 in hold will equal a 0 on return. Note how we used the mask value and the & operator to extract the value of a single bit.

In Section 7.1, we talked about splitting a single word of memory into two significant quantities. Figures 7-12 and 7-13 and Program Listings 7-1 and 7-2 illustrate two functions that do just that. A single 16-bit integer is a combination of a 4-bit bank and a 12-bit address or offset in that bank. Our two tasks are;

1. To combine a bank and an address value into a single integer
2. To take an integer and extract these two quantities

Figure 7-12 schematically shows the operation of creating the compound value:

1. Start with two quantities, bank and adr.
2. Shift bank left to the 12-bit position.
3. Combine this with addr into a new quantity.

This new quantity takes its leftmost 4 bits from bank and the rightmost 12 bits from adr. Figure 7-13 charts the reverse process and extracts these two quantities:

1. The leftmost four bits are extracted from the composite word.
2. These bits are right shifted 12 bits; this is the bank number.
3. The rightmost 12 bits become the address.

The process is complete.

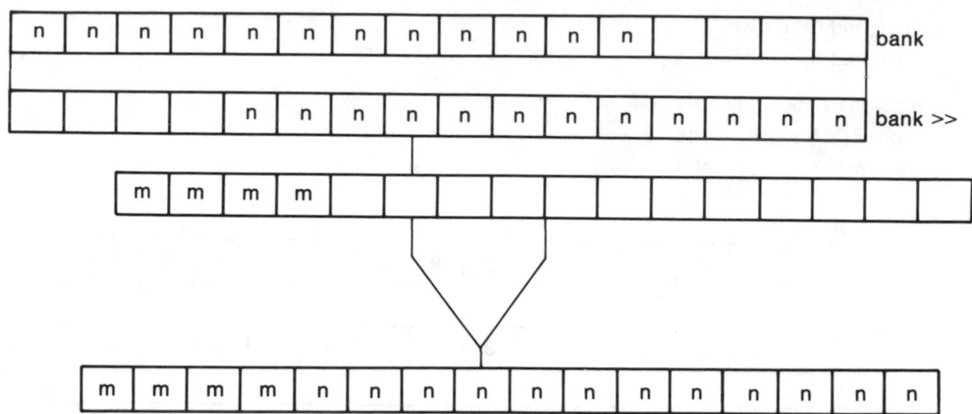

Figure 7-12. Combining bank and sddr into a single address. (function fold_adr())

Program Listing 7-1 contains the function fold_adr(). This function will accept the bank and address values and will return the composite quantity. With the function we have declared four variables: temp0 and temp1, to hold intermediate results; and l_mask and r_mask.

The variables l_mask and r_mask are initialized with bit patterns that allow us to combine our two quantities. Variable L_mask is initialized with the bit pattern

```
1111000000000000
```

Temp0 contains the result of an & operation on this word and the bank value sent in as a parameter. Note, however, that we first shift bank so that the value resides in the leftmost position of temp0. The rest of this variable is filled with 0s. Temp1 is created by applying the & operator to the addr parameter and r_mask.

Variable r_mask has been initialized to the bit pattern

```
0000111111111111
```

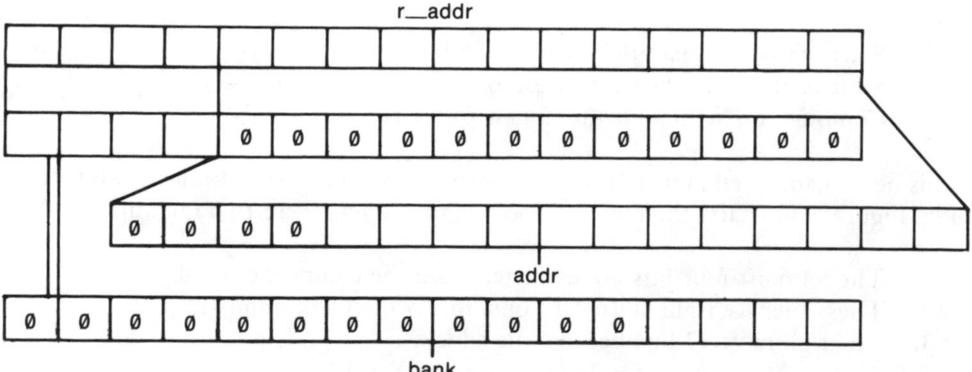

Figure 7-13. Extracting bank and addr from raddr in function extract_adr().

```
unsigned fold_adr(bank,addr)
unsigned bank,addr;
{
 unsigned l_mask=ØXFØØØ,r_mask=ØXØFFF,tempØ,temp1;

 tempØ=l_mask & (bank << 12);

 temp1=r_mask & addr;

 return(tempØ | temp1);

}
```

Program Listing 7-1. A function that will concatenate two address components into a single address.

```
extract_adr(r_addr,bank,addr)
unsigned r_addr,*bank,*addr;
{
 unsigned l_mask=ØXFØØØ,r_mask=ØXØFFF;

 *bank=(r_addr & l_mask) >> 12;

 *addr=(r_addr & r_mask);

}
```

Program Listing 7-2. A function that will divide a composite address into two parts.

The result in temp1 is an integer with 0 in the leftmost 4 bits and the value of addr in the remaining 12. By applying | to these two variables, we can return our composite value.

The function extract_adr is shown in Program Listing 7-2. This function will accept a composite address word and will return two values: the bank value and the address. It returns these through the pointers, bank and addr. The function declares two mask variables, l_mask and r_mask, and initializes them to the same bit patterns as the previous fold_adr() function. The bank number is extracted by applying & to the composite address word, r_addr and l_mask. This gives us the leftmost 4 bits which are then shifted down to the right. The result is put in the location pointed to by bank. The address value is decoded by using & on r_addr and r_mask; this zeros out the leftmost 4 bits, thus leaving us with the desired address value.

7.5. Bit Fields

So far, our bit manipulation capability has mirrored that of assembly language. Each operation has a comparable one specific to the machine. We can shift bits in C, we can perform shifts in assembler, we can perform a logical "and" in C; so, also, in assembler. In fact, C's bit operations are really a subset of those found in any complete assembly language package. We also have at our disposal another way to accomplish many of these bit-level tasks. C supplies us with a high-level structured data type, the bit field, that allows us access to individual bits and combinations of bits within a word or other integer data type.

The bit field is actually another variation on the structure data type. Its form follows the general form of a structure definition

```
struct ⟨name⟩  {
  ⟨type⟩ ⟨field_name⟩ : ⟨bits⟩;
  ⟨type⟩ ⟨field_name⟩ : ⟨bits⟩;
                :
                :
  ⟨type⟩ ⟨field_name⟩ : ⟨bits⟩;
 };
```

where ⟨name⟩ is a legal identifier for the structure type, ⟨type⟩ is any integer type, ⟨field_name⟩ is a legal variable identifier, and ⟨bits⟩ is an integer constant. ⟨field_name⟩ identifies a group consisting of ⟨bits⟩ bit positions, and ⟨type⟩ informs the compiler which type of integer word to use to create these bit fields. As with any structure definition, variables must also be declared to be of this new type before any memory is allocated. Thus,

```
struct b_example  {
    int f0 : 1,
        f1 : 1,
        f2 : 1,
        f3 : 1,
        f4 : 12:
             }b_demo, *b_ptr;
```

will set up a new type, b_example, that will divide an integer into four 1-bit fields and one, 12-bit field. B_demo is declared as a variable of this type, and b_ptr is a pointer to it. Access to individual fields is the same as any structure access. Using the example just shown

```
b_demo.f0
b_ptr->f0
```

will both work.

When a bit field variable is declared, the system will attempt to fit the declared fields into one integer, character, or whatever was specified in the definition. It will not, however, split a bit field across a data object boundary; if it cannot fit it in the space remaining, it will start again with a new object. Consider the following definition

```
struct b_field  {
    int f0 : 3,
        f1 : 3,
        f2 : 9,
```

```
        f3 : 5,
    }b_demo;
```

The parameters f0, f1, and f2 will all be assigned to a single integer; when we add up their size, we get 15 bits; this will easily fit into one 16-bit integer. However, no room is left over for field f4, so it will be placed in a new integer value. Note that on another machine, one with a larger integer—say 32 bits—this wouldn't be the case. The address of an individual field or arrays of fields is not permitted.

The chief advantage of a bit-field variable is that once we've defined it, we can set it and access it in the same way we access ordinary variables. Recalling the previous example,

```
b_demo.f0=1;
b_demo.f1=1;
if(b_demo.f2==200)
    printf("%d",x);
```

are all legal expressions. Through the bit field we can get at the bit positions in the word without using the sometimes awkward bit manipulation operators.

There is one caution that must be sounded. How a bit field definition and declaration will pack the bits in the word is implementation dependent—mostly on the hardware design. Some systems allocate bit positions from right to left, others allocate space left to right. This difference could cause some portability problems if we try some tricky programming: for example, defining a set of bit fields, setting them, and then using a typecast to treat the data object as a simple type. If we stick to accessing the bit fields through the structure format, we should have no difficulties.

Program Listing 7-3 lists a simple bit-map function. We have a static array of eight-character string buffers, buf[], and a bit map, buf_map, that associates a 1 bit field with each buffer. A zero value in the field indicates a free buffer, a value of one tells us the buffer is in use. Our function, store_line(), accepts a character string and searches through the bit map until it finds a free buffer, sets that bit to indicate the buffer is in use, copies the imported string to the buffer, and returns a 1 to the calling function. If no buffers are free, the function returns a 0.

7.6. Summary

In this chapter, we have discussed C's bit manipulation facilities. C supplies us with a number of operators that let us get inside the basic memory unit and directly access the bits found there. In this, C is more closely akin to assembly language than to other high-level languages.

For direct manipulation, C offers us the complement operator which will flip the value of an individual bit location; and the shift operators, which will move bits left or right within a word. We're also supplied with a complete set of logical operations: & (and), | (or), and ^ (exclusive or). These operators are a subset of those typically found in assembly language programming.

```
struct  {
   int  b0 : 1,
        b1 : 1,
        b2 : 1,
        b3 : 1,
        b4 : 1,
        b5 : 1,
        b6 : 1,
        b7 : 1;
   } buf_map;

static char buf[8][80];

store_line(ch)
char *ch;
{
 if(buf_map.b0==0)   {
   buf_map.b0=1;
   strcpy(buf[0],ch);
   return(1);
  }
 else if(buf_map.b2==0)   {
   buf_map.b2=1;
   strcpy(buf[2],ch);
   return(1);
  }
 else if(buf_map.b3==0)   {
   buf_map.b3=1;
   strcpy(buf[3],ch);
   return(1);
  }
 else if(buf_map.b4==0)   {
   buf_map.b4=1;
   strcpy(buf[4],ch);
   return(1);
  }
 else if(buf_map.b5==0)   {
   buf_map.b5=1;
   strcpy(buf[5],ch);
   return(1);
  }
 else if(buf_map.b6==0)   {
   buf_map.b6=1;
   strcpy(buf[6],ch);
   return(1);
  }
 else if(buf_map.b7==0)   {
   buf_map.b7=1;
   strcpy(buf[7],ch);
   return(1);
  }
 else
   return(0);
}
```

Program Listing 7-3. A simple bit map function.

C also has a high-level structured data type that allows us access to the lowest level of the machine. By defining a bit field structure, we can set up individual data objects that are made up of one or more individual bits. These objects are addressed in the same fashion as ordinary variables, thus simplifying access.

We have only been able to touch the surface of this low-level capability. Programs and functions using these operators and data types tend to be problem and even machine specific; but, at least we've gotten a good start on their use.

8

A Data Base Manager

This is the book's ultimate example project. The aim of this chapter is twofold:

1. *to tie together all the material discussed in the book in a practical piece of software, and*
2. *to give the reader insight into the development process as it applies to a very large and complex program.*

A data base manager is an ideal choice for this kind of example: It's big and complex and calls for most of the techniques covered in earlier chapters, and it must be designed and implemented in a step-by-step fashion requiring the diligent application of stuctured techniques and modular programming. You will also be introduced to some of the basic notions and structures that underlie the theory of relational data bases including: the data dictionary and query processing. As in the earlier examples, structured design techniques will be stressed.

Goals:

- To understand the basic principles involved in designing a data base management system
- To demonstrate the design process as it relates to a very large and complex program
- To understand implementation difficulties and trade-offs
- To demonstrate the principles and rules-of-thumb involved in debugging a very large, multifaceted program

8.1. Using C

One of the primary goals of studying a programming language like C is to develop the skill and insight into its working peculiarities and to do significant programming work using it as a medium. This means working through large projects, the kind that require more than one afternoon session at the computer terminal. This chapter will walk you through such a moderately involved project spread across four programs.

We have chosen for this project a small data base manager. This system of programs will allow us to create and use a data base of one record type supporting any key value. The model for data storage we will use is the relational one.

Our primary goal in this chapter is to apply some of the advanced statements, multistatement forms, and concepts we have discussed in the preceeding pages to the kind of real problem that challenges the programmer. By seeing these principles in action, we will begin to develop the thought patterns and problem analysis templates that characterize the so-called but misnamed "intuitive" programmer. This is precisely what we must do, learn to analyze a problem, develop a solution set consisting of an algorithm—or algorithms—and data structures and then create an implementation instrument consisting of the appropriate C elements. What's more, we have to develop a sufficient feel for the interaction between these three realms—world, algorithm, and implementation (so that we can come up with alternate formulations of the implementation plan to suit special situations and unusual resources).

A secondary goal is to demonstrate the desirability and necessity of modularization and planning in producing good software. We will see conclusively that the process of programming is one of design, not discovery. Programs, at least good ones, do not just grow from the computer; they are constructed, built by human intervention upon the basic elements ofered by the computer. Programming is a deliberate and not an intuitive process.

On the other hand, even though we will be studying some of the same concepts frequently listed under the name "structured programming," we will not be studying them within the context of a unified, theoretical body of principles, but rather as they aid in the implementation stage of our project. We will not be applying these principles in a consistent, conscious fashion, but only as they directly relate to an issue that we face in our specific design process. By this approach, we do not mean to denigrate the notions embodied in this notion of "structured programming" and the other recent and fruitful research done and still continuing in programmer productivity. However, these principles in their full formality are more appropriate to a full-blown project with a long time frame and many participants. Our aim is to reach the lone programmer or the small programming group—two or perhaps three individuals. Individuals such as these must eschew the full formalism of structured techniques or risk getting bogged down in details—with a three-person crew, communication need not and, in fact, cannot be formal and structured. In spite of this, the underlying principles must still be honored. What is needed is a set of informal structured rules.

We must, of course, approach this project chapter with our usual cautionary attitude. In all but the very simplest programs, everyday details and quirks of the environment force us to produce code that is not as simple and elegant as our design would have indicated. Details must always be dealt with that have nothing to do with the algorithm. Sometimes the combination of a particular machine, a particular operating system, and a certain combination of C statements will just not work in the way that it should; this is another reason why we must cultivate an insight into alternative implementations for a given algorithm. The transition from design to program will not always be a one-to-one translation, nor will it be a particularly smooth one.

8.2. Data Bases

Keeping information on a computer for easy access and updating is one of the ubiquitous problems in programming. Anyone who has written more than the barest minimum of programs has, at one time or another, coded a program that moved some kind of value—numeric or character—between main memory and a disk or other kind of secondary storage device. These programs are popular for a reason: easy access to information is one of the most significant new technological developments of the twentieth century, and at the heart of this revolution are programs to store and retrieve data.

One common approach to this problem is to create a data structure called a "file" and design an algorithm that will

1. get the appropriate data into this data structure
2. put the values from it into a disk file
3. display the values stored on a display terminal

These are broad descriptions that hide many details. The drawback to this approach is that data structure, algorithm, and ultimately program are all specific to one particular set of values, organized in one particular way. This is fine for many kinds of situations. Relatively stable sets of data and processing requirements would be served just fine by such programs. An added advantage is that performance of the programs can be tuned to an optimal state. Most business data processing still depends on software customized to the data.

Unfortunately, the flood of information that needs to be organized and put "online" has far outstripped the capacity of the industry to supply customized programming. Also, the marginal value of much of this data falls in the range where justifying the high cost of programming is problematical. What is needed is a tool that will allow the user of the data to automatically produce software that will automate access to the data. This need is answered by a data base management system. Such a system will allow the user to specify

- the range of data
- its organization
- access paths to it

The specification will be used to build a system that will allow the same kind of access as a customized program would produce.

We must be careful not to oversimplify the situation. There are many significant advantages beyond the economic argument for creating and using a data base management system instead of a file program. One advantage to a data base system that has generated much interest is the possibility of combining and connecting different data sets and of creating new ones with new organizations without having to create new physical files (*see* Figure 8-1). Another advantage is that the data base system allows the privacy and security of individual file systems but the consistency and ease of maintenance of a single, unified file system.

Our goals here are more modest. We seek to set up a simple system that will allow us to specify a data base record by listing the

- data items
- their sizes
- their names

Our program will then take this information, create a data base, and allow us both read and write access to it. When we finish, we will have a tool that will produce the same kind of access to any specified set of data values.

Our data base system will consist of two main files

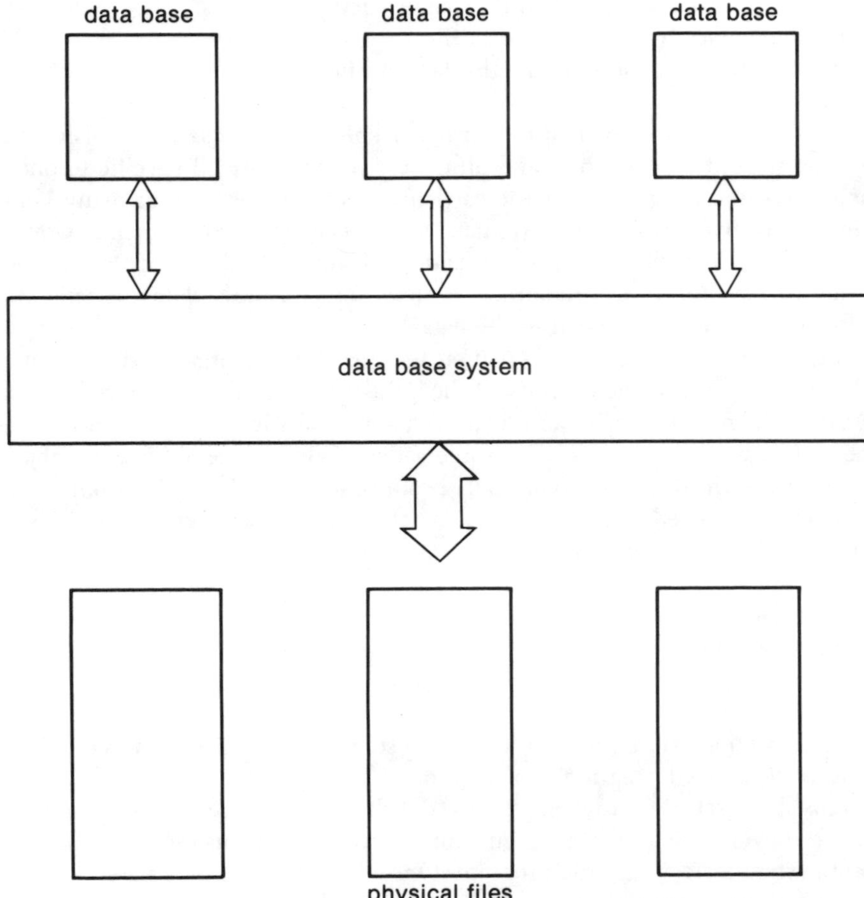

Figure 8-1. A data base system allows the creation of different data bases using the same physical files.

1. the data dictionary
2. the data files

and four programs:

1. the data dictionary compiler
2. the data base filler
3. the update/delete program
4. the query processor

All of these programs are tied together by a menu program. Figure 8-2 displays a schematic diagram of the data base system.

8.3. The Data Dictionary

The heart of our data base system is the data dictionary; this is a data base about the data base. More specifically, it contains the specification of the data base record:

- the name of the data file
- the names of the fields within the data base record
- the number of bytes that each of these fields will occupy in the main data file

These are kept available in a file in a form readily usable by any of our data base programs. Program Listing 8-1 shows the general form of this file and gives a specific example.

```
<file_name>
<field_name>
<field_size>
<field_name>
<field_size>
    :
    :
    :
<field_name>
<field_size>
```

(a)

```
personal.dat
first_name
2Ø
last_name
3Ø
street
2Ø
city
2Ø
   :
   :
```

(b)

Program Listing 8-1. (a) The layout of the compiled data dictionary. (b) An example dictionary.

Any access of the data in the main file must first go to the data dictionary to find the storage format. It must also get from the dictionary the names of the data fields for display to the terminal screen. It is the data dictionary that converts the general purpose file access routines comprising the data base manager into specific access routines for a particular data base design.

The data base dictionary begins as a source file. This file lays out the requisite information in a way more appropriate for the user. Program Listing 8-2 shows the form of a data dictionary source file. Such a file is an ordinary text file produced by any convenient editor or word processing program.

It is the job of the data dictionary compiler program to read through the source file and produce the data dictionary. In our case, the processing is simple and straightforward but it can be arbitrarily complex, approaching the scale of a language compiler—this shouldn't surprise us. The statements in the data dictionary are defining a new programming language—not a general purpose one but a highly specialized one—but, for all that, still a programming language because it tells the computer to do things. The compiler program is translating the statements in this language into a form that the other programs in the data base system can utilize (*see* Figure 8-3).

The file where the actual data values are stored has no inherent structure at all. It is, in essence, one long string of characters. All format information lies solely in the data dictionary file. This is necessary if we are to design an access algorithm that will work for an arbitrary series of data sets. The interface between the file and the program will be a character by character one. We will move an arbitrary number of bytes from the file to main memory; only then will we structure this data.

Of course the structure of the data doesn't exactly disappear when the values are put, byte by byte, on the file. That part of the program that brings the values in can't recognize any structure beyond the character level, but we stored the values on that file with an eye to recovering them with the data dictionary. Thus, the records, even the fields are all the same size, they are all stored in the proper relationship to one another, and all characters are there—no spaces or repeating values have been "squeezed" or otherwise eliminated. Once we move a chunk of the file into memory, we can begin to recapture its internal structure.

8.4. Functional Decomposition

Once we have figured out the file layout our next step is to identify the necessary functions for the given tasks and to design algorithms that will embody these functions. The key words to note here are "identify" and "design." These two concepts are sometimes collapsed into a vague notion of "discovery" or "intuition." Whatever part intuition or insight may take in the process of producing software systems, most of the job is done by thoughtful and deliberate human action. Programs do not write themselves nor do the interconnections between the syntactical elements spring to light through some inspirational process.

The first stage is to identify the functions that need to be performed in order to accomplish our stated goal or goals. This is an iterative process; it will require several

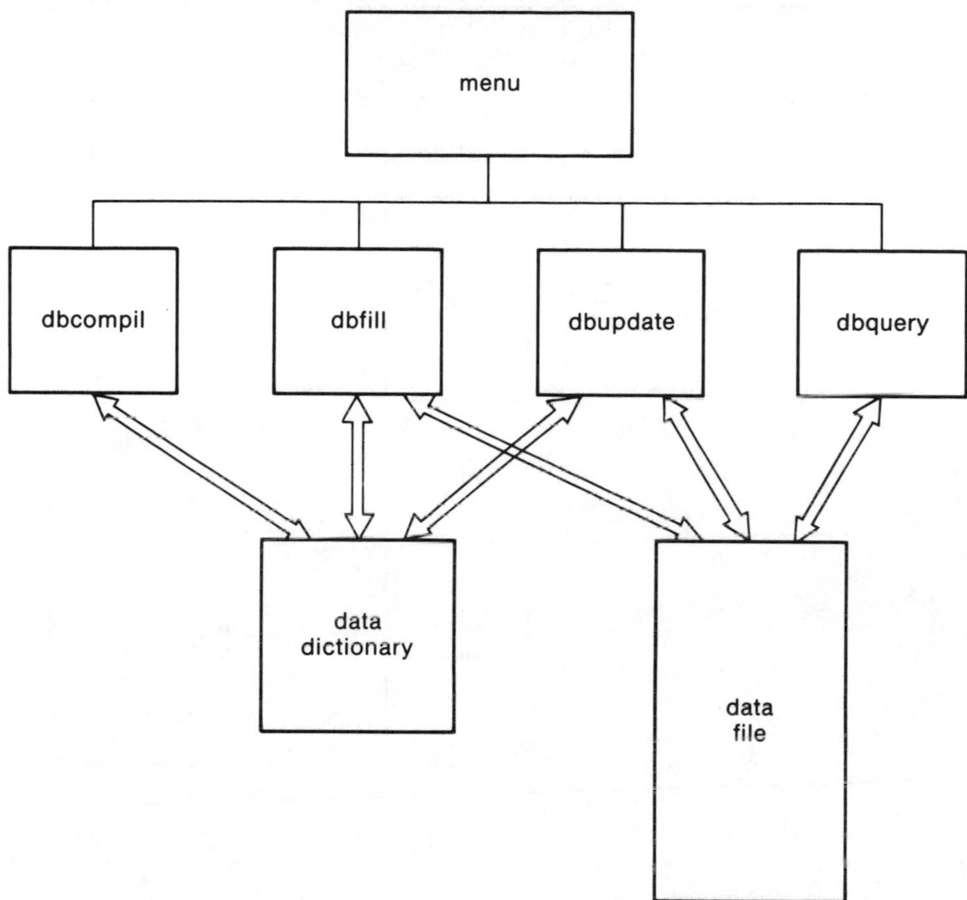

Figure 8-2. A schematic diagram of the data base system.

```
file=<file_name>
<field_name> size=<size>
<field_name> size=<size>
        :
        :
        :
<field_name> size=<size>
```

(a)

```
file=personal.dat
first_name size=20
last_name  size=30
street     size=20
city       size=15
state      size=2
```

(b)

Program Listing 8-2. (a) The layout of the data dictionary source file. (b) An example of a data dictionary source file.

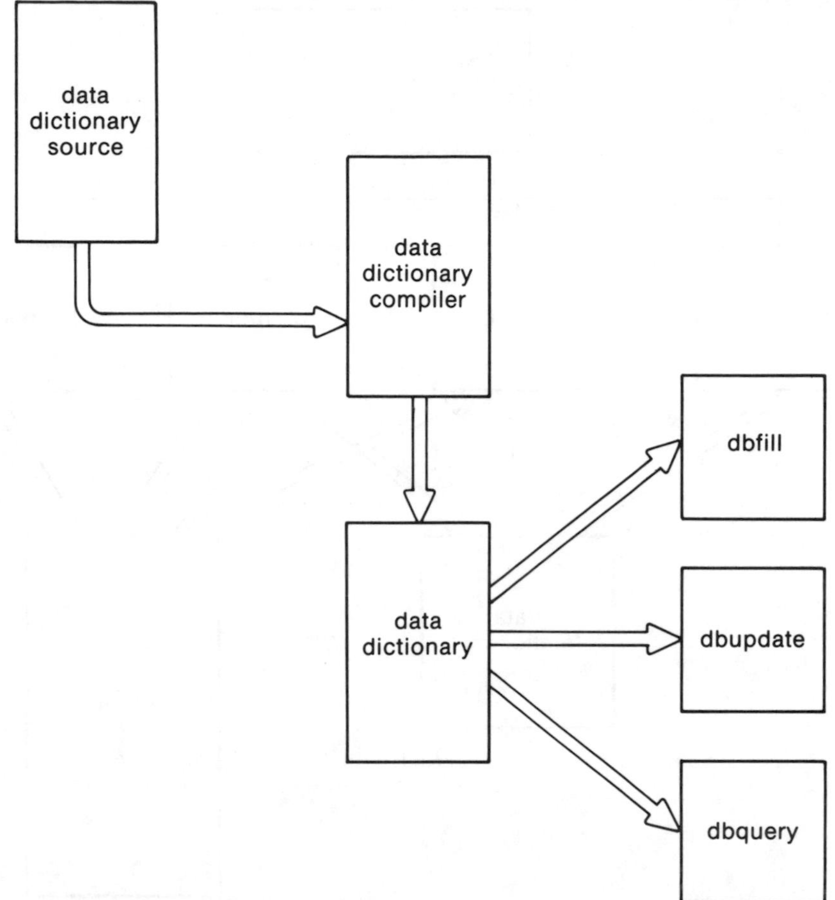

Figure 8-3. Illustrating the process of creating a data dictionary.

passes over the material to identify all of the necessary tasks, and the list will always be open to revision as the planning stages progress. We start by identifying the major divisions of our program. If we don't mind the risk of getting bogged down in terminology, we might call these our major subsystems. We've already done this for our project

- dbcompiler
- dbfill
- dbupdate
- dbquery
- dbmenu

At this point, it can be useful to draw an organizational chart indicating the relationship of each of these subsystems. As more and more functions are identified, they can be placed in their appropriate spot on the chart, and eventually a complete map of the project will emerge. Figure 8-4 shows a chart for our project so far. A word of caution, this chart is not a flow chart nor even a flow chart derivative; it doesn't contain the detailed information that a flow chart claims to have, nor does it indicate anything about the flow of control within the program. It contains the same kind of information as would be found in an organizational chart for a business, the relative position of each element and its interconnection or lack of interconnection to every other element.

There is another piece of documentation that is appropriate at this point in the design process. For each of the major functions, we should write a brief paragraph describing the operation of that function. Within our stated context, this need not be a very formal document, just a few lines detailing expected input values, expected output values, and what transformations will be accomplished while in the function. This kind of document may seem unnecessary for the individual working alone or in a small group, but as work on the project continues, the focus will shift to a more and more detailed level, and our attention will also shift from a macro- to a microscopic level. It will be valuable to us to have this document and the function map to help us quickly shift back to the level of the design as a whole so that we can keep our programming work in perspective. Table 8-1 lists these descriptions for our project. Whether we continue to produce such descriptions for all the functions as we identify them is specific to the circumstances. At some level the function becomes so simple that a description, even as brief as this, becomes an unprofitable exercise, but when this point is reached depends on many of the intangible details of the project and on personal style.

On the next pass through the design, it is necessary to go through each subsystem and find the functions necessary for its operation. Each branch of the diagram in Figure 8-4 will generate its own diagram; these are illustrated in Figures 8-5 through

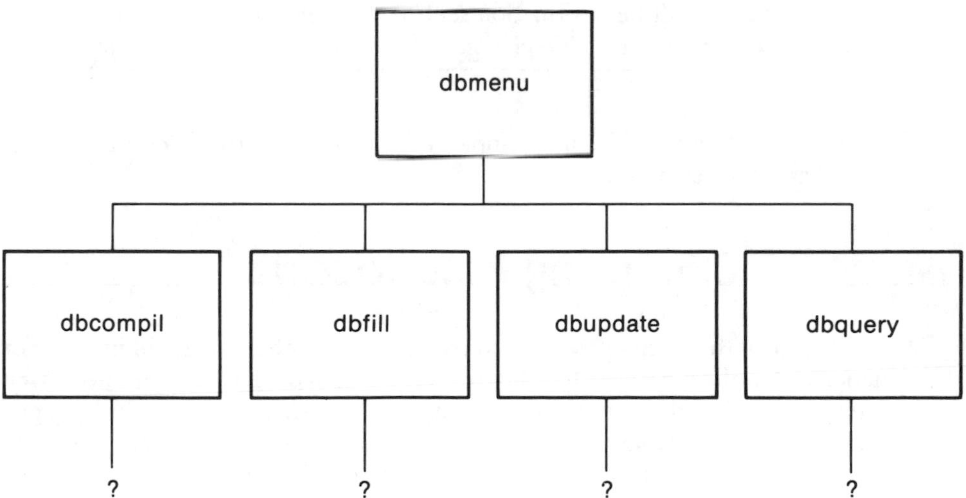

Figure 8-4. A first pass at a system organization chart.

Table 8-1. Major subsystems of the data base management system.

Subsystem	*Description*
dbmenu	This function is the user's entry point into the data base system. It will display the available functions, accept the user's choice, and call the appropriate program. At the end of each subsystem, control will be returned to this program.
dbcompil	This function will accept as input the data dictionary source file, a text file produced outside the data base system. It will produce the compiled data dictionary file as output. The entries in the source file will be transformed into a form usable by the data base system. This function will automatically create the data dictionary file. If a file by that name already exists, it will be overwritten.
dbfill	This function will allow the user to add new entries to a created data base. It will accept as input the name of the data dictionary and the values for each data base record from the user; it will put a new record at the end of the data file. In the case of a new data base, this function will automatically create the data file.
dbupdate	This function will allow the user to change the values in an individual data base record or to mark a record as deleted. It will take as input a search value used to find the desired record and will produce changes to the data base's data file.
dbquery	This function will accept from the user a query request and will display the requested information from the data base. Input will be a program written in the data base system's query language. Output will be information sent to the user terminal. No change to the user terminal. No changes to the data base will be made.

8-8. The menu function is sufficiently simple and straightforward in design so that it doesn't need any further decomposition.

8.5. Using Pseudocode

The next stage in the design process is to create the algorithms that will implement the functions identified previously. But before we can proceed to this necessary stage, we must address the issue of a medium for expressing our algorithm design. What vocabulary is available to us to communicate our concepts apart from the actual program code? Both formal and informal methods present themselves, several possibilities are available in each category.

Graphical techniques other than our simple function diagrams are either too experimental to be of much use to the lone programmer or small project group or are

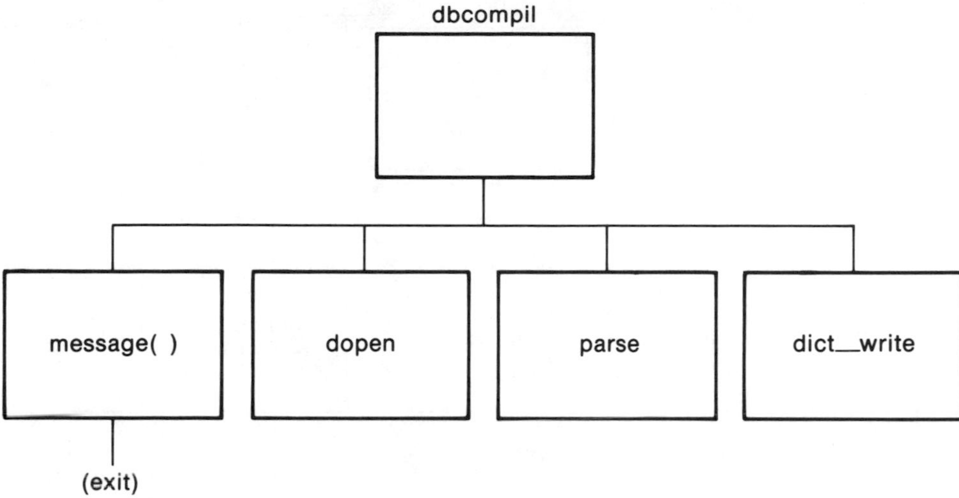

Figure 8-5. Decomposition of the compiler subsystem.

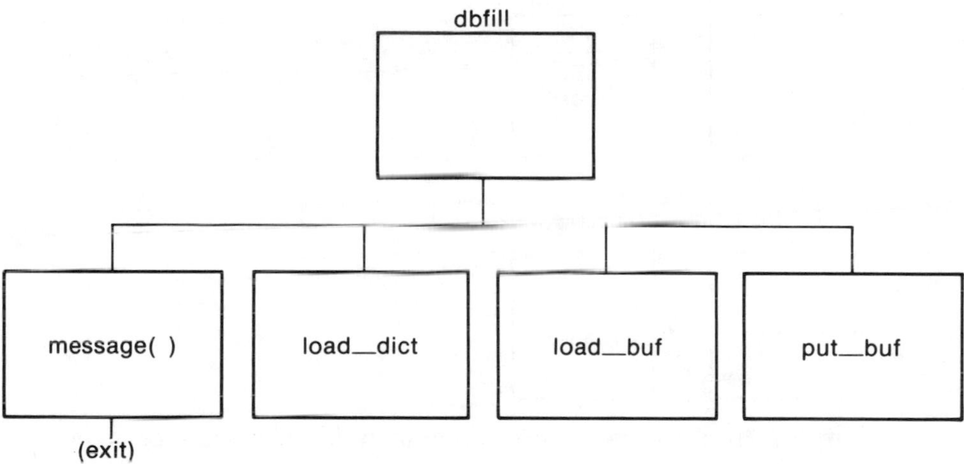

Figure 8-6. Functional decomposition of the fill subsystem.

inappropriate to the C syntax. The latter is exemplified by the ubiquitous (infamous?) flow chart whose basic symbols are too poor in content to model the subtleties of C. Graphical techniques are suspect in general. They add an additional layer of complexity to accommodate the extra modeling effort necessary to transpose our design to a different medium; this is an excellent spawning ground for subtle, hard-to-find errors.

Another possibility for algorithm design is to use a form of programming language itself, but one which doesn't require attention to detail that is normally associated with programming. Such a language is known as pseudocode, and it can run the gamut from a very strict form, almost as stringent as an ordinary programming

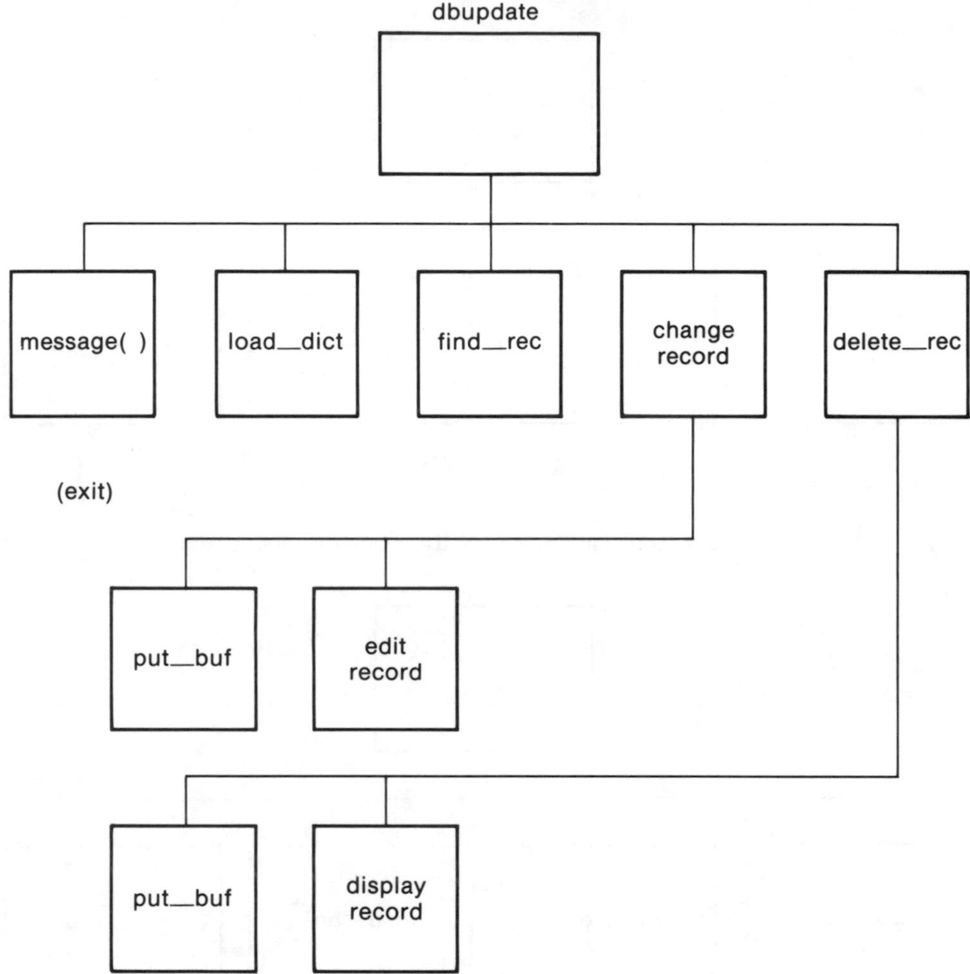

Figure 8-7. Functional decomposition of the update/delete subsystem

language, to a loose and idiosyncratic form peculiar to the individual designer. It can also vary this way across time: starting out loose and undisciplined and evolving, through stages of design, to a formal document.

It is this evolutionary quality that makes pseudocode attractive as a design tool. During the preliminary design phase when details are limited and only the broad outline of the algorithm is available, the pseudocode is correspondingly informal. Through the several iterations of the design phase, the language used becomes ever tighter and more formal, until, during the final design phase, the pseudocode becomes virtually indistinguishable from actual program code. The advantage of pseudocode over any graphical technique is this quality of evolving with a design and at the end of the process having an object that is very easy to translate into legal programming statements.

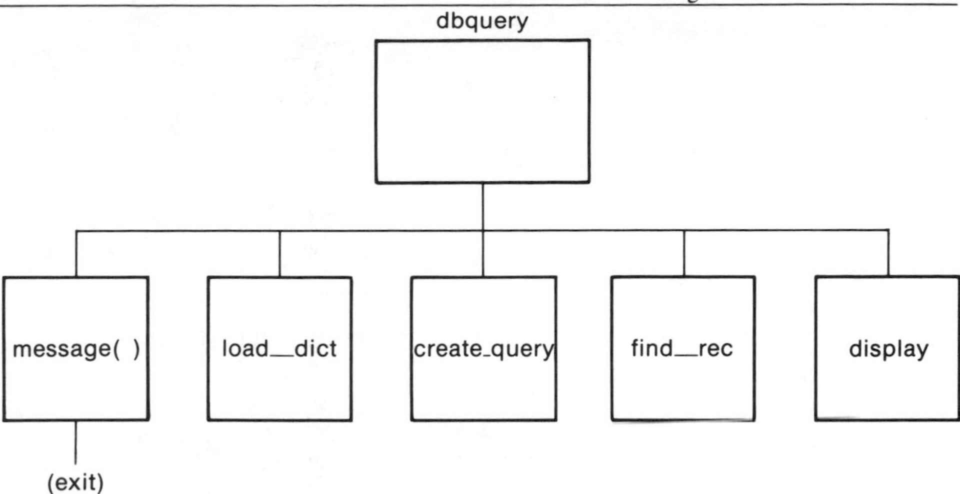

Figure 8-8. Functional decomposition of the query processing subsystem.

Most modern programming languages share a common set of concepts and constructs. Conditional branches, do-while and do-until loops, for example, are either found in, or can be readily implemented in all general purpose programming languages. It's necessary to be able to use these constructs in our pseudocode, but what form will they take? Pascal has become an unofficial pseudocode throughout the programming literature. There is some justification for this:

- Pascal is widely known in the computer community.
- Even among those who don't program in it, it is usually sufficiently well understood to serve as a description language.
- Pascal is complete enough to cover all programming situations.

Because Pascal is a fully developed programming language and was designed quite deliberately to be a teaching language, might be arguments enough to adopt it as our pseudocode. However,a Pascal-like pseudocode is fine only if you're programming in Pascal or a similar language. C is not such a language. There are major differences in both style and content between these two, enough to make the fit between a Pascal pseudocode description and a C function an ill fit.

First, the essential nature of a C program is that it is a collection of equal functions, some of which might be in external files. Pascal can never capture this. As a matter of fact, Pascal cannot describe most of the subtle operations that make C an attractive choice for programming. In Program Listing 8-3, we see a typical pair of functions that implement a stack data structure. We have an array, stack[], to hold the actual values and a variable, top, which marks the current position in the stack. Both of these are declared as static so they will be hidden from the rest of the program. Our two functions, push() and pop(), implement operations on the stack. Program Listing 8-4 shows an attempt to capture these two functions with a Pascal-like pseudocode.

```
static stack[100],top=0;

push(x)
int x;
{
 if(top<100)
   return(stack[++top]=x);
}

pop()
{
 if(top>0)
   return(stack[top--]);
}
```

Program Listing 8-3. A set of simple stack manipulation functions.

```
function push(var stack:iarry;var top:integer):integer;
begin
  if(top<100)
   then
       begin
           top:=top+1;
           stack[top]:=x;
           push:=x
       end
end;

function pop(var stack:iarray;var top:integer):integer;
var
  x:integer;
begin
  if(top>0)
    then
        begin
          x:=stack[top];
          top:=top-1;
          pop:=x
        end
end;
```

Program Listing 8-4. The two stack functions mentioned in Program Listing 8-3 described in Pascal.

Second, while it might be argued that these two are functionally equivalent, none of the subtlety of the C program is evident in the Pascal description. We can't specify data hiding through our stack declaration. We can't create a variable global to a region of the program, but we must let it range over the entire program getting into whatever mischief it can find.

Finally, look how much more awkward the description is than the actual code. It's clear that if we use Pascal as a description language for C, we will still have as much of a leap from pseudocode to code at the end as we had at the beginning.

What we propose to do here is to use C as its own pseudocode. We will design algorithms by using a mixture of C statements and ordinary English ones. The transition from pseudocode to program code reduces to a task of replacing the remaining English sentences with appropriage C statements.

Before closing out this topic, we should duly recognize that design specification is a highly eccentric thing. Some designers even find flowcharts useful. All of us develop our own little quirks and favorite methods. Once we recognize these eccentricities, we should stick with them. The whole point of programming is to produce software. Any way that enables us to produce programs effectively and, above all, reliably is the right thing to do.

Program Listings 8-5 through 8-22 list the pseudocode for each of our proposed functions. The most striking thing to notice is that there is a wide range of levels of detail. With the smallest and most straightforward functions, the pseudocode algorithm is almost legal C. Message(), for example, needs only the list of error messages and a specification of the fatal error cutoff value to be legal code (*see* Program Listing 8-7). With the more complex functions, there are more statements about what we want to do and fewer legal C constructions. The change_rec() function (Program Listing 8-16) is a good example of the latter. This mixture of detail level is indicative of the design process: it is not monolithic and precise but, rather, iterative and evolutionary. Some functions, because they're small or similar to functions that we've coded in the past, can be written down immediately in a form that's nearly complete. Others require more thought and more planning—more passes. Size is not always an indicator of complexity. Put_buf() is a relatively short function, yet in our pseudocode document, it is far from finished (*see* Program Listing 8-14).

```
struct field_buf  {
  char name[41];
  int size;
 };
struct dict_buf  {
  char filename[15];
  struct field_buf field[10];
  int tsize;
};

struct qfield_buf {
  char name[41];
 };

struct query_buf  {
   struct qfield_buf qfield[10];
   char key[41],
        value[81];
  };
```

Program Listing 8-5. Data structures used by the pseudocode representation.

```
externs
  err_number
  buffer

dbcompil()
{
 get source file name

 if(!dopen())
    message();

 parse()

 dict_write()

}
```

Program Listing 8-6. Dbcompil() algorithm in pseudocode.

```
externs
   err_number
   static char *mess={ list of system wide error messages}

message()
{
  if(err_number is null)
    return;

  if(err_number < CUT_OFF)
    print it
    return();

  print it
  exit()
}
```

Program Listing 8-7. Message() algorithm in pseudocode.

```
dopen()
{
  take source file
  make dictionary object file
  return();
```

Program Listing 8-8. dopen() in pseudocode.

```
externs
  buffer

parse()
{
 while (not end of file)
   {
    read line form source file.

    if(line="filename=")  {
      set filed name in buffer
      set size in buffer;
     }
   }
  return;
}
```

Program Listing 8-9. Parse() algorithm in pseudocode.

```
dict_write()
{
  put buffer.filename to destination file;
  for(i=Ø;i<1Ø;i++)   {
    put buffer.field to destination file;
    put buffer.size to destination file;
  }
  return;
}
```

Program Listing 8-10. Dict_write() algorithm in pseudocode.

```
externs
  err_number

dbfill()
{
 if (!load_dict())
    message();

 load_buf();

  if(!put_buf())
     message();

}
```

Program Listing 8-11. Dbfill() algorithm in pseudocode.

```
externs
  dict
  err_number

load_dict()
{
  if(can't open dictionary file)   {
     set err_number;
     return(Ø);
    }

   get(filename from dict_file)

    while(!eof)
       get(dict.fieldname[++1];

     return(1);
}
```

Program Listing 8-12. Load_dict algorithm in pseudocode.

```
externs
    dict;
    err_number;
    buffer;

load_buf()
{
 for(i=Ø;i<=total number of fields;i++)   {
    display the fieldname and prompt;
    get the field value into the buffer;
    fill out the field to dict.size with blanks.
  }
 return(1);
}
```

Program Listing 8-13. The load_buf() algorithm in pseudocode.

```
externs
   dict;
   err_number;
   buffer;

put_buf()
{
 if(can't open data file )   {
   set err_number;
   return(Ø);
  }

 put the buffer at the end of the datafile

 close the data file;

 return(1);

}
```

Program Listing 8-14. The put_buf() algorithm in pseudocode.

```
externs
   err_number;

dbupdate()
{

 if(!load_dict())
   message()

 if(!find_rec())
   message();

  if(delete)
    delete_rec();
  else if(change);
     change_rec()
  else  {
    set err_number;
    message();
  }
}
```

Program Listing 8-15. Dbupdate() alogorithm in pseudocode.

```
externs
   dict;
   err_number;
   buffer;

change_rec()
{
  display dict.field.names and values from buffer

  if(no change)
    return(1);

  get fieldname, new_value from terminal.

  edit(fieldname,new_value)

  redisplay dict.field.names and values from buffer;

  if(!put_buf)  {
    set err_number;
    return(Ø);
  }
}
```

Program Listing 8-16. Change_rec() algorithm in pseudocode.

```
externs
   err_number;
   dict;
   buffer;

delete_rec()
{
  display dict.field.name and values from.buffer;

  if(delete O.K.)  {
    change put "***" in the first three charecters of buffer;

  if(!put_but())
    message();

  return(1);
 }
 return(1);
}
```

Program Listing 8-17. Delete_rec algorithm in pseudocode.

```
externs
    err_number;
    dict;
    buffer;

find_rec()
{
  display prompt;
  get key_field and field value;

  if (can't open dictbuf.filename)  {
    set err_number;
    return(Ø);
   }

  match key_field to dict.field.name
  calculate offset using dict.field.name and dict.field.size

  while(!eof)  {
     set record location;
     get record into buffer from dict.filename;
     match field_value to buffer.field_value;

     if(they match)  {
        close file;
        return(Ø);
       }
    }

  close file;
  set err_number;
  return(Ø);
}
```

Program Listing 8-18. Find_rec algorithm in pseudocode.

```
externs
    dict;
    buffer;

edit_rec(field_name,new_value)
{
  match field_name to dict.field.name;
  calculate offset using dict.field.size;

  put new_value into buffer at offset location;
  fill out space with 'Ø' using dict.field.size;

  return(1);

}
```

Program Listing 8-19. Edit_rec() algorithm in pseudocode.

```
externs
    err_number;
    buffer;
    record_loc
    dict;

put_buf()
{
  if(can't open dict.filename)  {
    set err_number;
    return(Ø);
   }

  position file cursor at record_loc;
  put buffer on file;

  close file;
  return(1);
}
```

Program Listing 8-20. Put_buf() algorithm in pseudocode.

```
externs
   err_number;
   dict;

dbquery()
{
  get dictionary name;
  if(!load_dict)
     message();

  if(!create_query())
     message();

  find rec();

  display_rec();
}
```

Program Listing 8-21. Dbquery() algorithm in pseudocode.

```
externs
   dict
   query;
   err_number;

create_query()
{
 while(line!='\n')  {
   if(line is "show" clause)  {
      while(line[i]!='\n')  {
         get next field name;
         if(it doesn't match a name in dict)  {
            set err_number;
            return(Ø);
          }
         query.field.name=fieldname;
        }
    else if(line is "where" clause)  {
      get fieldname;
      if(field.name doesn't match a field.name in dict)  {
          set err_number;
          return(Ø);
        }
      query.key=fieldname;
      get field_value;
      query.value=field_value;
    }
  return(1);
}
```

Program Listing 8-22. Create_query() algorithm in pseudocode.

In speaking of the design process, we are no longer in the neat, precise world of the computer. We now inhabit a hit and miss realm where trial and error are the modus operandi. To design a complex algorithm, we must start with a clear picture of our goal, one without all the details of implementation to cloud our vision and obscure the task. That's why we use ordinary language statements in place of programming instructions: to hide unnecessary details and focus on the operation itself. Thus,

put the buffer at the end of the data file

is more to the point than

```
fseek(file_ptr,0L,2);
fwrite(buffer,size,1,file_ptr);
```

This example is small, sometimes we can use a single sentence to cover a long and complex series of statements or even an entire algorithm. In find_rec() (*see* Program Listing 8-18) the sentence

```
match key_field to dict_buf.field.name
```

stands in for the sequence

```
for(i=0;i < MAXFIELD; i++)
   if(dict_buf.field[i].name[0]==FILL)  {
      err_number==NOFIELD;
```

```
        return(0);
    }
    else if(!strcmp(key_field,dict_buf.field[i].name)
        break;
```

which is really a subalgorithm. If we placed this latter set of statements in our algorithm design, it would tend to obscure the logic flow of the overall design, especially in conjunction with other such subalgorithms in the function.

Adding too much detail, too quickly is a trap that many novice programmers make. Since some simple functions can be programmed in their entirety at once, it is tempting to believe that all functions can be dealt with in this fashion. Design is abandoned in favor of immediate coding. But if the function has a complex algorithm, we run the danger of bogging down in detail, perhaps getting stuck in one of the subalgorithms. Code like this requires much patching and awkward juxtapositions of statements to get it to work at all, the desire for excellence having long since been abandoned. If, in contrast, we have a design that has been developed in stages, we have two important advantages:

1. an overview of the logical flow of the function
2. a prior level with fewer details to return to if we do get bogged down

A design gives us a coherent structure, built up in layers that we can flesh out with C statements and collections of statements.

The alogrithmic descriptions in these program listings represent a first pass at the the design. An important question to ask is: How far do we take this process? Do we need one, two, or three more iterations to get to the final code? At what point do we make the leap from the design language to one that the machine understands?

Answers vary. Some functions are ready almost immediately; our message() is such a function. A more significant answer involves the more complex functions. This is a gray area where the more strident advocates of structured technique often come to grief. There is no absolute answer; it depends on the function, the style of the designer/programmer, and even the time constraints of the project. A large multiprogrammer project must be relatively formal, and all details must be settled before coding begins otherwise it will be difficult to keep each piece of the program consistent. In this environment, several passes through the design phase will be necessary until all aspects of the program or system of programs have been worked out, and every potential trouble spot has beem identified. An individual working alone or in a small group can get by with a more informal design environment. Here one or two iterations of the algorithm design are all that are necessary to arrive at the code-producing stage. Perhaps one or two particularly recalcitrant functions might require more design; but, many functions will be in code form after the first design iteration.

Program Listing 8-23 lists the results of a second design pass for the load_buf() function first listed in Program Listing 8-13. We've added some of the local variable declarations and the final form of the main control logic. We've deferred some of the detail to the next pass—the formats for scanf() and printf()—and one tricky section of code—fill out the buffer with zeros to maintain a fixed length to each record in the data file. Depending on the factors we just discussed, this function could go through another iteration or directly to code.

```
externs
     dict;
     err_number;
     buffer;

load_buf()
{
 int i;
 char field_value[81];
 for(i=Ø;i<=TOTALFIELDS;i++)
   if(dict.field[i].name is zero)
     return(1);
   else  {
     printf(dict.field[i].name.'>');
     scanf(field_value);
     add dict.field[i].size-sizeof(field_value) Ø's to field_value);
     strcat(buffer,field_value);
   }
  return(1);
}
```

Program Listing 8-23. The result of a second pass at algorithm design for the load_buf() function.

8.6. Source Code

The following section contains a first pass at "runable" code based on our earlier discussions, diagrams and pseudocode. Our planned subsystems have generated the following files:

The compiler subsystem:
- dbcompil.c (Program Listing 8-24)
- message.c (Program Listing 8-36)
- parse.c (Program Listing 8-25)

The fill subsystem:
- dbfill.c (Program Listing 8-26)
- message.c (Program Listing 8-36)
- dictload.c (Program Listing 8-37)
- load.c (Program Listing 8-27)

The update subsystem:
- dbupdate.c (Program Listing 8-28)
- message.c (Program Listing 8-36)
- dictload.c (Program Listing 8-37)
- findrec.c (Program Listing 8-29)
- update.c (Program Listing 8-30)

The query subsystem:
- dbquery.c (Program Listing 8-31)

message.c (Program Listing 8-36)
dictload.c (Program Listing 8-37)
create.c (Program Listing 8-32)
find.c (Program Listing 8-33)
display.c (Program Listing 8-34)

The menu subsystem:
dbmenu.c (Program Listing 8-39)

Dictload.c and message.c are files that are common to many of the programs.

Note that the final code is different in many respects from the pseudocode descriptions. This is to be expected. The pseudocode was only a rough approximation. Note particularly that the function dict_write() disappeared into a larger and more complex parse(). The edit_rec() function, in contrast, was spread out into find_rec(), calc_offset(), match(), and change(). Other changes will be apparent. These programs work but could easily be improved. The reader is invited to use them as a model to create more robust and complete examples.

```
#include <stdio.h>

int err_number;

main(argc,argv)
int argc;
char *argv[];
{
 char source[11],dest[15],*dopen();

 if(argc<2)  {
      printf("dictionary source file->");
      scanf("%s",source);
   }
 else
   strcpy(source,argv[1]);

 if(!parse(source,dest))
   message();
}
char dopen(file)
char *file;
{
 char *ext,file0[15];

 strcpy(file0,file);

 if((ext=index(file0,'.'))!=0)   {
      *(++ext)='d';
      *(++ext)='i';
      *(++ext)='c';
   }
 else
     strcat(file0,".dic");

 return(file0)
}
```

Program Listing 8-24. The contents of file dbcompil.c.

```
#include <stdio.h>

extern err_number;
struct field_buf  {
   char name[41],
        size[5];
  };
 struct dict_buf  {
   char  filename[15];
   struct field_buf field[10];
  };
static struct dict_buf dict;

parse(file0,file1)
char *file0,*file1;
{
 char line[81],*ptr;
 int i;
 FILE *s_ptr,*d_ptr,*fopen();

 if((s_ptr=fopen(file0,"r"))==NULL)  {
     err_number=1;
     return(0);
   }
 for(i=0;i<10;i++)  {
    if(feof(s_ptr))  {
       fclose(s_ptr);
       break;
      }
    fgets(line,81,s_ptr);
    if(!strncmp(line,"file=",5))  {
       ptr=index(line,'=');
       strcpy(dict.filename,++ptr);
      }
     else  {
       ptr=index(line,'=');
       strcpy(dict.field[i].size,++ptr);
       *(ptr-=5)='\0';
       strcpy(dict.field[i].name,line);
      }
    }
 fclose(s_ptr);

 if((d_ptr=fopen(file1,"w"))==NULL)  {
     err_number=2;
     return(0);
   }
 fprintf(d_ptr,"%s",dict.filename);
 for(i=0;i<10;i++)  {
    fprintf(d_ptr,"%s",dict.field[i].name);
    fprintf(d_ptr,"%s",dict.field[i].size);
   }
 return(1);
}
```

Program Listing 8-25. The contents of file parse.c.

```
#include <stdio.h>

extern err_number;

main(argc,argv)
int argc;
char *argv[];
{
 char fname[15],*get_file();

 strcpy(fname,get_file(argc,argv));

 if(!load_dict(fname))
      message();

 if(!load_buf())
      message();

 if(!put_buf())
      message();
}
get_file(x,y)
int x;
char *y[];
{
 char fname[15];

 if(x<2)   {
    printf("dictionary name->");
    scanf("%s",fname);
   }
 else
   strcpy(fname,y[1]);
 return(fname);
}
```

Program Listing 8-26.The contents of file dbfill.c.

```
#include <stdio.h>
#include "dict.h"

extern err_number;
extern struct dict_buf dict;

char buffer[512];

load_buf()
{
 int i,j,a_size;
 char *b_ptr;

 b_ptr=buffer;

 for(i=0;i<10;i++)
    if(dict.field[i].name[0]==0
      break;
    else  {
        printf("%s->",dict.field[i].name);
        scanf("%s",b_ptr);
        a_size=strlen(b_ptr);
        b_ptr+=a_size;
        for(j=0;j<dict.field[i].size-a_size;j++)
            *(b_ptr++)='*';
      }
 return(1);
}
put_buf()
{
 FILE *d_ptr,*fopen();
 int i;

 if((d_ptr=fopen(dict.filename,"a"))==NULL)   {
    err_number=5;
    return(0);
   }
 for(i=0;i<dict.tsize;i++)
     putc(buffer[i],d_ptr);
 fclose(d_ptr);
 return(1);
}
```

Program Listing 8-27. The contents of file load.c.

```
#include <stdio.h>

extern err_number;

main(argc,argv)
int argc;
char *argv[];
{
 char fname[15],*get_file();
 char mark[20];
 long position,find_rec();

 strcpy(fname,get_file(argc,argv));
 if(!load_dict(fname))
      message();
 if((position=find_rec())==-1L)
      message();
 printf("position=%d\n",position);
 printf("c(hange) of d(elete)->");
 scanf("%s",mark);
 printf("mark=%s\n",mark);

 if(mark[0]=='c')
      change(position);
 else if(mark[0]=='d')
      delete(position);
 else  {
      err_number=11;
      message();
    }
}
get_file(x,y)
int x;
char *y[];
{
 char fname[15];

 if(x<2)  {
     printf("dictionary name->");
     scanf("%s",fname);
    }
 else
    strcpy(fname,y[1]);
 return(fname);
}
```

Program Listing 8-28. The contents of file dbupdate.c.

```
#include <stdio.h>
#include "dict.h"

extern err_number;
extern struct dict_buf dict;

char buf[1024];
int offset;

long find_rec()
{
 int field_no;
 long match();
 char key[81];

 field_no=display_prompt(key);
 offset=calc_offset(field_no);
 return(match(key,offset));
}
display_prompt(key)
char *key;
{
 int i,field_no;

 for(i=0;i<10;i++)
     if(dict.field[i].name[0]==0)
        break;
     else
        printf("%s\n",dict.field[i].name);
 printf("key field->");
 scanf("%d",&field_no);

 printf("key value->");
 scanf("%s",key);

 return(field_no);
}
calc_offset(field_no)
int field_no;
{
 int i,offset=0;

 for(i=0;i<field_no;i++)   {
     printf("***%d\n",dict.field[i].size);
     offset+=dict.field[i].size;
   }
 return(offset);
}
long match(key,offset)
char *key;
int offset;
{
 FILE *s_ptr,*fopen();
 long position;

 if((s_ptr=fopen(dict.filename,"r"))==NULL)   {
     err_number=5;
     return(-1L);
   }
 while(! feof(s_ptr))   {
    position=ftell(s_ptr);
    fread(buf,dict.tsize,1,s_ptr);
    printf(">>%d\n",strncmp(key,&buf[offset],strlen(key)));
    if(!strncmp(key,&buf[offset],strlen(key)))
        return(position);
   }
 err_number=13;
 return(-1L);
}
```

Program Listing 8-29. The contents of file findrec.c.

```
#include <stdio.h>
#include "dict.h"

extern err_number;
extern struct dict_buf dict;
extern char buf[];
extern offset;

delete(position)
long position;
{
 buf[offset]=27;

 if(!altfile(position))
    return(0);
 return(1);
}
change(position)
long position;
{
 char xbuf[81];
 int i;

 printf("new value->");
 scanf("%s",xbuf);

 for(i=0;i<=strlen(xbuf);i++)
    buf[offset++]=buf[i];

 if(!altfile(position))
    return(0);
 return(1);
}
altfile(position)
long position;
{
 int spr;
 if(spr=open(dict.filename,2)==-1)  {
     err_number=5;
     return(0);
   }

 lseek(spr,position,0);
 write(spr,buf,dict.tsize);

 close(spr);
 return(1);
}
```

Program Listing 8-30. The contents of file update.c.

```
#include <stdio.h>
extern err_number;

main(argc,argv)
int argc;
char *argv[];
{
 char fname[15],*get_file();

 strcpy(fname,get_file(argc,argv));
 if(!load_dict(fname))
   message();
 if(!create_query())
   message();
 if(!find())
   message();
 else
   display();
}
char *get_file(x,y)
int x;
char *y[];
{
 char fname[15];

 if(x<2)   {
        printf("dictionary->");
        scanf("%s",fname);
    }
 else
    strcpy(fname,y[1]);
 return(fname);
}
```

Program Listing 8-31. The contents of file dbquery.c.

```
#include <stdio.h>
#include "dict.h"
#include "query.h"

extern err_number;
extern struct dict_buf dict;
struct query_buf query;

create_query()
{
 char line[81],field[41],xval[81];
 int i=1,fd;

 while(strncmp(line,"where",5))  {
     printf(">>");
     gets(line);
     if(!strncmp(line,"where",5))  {
        if(!parse_line(&line[5],field,xval))
           message();
        if((fd=match(field))==-1)
           message();
        query.key=fd;
        strcpy(query.keyval,xval);
        return(1);
       }
      else
        if((fd=match(line))==-1)
           message();
        else
           query.fd[fd]=1;
   }
}
parse_line(line,x0,x1)
char *line,*x0,*x1;
{
 char *val0,*val1;
 strcpy(val0,line);

 if((val1=index(val0,'='))==0)  {
      err_number=8;
      return(0);
   }

 *val1='\0';

 if(*(++val1)=='\n')  {
      err_number=9;
      return(0);
   }

 while(*(++val0)==' ')
    ;
 if(*val0=='\0')  {
      err_number=10;
      return(0);
   }
 strcpy(x0,val0);
 strcpy(x1,val1);
 return(1);
}
match(field)
char *field;
{
 int i;
 for(i=0;i<10;i++)  {
    if(!strncmp(dict.field[i].name,field))
       return(i);
   }
 err_number=7;
 return(-1);
}
```

Program Listing 8-32. The contents of file create.c.

```
#include <stdio.h>
#include "dict.h"
#include "query.h"

extern err_number;
extern struct dict_buf dict;
extern sturct query_buf query;

char buf[1024];

find()
{
 int field_no,offset;

 field_no=query.key;
 offset=calc_offset(field_no);
 return(fmatch(query.keyval,offset));
}
calc_offset(field_no)
int field_no;
{
 int i,offset=0;

 for(i=0;i<field_no;i++)
    offset+=dict.field[i].size;
 return(offset);
}
fmatch(key,offset)
char *key;
int offset;
{
 FILE *s_ptr,*fopen();

 if((s_ptr=fopen(dict.filename,"r"))==NULL)  {
    err_number=5;
    return(0);
  }
 while(!feof(s_ptr))  {
    fread(buf,dict.tsize,1,s_ptr);
    if(!strncmp(key,&buf[offset],strlen(key)))
       return(1);
  }
 err_number=13;
 return(0);
}
```

Program Listing 8-33. The contents of file find.c.

```
#include <stdio.h>
#include "dict.h"
#include "query.h"

extern struct dict_buf dict;
extern struct query_buf query;
extern char buf[];

display()
{
 int i,cursor=Ø,next;

 for(i=Ø;i<1Ø;i++)  {
      if(query.fd[i])  {
           next=cursor+dict.field[i].size;
           printf("%s->",dict.field[i].name);
           for(;cursor<next;cursor++)
                printf("%c",buf[cursor]);
           printf("\n");
         }
      else
          cursor+=dict.field[i].size;
}
```

Program Listing 8-34. The contents of file display.c.

```
struct query_buf  {
   int fd[1Ø],key;
   char keyval[81];
 };
```

Program Listing 8-35. The contents of file query.h.

```
#include <stdio.h>
#define CUT_OFF Ø

int err_number;

static char *mess[]={"*nop*",
                     "Can't open dictionary source file",
                     "Can't open dictionary object file",
                     "Write to dictionary object file failed",
                     "Can't open dictionary",
                     "Can't open data file",
                     "No 'where' clause in query",
                     "Field name not found in dictionary",
                     "Incomprehensible 'where' clause",
                     "No key field offered",
                     "Too many fields in query",
                     "Change or delete are the only options available",
                     "Record not found',
                     "*nop*"};
message()
{
 if(!strcmp(mess[err_number],"*nop*"))
     return;
 printf("%s\n",mess[err_number]);
 if(err_number>CUT_OFF)
     return;
 exit();
}
```

Program Listing 8-36. The contents of file message.c.

```
#include <stdio.h>
#include "dict.h"

struct dict_buf dict;
extern err_number;

load_dict(fname)
char *fname;
{
 FILE *s_ptr,*fopen();
 int i;

 if((s_ptr=fopen(fname,"r"))==NULL)   {
     err_number=4;
     return(Ø);
   }
 fscanf(s_ptr,"%s",dict.filename);
 for(i=Ø;i<1Ø;i++)
      if(feor(s_ptr))
         break;
      else  {
        fscanf(s_ptr,"%s",dict.field[i].name);
        fscanf(s_ptr,"%d",&dict.field[i].size);
        dict.tsize+=dict.field[i].size;
       }
 fclose(s_ptr);
 return(1);
}
```

Program Listing 8-37. The contents of file dictload.c.

```
struct field_buf   {
  char name[41];
  int size;
 };
struct dict_buf   {
  char filename[15];
  struct field_buf field[1Ø];
  int tsize;
 };
```

Program Listing 8-38. The contents of file dict.h.

```
#include <stdio.h>

main(argc,argv)
int argc;
char *argv[];
{
 char cmd[41];

 if(argc<2)  {
    printf("command...");
    scanf("%s",cmd);
   }
 else
   strcpy(cmd,argv[1]);

 if(!strcmp(cmd,"compile"))
    system("dbcompil");
 else if(!strcmp(cmd,"fill"))
    system("dbfill");
 else if(!strcmp(cmd,"update"))
    system("dbupdate");
 else
    system("dbquery");
}
```

Program Listing 8-39. The contents of file dbmenu.c.

8.7. Summary

In this chapter we have put our newly expanded knowledge of C to work. Specifically, we have explored the ways that C coupled with a judicious use of structured programming concepts can be utilized as a medium for the production of moderate-to-large scale software projects. We have seen the role that pseudocode plays in the design process and the way we can use pseudocode descriptions to plan and design a program through various stages until a point is reached where actual coding can begin. We have also touched upon other techniques for program planning.

We have also planned, designed, and implemented a small data base management program. In the process we have studied some of the notions involved in information storage and retrieval and query processing. Data base programs are and will continue to be one of the mainstays of the programming profession. Our exercise has a practical as well as a pedagogical value.

This final chapter wraps up the book with a practical exercise. It will serve to underscore the utility and the practical nature of the C programming language and will point the reader to future projects and utilities.

Index

A

address of operator 103
and operator 115
  & and && compared 115
architecture of memory 96
arrays 69-73
  declaration 69
  as a function parameter 70-71
  to allocate memory 72-73
arrays and pointers 112-113, 115
arrays of pointers 116
arrays of structures 87

B

bitfields 165-167
  fitting into datatypes 166
buffered and unbuffered file I/O 39, 136-147
  open() 136-137
  creat() 136-138
  close() 137-138
  fopen() compared to open() 137
  read() and write() 139-140
  lseek() 142
  unlink() 147

C

C
  as a complex tool 2
  as an extensible language 32
  as a mid level language 152
  as its own pseudocode 182
call by reference 100-101, 104-105
character I/O 45-46
  conversion 50-51
character strings 48, 74-78
  converstion 48
  dynamic nature 74
  functions 75-78
complement operator 154
conditional compilation 6-7
criteria for function definition 15
customized file systems 171

D

data abstraction 19
data base management systems 171
data dictionary 173-175
  compiler 175
data types 67-68, 74
  as a passive notion 67
  influencing algorithm design 68
  as a method of access 68, 74
defining regions of the program 11
design 13-14, 191
  as an iterative process 13-14
  vs. immediate coding 191
device files 44
dynamic memory allocation 119

E

eccentric nature of specification 183
errno 148
exclusive or operator 159
extern storage class 25

F

files 39-43, 57-58, 86, 133, 136
  FILE data type 42, 86
  file descriptor 136
  file management subsystem 133
flat structure of C 22
flexibility of the I/O library 36
formatted I/O 52-56
functional decomposition 10-11
functions 16, 101, 126-129, 177
  as building blocks 16
  as parameters 101, 126-129
  simplify code 16
  specification 177

G

graphical specification techniques 178-179

I

identifying necessary functions 175-178
indirect addressing 97-98
indirection operator 104-105, 111
  symmetry of * and & 105
  with increment and decrement operators 111
I/O library enhances portability 37

L

left shift operator 155-156
levels of functions 14
linked data types 67
linked lists 100, 117-120
  comparison to an array 118
  structure node 118

M

malloc() 119
mapping objects 64
modularity in programming 170
modularity of I/O 38
multidimensional arrays 88
multiple returns from functions 46-47

N

NULL pointer 107

O

operating system 132-133
  tasks 132
  as a service provider 133
or operator 158-159
  | and || compared 159

P

passing details to lower levels 19-20
perror() 148
pointers 99-115, 129-130
  and dynamic data structures 99-100
  and relational expressions 111
  declaration 102
  overruning alloted space 115
  scaling of arithmetic operations 108
  with character strings 113-114
  with register storage class 129-130
portability issues 133
problem breakdown 11
problems requiring bit manipulation 152, 154
  status words 152
  bit maps 154
problem solving environments 34
program as a collection of functions 16
project definition 169-170
preprocessor 4-8
  #include 4
  #define 5-8
  #undef 6
  #if, #ifdef, #ifndef 7
  #else, #elseif 7
  #line 8
pseudocode 179-181
  Pascal as a pseudocode 181

R

reassigning files 44
restricting the scope to a single file 26
right shift operator 156-158
  zero fill vs. sign extension 157-158

S

scope as part of the design process 20
sensible arithmetic on characters 50
separate compilation 25, 32
sizeof 119
source code for the data base manager 192-205
specialized function libraries 32
stack data type 100, 124-126
structured programming 10, 170
structures 80-83
  definition 80-81
  dot notation 81
  nested structures 82-83
structures and pointers 117
subtracting pointers 108-109
sys_list 148
sys_nerr 148
system() 134

system calls compared to functions 139

T

trading complexity for overhead 18
type cast 119
typedef 85-86, 88-89

U

unpacking a value 163
using hexadecimal or octal constants to set bits 159-160
using int for character I/O 45
using the array to set aside memory 115-116

V

variables global to a region of the program 22
virtual devices 140
virtual memory 96-97, 107

W

word as the basic unit of storage 65-66

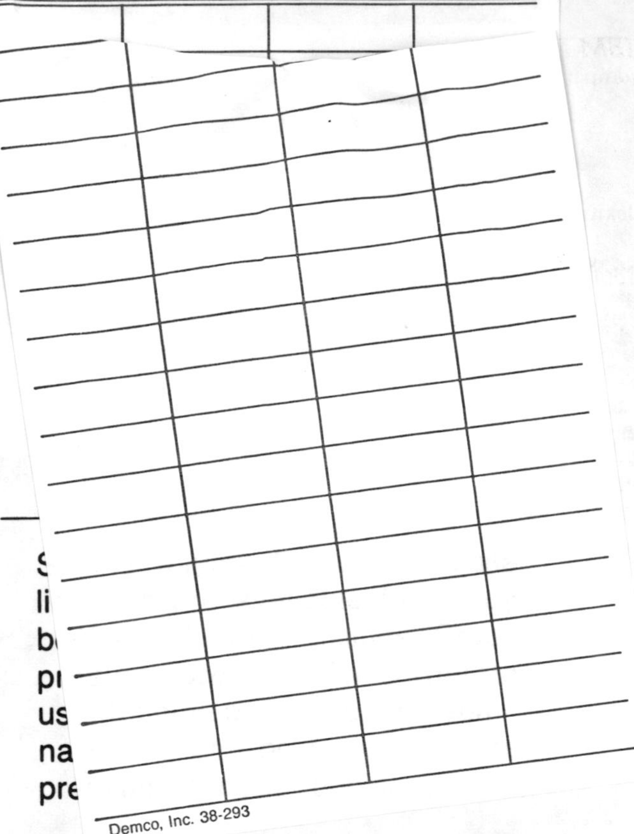

S
li
b
p
us
na
pre

For information, please contact: Director of Special Sales, Brady, Simon & Schuster, Inc., New York, NY 10023 (212) 373-8232

Related Resources Shelf

Inside the IBM PC, revised & enlarged Peter Norton

This best-seller has been thoroughly updated and expanded to include *every* model of the IBM microcomputer family! Detailed in content, yet brisk in style, INSIDE THE IBM PC provides the fascinating tour inside your machine that only the renowned Peter Norton can give. He'll lead you into a complete understanding of your IBM—knowing what it is, how it works, and what it can do. First review the fundamentals, then move on to discover new ways to master the important facets of using your micro to its fullest potential. Definitive in all aspects.

☐ 1986/400 pp/paper/0-89303-583-1/$21.95

Creating Utilities with Assembly Language: 10 Best for the IBM PC & XT
Stephen Holzner

With assembly language as its foundation, this book explores the most popular utility programs for the IBM PC and XT. For the more advanced user, this book unleashes the power of utilities on the PC. Utilities created and discussed include PCALC, ONE KEY, CLOCK, FONT, DBUG SCAN, DSKWATCH and UNDELETE. The author is a regular contributor to *PC Magazine*.

☐ 1986/352 pp/paper/0-89303-584-X/$19.95

Artificial Intelligence for Microcomputers: A Guide for Business Decision Makers Mickey Williamson

This book discusses artificial intelligence from an introductory point of view and takes a detailed look at expert systems and how they can be used as a business decision making tool. Includes step-by step instructions to create your own expert system and covers applications to cost/benefit analysis, personnel evaluations and software benchtesting.

☐ 1986/216 pp/paper/0-89303-483-5/$17.95

Assembly Language Programming with the IBM PC AT Leo J. Scanlon

Author of Brady's best-selling IBM PC & XT ASSEMBLY LANGUAGE: A GUIDE FOR PROGRAMMERS (recently revised and enlarged), Leo Scanlon is the assembly language authority. This new book on the AT is designed for beginning and experienced programmers, and includes step-by-step instructions for using the IBM Macro Assembler. Also included is a library of 30 useful macros, a full description of the 80286 microprocessor, and advanced topics like music and sound.

☐ 1986/464 pp/paper/0-89303-484-3/$21.95

To order, simply clip or photocopy this entire page, check your order selection, and complete the coupon below. Enclose a check or money order for the stated amount or include credit card information. Please add $2.00 per book for postage & handling, plus local sales tax.

Mail to: **Prentice Hall Press, c/o Prentice-Hall Mail Order Billing, Route 59 at Brook Hill Drive, West Nyack, New York 10994.** To order by phone, call 201-767-5937.

Name ____________________

Address ____________________

City/State/Zip ____________________

Charge my credit card instead: ☐ MasterCard ☐ Visa

Credit Card Account # ____________________ Expiration Date ______ / ______

Signature ____________________

Dept. Y D5831-BB

Prices subject to change without notice.

BRADY Knows Programming

1. Beyond the basics, this guide explores new structured concepts to analyze and solve problems in C with tools of modularity, input and output functions, arrays and structures, and bit manipulation. $21.95

2. You learn by example with this guide through hundreds of subroutine listings. Discover how to enhance high level language programs (esp. BASIC) to quickly manipulate and sort large data files, generate graphics, integrate arrays, and use interrupts to access DOS. $17.95

3. Learn the techniques used for creating assembly language utilities. Includes 10 of the most popular utilities such as DBUG SCAN, CLOCK, UNDELETE, ONE KEY, PCALC calculator and notepad and five others. $19.95 (Disk available)

4. Includes code listings for three working debuggers including single-stepping, cross referencing, and mapping utilities. $17.95 (Disk available)

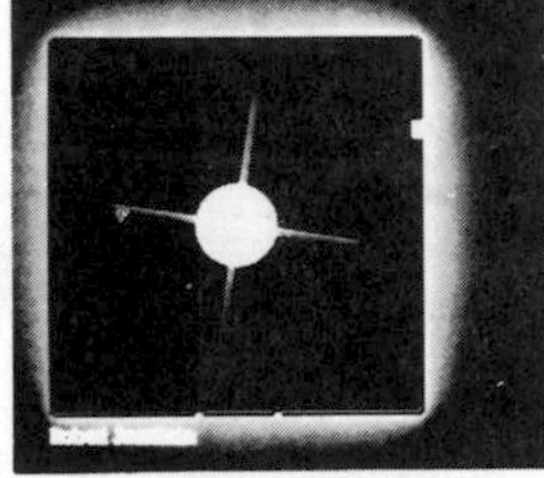

5. A definitive reference text for advanced programmers. You'll find over 150 discussions of common hardware-control tasks (in BASIC, Pascal, or C) as well as assembler overlays, drivers, and real-time operators. $22.95

6. Perfect for both beginners and experienced programmers, you'll find everything from the basics of computer numbering through to step-by-step instructions for using the IBM Macro Assembler. With complete coverage of BIOS and a library of over 30 macros for faster programming. $21.95 (Disk available)

7. Here's a compendium of many of the most useful, but often neglected, advanced programming concepts. A tutorial in format that uses BASIC for examples, it covers techniques such as: linked data structures; recursion; pipelining; and dynamic storage allocation. Includes listings for 25 subroutines. $21.95 (Disk available)

8. The title might say "advanced" but you'll find a guide that begins with the fundamentals of BASIC graphics and takes you through truly sophisticated 3-D assembly routines. Includes block graphics, creating a graphics editor, directly programming IBM's color graphics adapter, and much more. $21.95

Now at your book or computer store.
Or order today: **201-767-5937**

Prentice Hall Press
c/o Prentice-Hall
Mail Order Billing
Route 59 at Brook Hill Drive
West Nyack, NY 10994

Circle the numbers of the titles you want below.
☐ Please charge my ☐ Mastercard ☐ Visa

Credit Card # ______________________ Exp. Date ________

Signature ______________________________
☐ Enclosed is my check or money order
☐ Bill me

Name ______________________________

Address ______________________________

City ______________ State ______________ Zip ________

Merchandise Total		
Add	sales tax for your state	
	12% postage + handling*	
Total; check enclosed		

*Publisher pays postage + handling charges for prepaid and charge card orders.

1 (0-89303-473-8)	2 (0-89303-409-6)	3 (0-89303-584-X)	4 (0-89303-587-4)
5 (0-89303-787-7)	6 (0-89303-484-3)	7 (0-89303-481-9)	8 (0-89303-476-2)